Peacemaking from Above,
Peace from Below

A VOLUME IN THE SERIES

Cornell Studies in Security Affairs

Edited by Robert J. Art, Robert Jervis, and Stephen M. Walt

A list of titles in this series is available at www.cornellpress.cornell.edu.

Peacemaking from Above, Peace from Below

Ending Conflict between Regional Rivals

Norrin M. Ripsman

Cornell University Press

Ithaca and London

First published 2016 by Cornell University Press

Printed in the United States of America

Library of Congress Cataloging-in-Publication Data

Names: Ripsman, Norrin M., author.
Title: Peacemaking from above, peace from below : ending conflict between regional rivals / Norrin M. Ripsman.
Other titles: Cornell studies in security affairs.
Description: Ithaca ; London : Cornell University Press, 2016. | ©2016 | Series: Cornell studies in security affairs | Includes bibliographical references and index.
Identifiers: LCCN 2015043910 | ISBN 9781501702471 (cloth : alk. paper)
Subjects: LCSH: Pacific settlement of international disputes. | Peace-building. | International relations—History—20th century.
Classification: LCC JZ6010 .R57 2016 | DDC 327.1/72—dc23
LC record available at http://lccn.loc.gov/2015043910

Cornell University Press strives to use environmentally responsible suppliers and materials to the fullest extent possible in the publishing of its books. Such materials include vegetable-based, low-VOC inks and acid-free papers that are recycled, totally chlorine-free, or partly composed of nonwood fibers. For further information, visit our website at www.cornellpress.cornell.edu.

Cloth printing   10 9 8 7 6 5 4 3 2 1

To my parents,
Michael and Toba Ripsman,
whose love, guidance, and values
are with me in all that I do

Contents

Acknowledgments

This book is the product of a two-decade obsession with the dynamics of interstate peacemaking. Beginning with my dissertation at the University of Pennsylvania, I have been troubled by the complexity of Robert Putnam's two-level game of international politics and its implications for peacemaking. Rarely do the two game boards align for rival states in order to compel the resolution of conflict. Instead, mutual distrust and insecurity are usually reinforced by domestic hostility toward the adversary, which undermines the prospects for peace and stability. How can peace be achieved and maintained, given this complexity? What roles do states and societies have in making peace and maintaining it?

Inspired by Benny Miller and T. V. Paul, two good friends and mentors, I reach beyond traditional paradigmatic boundaries to investigate these questions, as the theories drawn from paradigmatic approaches are insufficient to explain the complex processes of peacemaking and peace stabilization. Consequently, consistent with eclectic approaches and, in particular, with neoclassical realism, in this book I combine insights and concepts from structural realism, liberalism, and constructivism to generate the explanatory leverage to explain the outbreak and maintenance of peace between regional rivals. Moreover, the book continues my commitment to careful primary source case studies to shed light on important theoretical questions.

Portions of this book were previously published as "Top-Down Peacemaking: Why Peace Begins with States and Not Societies," in *International Relations Theory and Regional Transformation*, edited by T. V. Paul, Cambridge University Press, 2012, and "Two Stages of Transition from a Region of War to a Region of Peace: Realist Transition and Liberal Endurance," *International Studies Quarterly* 49, no. 4 (December 2005).

Many colleagues and friends gave me comments and suggestions on various aspects of this manuscript. I would particularly like to acknowledge Bob Art, the late Yaacov Bar Simantov, Dale Copeland, Oded Haklai, John Hall, Eric Hamilton, Yair Hirschfeld, Pat James, Arie Kacowicz, Korina Kagan, Jack Levy, Michael Lipson, Steven Lobell, Sean Lynn-Jones, David Mares, Benny Miller, Steven Miller, T. V. Paul, Charles Pentland, Vincent Pouliot, Galia Press-Barnathan, Larry Rubin, Jeff Taliaferro, Monica Duffy Toft, and Steve Walt for their useful suggestions. I'm particularly grateful to Steven Lobell and Jeff Taliaferro, with whom I have worked closely on numerous projects. Their advice, guidance, and moral support during our biweekly Skype calls have helped this book immensely.

I have also benefitted from feedback on presentations of this work in progress at the Belfer Center for Science and International Affairs at the Harvard Kennedy School, the University of Colorado at Boulder, the School of International Studies at the University of Southern California, Georgia Tech University, Queen's University, the University of Haifa, the Hebrew University of Jerusalem, Florida International University, the University of Massachusetts at Lowell, and Northern Illinois University. I am also grateful for the research funding I received for the project from the Social Science and Humanities Research Council and the Fonds de recherche du Québec: Société et culture.

Over the years, several excellent research assistants at Concordia University have helped me with this book. I thank Eugenia Yupanqui Aurich, Shaun Cavaliere, Nadine Hajjar, Sandra Helayel, Sebastien Mainville, Shoghig Mikaelian, and Aleksandra Vuldzheva for all their hard work.

It has been wonderful to work with Roger Haydon of Cornell University Press on this book. I value his professionalism and judgment. His production team, including Susan Specter and Katy Meigs, did a superlative job with the copyediting and guiding me through the production process. The editors of the Cornell Studies in Security Affairs series, Bob Art, Robert Jervis, and Steve Walt, also provided excellent guidance, which helped improve the final product.

Finally, I must acknowledge the immense contribution of my family to this book. My parents, Toba and Michael Ripsman, have supported me in all my endeavors and encouraged me to work hard to achieve any goal I set for myself. My beautiful daughters, Shira and Dafna, inspired me to help advance our understanding of the causes of peace in the hope that they may live in a more peaceful world. I appreciate their sacrifice, as they had to live without their Daddy for extended periods, while I conducted research in archives, interviewed diplomats overseas, or buried myself in my basement office writing this book. And I cannot thank my wife, Nathalie, enough. Her contribution to this book is in the methodological advice she gave me, the times she served as a sounding board for half-baked ideas, the moral support she offered when the project moved slowly, her willingness to tolerate long research trips abroad and long periods of writing while locked in my office, and her joy at its completion. I share this book with her, as I share everything in life.

Peacemaking from Above, Peace from Below

Top-Down Peacemaking, Bottom-Up Peace

Neighboring states wage war far more frequently than other states. This makes sense given that they have frequent interaction and, thus, increased opportunities for conflict. It is also much easier to project force across shorter distances than longer ones, making war more likely within geographically defined regions than across them. For this reason, regional rivalries—geographically proximate states with a history of war and protracted hostility that participate in a well-recognized regional geopolitical security dynamic—account for a large percentage of interstate violent conflicts. Resolving regional rivalries, therefore, would reduce the incidence of interstate war and contribute greatly to international stability. The central focus of this book is how to promote peacemaking between regional rivals and how to sustain peace agreements reached between them.

What makes regional rivals with a history of mistrust and violent conflict make peace? Why do some states with intense regional rivalries negotiate peace treaties to end their conflict? How can third parties, both states and international institutions, promote peacemaking between regional rivals? Why do some peace treaties between regional rivals endure and transform relations between the former enemies, while others are only short lived? These are questions of fundamental theoretical importance. Presently, they are also of great practical importance as the international community seeks to forge lasting peace and stability in South Asia and the volatile Middle East, regions with longstanding rivalries that contain the potential to escalate to the nuclear level.

The international relations theory literature suggests two possible paths to peace between regional rivals. A bottom-up approach, drawn largely from liberal and constructivist theories, suggests that peace could result from societal pressures to end a destructive and economically irrational rivalry. In this model, for self-interested or normative reasons, key societal actors or the public at large in belligerent societies drive the process of

1

peacemaking, compelling their reluctant states to de-escalate the conflict and, ultimately, resolve it. This bottom-up approach would then expect that once societal attitudes are changed and states overcome their mutual hostility the peace settlement is likely to endure.

In contrast, a top-down approach, drawn from realist and statist theories, suggests that the engines of peacemaking might be the states themselves (i.e., the leadership and governmental apparatus) for geostrategic reasons and to preserve their power positions. This model posits that states, being more pragmatic than society, may pursue peace settlements with rival states in response to changes in the state's strategic situation and domestic threats to regime survival, often despite intense societal opposition and deep-seated public animosity toward the adversary. Nonetheless, given that state interests change over time, peace treaties should endure only as long as states maintain an active interest in preserving them.

My central conclusion in this book is that neither approach satisfactorily explains the transition to and entrenchment of regional peace. Peacemaking, when it works, proceeds in two stages. In the first stage (the *transition*) peacemaking is a top-down process led by state leaders, often over societal objections. Leaders engage in peace negotiations for a variety of statist motivations, including concerns about third states that pose greater threats to one or both of the regional rivals, pressure from powerful external actors—especially the global hegemon in a unipolar international system or the predominant power within a given region—and domestic economic troubles exacerbated by the conflict that threaten the regime's hold on power. Societal pressures, whether mass democratic pressures, lobbying from business interests, or normative pressures filtered through society as a result of participation in cooperative international institutions, do not lead states to embark on rivalry termination.

In contrast, the stability of a peace settlement depends on the degree to which it obtains societal buy-in during the second stage (the *post-transition* phase). Treaties are most likely to be stable when the formerly belligerent states, together with outside actors, socialize key interest groups and the public at large with strategies derived from bottom-up approaches: by providing an economic peace dividend, fostering cross-national economic and cultural ties, and participating together in cooperative regional institutions. Furthermore, if nondemocratic rivals undergo a democratization process, making the leading regional participants democratic states, that further builds societal trust and enhances stability, as do efforts to reunite dispersed ethnic groups and grant self-determination to stateless minorities. In essence, if the treaty continues to be respected only because of statist calculations, it will be fundamentally unstable and potentially vulnerable to changes of government or regime or changes to the conditions that motivated the treaty. Thus, it may endure without underlying stability if the states involved continue to face powerful geostrategic or regime survival motives to honor it. If statist motives for peace erode, then, absent societal entrenchment of the agreement, the peace settlement will remain only a temporary expedient and will unravel.

I reach these conclusions based on detailed case studies that rely on personal interviews, archival research, and secondary sources of the peace treaties between France and the Federal Republic of Germany (1954), Egypt and Israel (1979), and Israel and Jordan (1994) and their aftermaths. In addition, I conduct brief analyses of all other peace treaties between regional rivals concluded in the twentieth century, to cover the universe of twentieth-century cases. I thus have great confidence that these results are not merely an artifact of case selection.

These findings are of more than merely theoretical importance. In the post–Cold War era, Western governments and international organizations have embraced bottom-up approaches to peacemaking, investing hundreds of millions of dollars on programs that engage conflict-ridden societies in an effort to build bridges between rival peoples and promote conflict resolution. The United States Agency for International Development (USAID), for example, has a Democracy, Conflict, and Humanitarian Assistance/ Conflict Management and Mitigation office, which has disbursed over $115 million to date through its People-to-People Reconciliation Fund to promote peacemaking and conflict resolution.[1] The US State Department also supports a variety of projects, including the Seeds for Peace camp, which brings Palestinian and Israeli children together to promote peace in the Middle East and Indian and Pakistani children together to do the same in South Asia.[2] The European Union also supports numerous people-to-people aid projects, including the Partnership for Peace program with an annual budget of €10 million, which attempts to engage Israeli and Palestinian society to promote reconciliation.[3] The government of Japan sponsored the Folding Together project, in which Israeli and Palestinian children made origami birds to create common ground.[4] And, the United Nations Development Programme sponsors a variety of intercommunity peace-building programs, including the intercommunity dialogue between East African pastoral communities.[5] To be sure, these initiatives—and many others like them—were not meant to replace state-to-state efforts to jump-start peace negotiations, but it bears asking whether the resources devoted to societal engagement are warranted prior to a peace agreement.

At the same time, Western leaders have evinced great faith in the power of democracy, economic exchange, and international institutions as means of promoting peace in troubled regions. US presidents George W. Bush and Barack Obama are united in the conviction that nondemocratic regimes allow grievances to fester, whereas democracies generate understanding and reconciliation.[6] President Bill Clinton's national security advisor, Anthony Lake, articulated a national security strategy of "enlargement" based on the concept that peace could be spread through the proliferation of democracy and market economics.[7] Former French president Nicolas Sarkozy proposed an economic union of Mediterranean countries with the explicit aim of promoting Arab-Israeli peace through economic interdependence.[8] US secretary of state Hillary Clinton has praised regional institutions, such as the African Union, for promoting peace and security in troubled regions.[9] It is worth investigating, therefore, whether spreading democracy, economic ties, and cooperative international institutions to foster reconciliation and understanding between troubled societies is truly the way to achieve peace between regional rivals. I suggest it is not. Instead, these strategies are best held in reserve until after an agreement is reached in order to help entrench it.

The Problem of Regional Peacemaking

Regional peacemaking is a complex and multifaceted problem. Disputes between regional participants frequently involve not only rival territorial claims but also those grounded in competing national, religious, and ideological world views. Resolving these competing claims in a manner such that all parties are satisfied and do not feel shortchanged is a heroic task. What then can we hope for in conflict resolution?

To some extent, conflict lies in the minds of human beings. Unless we can change those minds, the dispute will remain and the recurrence of war will be possible. Frequently, the best we can hope for, at least in the short term, is conflict management, using incentives and disincentives—mainly provided by outside actors—to prevent the rivals from using force to resolve the conflict and, in general, to limit the level of violence, at least in the short to medium term.[10] This was the approach taken in the Arab-Israeli conflict in the late 1960s and early 1970s, in which the parties reached disengagement agreements involving demilitarization or force reductions in particular zones, monitoring by outside parties, and occasionally the presence of foreign peacekeeping troops.[11] These agreements do not constitute peace agreements as they do not aspire to end the conflict but merely to manage and stabilize it. They encompass what Benjamin Miller calls "cold war" or what Alexander George labels "precarious peace" and "conditional peace."[12] In a precarious peace, the parties reach a temporary, possibly extended absence of hot war due to deterrence or the short-term inability of one or both parties to gain through active hostilities. In a conditional peace, because of general deterrence or conflict management, active hostilities are less likely, except during crises. Neither party views the use of force as illegitimate; therefore, war can recur whenever one side believes it has an advantage.

In some instances, however, rivals proceed from conflict management to peacemaking in which they seek a peace treaty with the goal of terminating the conflict and putting bilateral relations on a different footing. A peace treaty might not resolve the underlying differences between the rivals but merely achieve a politically acceptable compromise for the medium to long term and, more important, rule out violence as a legitimate recourse for either party. Instead, such a settlement might spell out political or diplomatic steps that need to be taken to resolve the conflict completely. The 1979 Egyptian-Israeli peace treaty, under which the parties not only foreswore the use of force but agreed to seek a broader comprehensive peace treaty between Israel and the Arab states and required satisfactory Israeli treatment of the Palestinian people, is a good example. Under these circumstances, the conflict might not be fully resolved, but the parties move from cold war to what Miller terms "cold peace." War is not likely in the foreseeable future, but it remains conceivable if underlying disagreements are not resolved and societal hostility were to boil over.

The ultimate state of peacemaking occurs when a treaty or its aftermath transforms bilateral relations by resolving the underlying dispute and eliminating societal antagonisms between the former rivals. The 1990 Treaty on a Final Settlement with Respect to Germany, in which Germany renounced all claims to territory east of the Oder-Neisse line, thereby resolving any residual conflict with Poland, provides a good example. The parties may then go on to develop what George terms "stable peace," in which neither party has any interest or desire to consider the use of force against the other. Stable peace encompasses both Miller's "normal peace" and "warm peace." In the former, the parties no longer harbor antagonism for each other but do not build a positive, cooperative future together. In the latter, the former rivals move from conflict to cooperation by enmeshing themselves in cooperative institutions and engaging in economic and security cooperation together.[13]

Any movement away from active hostilities to conflict management, cold peace, or stable peace is constructive and desirable. Even if all that can be achieved is conflict management, that still can yield important goals, such as the short-term prevention of war, a reduced risk of conflict spreading to other states, and a reduction in human casualties on all sides. Moreover, stabilizing the conflict may create openings for peacemaking.[14] In this book, however, I focus on peacemaking itself or the negotiation of a peace treaty (or its equivalent) that begins either a cold peace or something more stable.

The Object of Study: Peace between Regional Rivals

The purpose of this book is to determine what brings about peace between states that are regional rivals, a subject of great importance. These rivalries are among the most intense international rivalries because geographic proximity increases points of dispute and raises the stakes of conflict, given the ease of power projection and the intensity of the security dilemmas vis-à-vis proximate states. Indeed, these rivalries typically involve core territory for one or both parties. Therefore, they may be more difficult to resolve than geographically dispersed rivalries. In this regard, even long-standing great power rivalries, such as the Soviet-American rivalry, which did not escalate beyond proxy wars and did not threaten either superpower's core national territory, typically do not match the fury of a regional rivalry. Consequently, the causes of the termination of less intense rivalries may not be a good guide for more intense rivalries such as the Arab-Israeli, the Franco-German, or the Sino-Japanese ones. The strategies that could de-escalate the more intense regional rivalries, however, should be able to gain traction over less intense rivalries, as well. Therefore, it makes sense analytically to concentrate on rivalries between regional states.[15]

A few caveats are in order. First, although the principles of peacemaking between rival states may apply in whole or in part to the resolution of civil wars or conflicts between states and nonstate actors, there is no reason a priori to assume so. These phenomena may be analytically distinct and subject to different logics.[16] After all, in intrastate wars the actors involved are of an inherently unequal character and quality, with states usually enjoying privileged status and resources. Therefore, I will restrict my analysis and any policy prescriptions that flow from it to conflicts between states. Many of the low-intensity conflicts in Africa, therefore, do not meet the criteria for inclusion in this book. Similarly, the peace agreement between Catholics and Protestants in Northern Ireland remains outside the purview of this book. Nor, due to the absence of a Palestinian state, does the Israeli-Palestinian conflict belong here. Instead, I focus on interstate rivalries, such as historical rivalries between France and Germany, Israel and Egypt, Greece and Turkey, and India and Pakistan.

Second, not all interstate rivalries are regional in nature. A region is characterized by both geographic coherence and routine geopolitical interaction in which security relations are characterized by a regional security complex that is distinctive to the region.[17] Because geographic proximity imposes a high degree of strategic interdependence on regional participants, in which the actions and strategic choices of one state affect the security of all the others, the strategic interactions between these states tend to be quite intense. Furthermore, proximity allows easy access that can increase the intensity of economic and cultural relations as well.[18] Because of these features, it is possible for outside observers to identify regions for analytical purposes, even if some regional participants would not identify themselves as belonging to such a region.[19] Thus, for example, we can talk meaningfully about a Middle East region that includes both Israel and the Arab states, because their security complex is dominated by the Arab-Israeli conflict, even if some Arab regimes would reject the notion of a Middle East region that includes Israel and some scholars would as well.[20] In this book, my understanding of region is very conventional, addressing rivalries in well-established regions, such as Western Europe, the Middle East, South America, East Asia, and others.

Although some scholars include geographically removed great powers that participate in a region's security affairs as members of the region—such as the United States as a member of the Western European or Asian security orders—I reject that approach as being at odds with the commonsense geographic understanding of the concept of "regions."[21] External great powers can play important roles in regional security dynamics, but they do so as extraregional actors, without the same intensity of interactions that geographic propinquity brings. Consequently, rivalries between the United States and North Korea or China do not constitute regional rivalries.

Finally, this book examines regional rivalries that terminate in peace settlements or formal peace treaties between the belligerents. Unlike Johan Galtung, who distinguishes between positive and negative peace, however, I do not make normative judgments about the content of the peace settlement.[22] The purpose of my research is to determine what makes peace settlements possible—whatever peace terms are negotiated and accepted by the rivals, regardless of whether these terms are truly fair and just. Although I do consider what leads these settlements themselves to vary in quality after treaties are signed, at least in terms of their stability and likely endurance, my focus here is not exclusively on settlements that completely eliminate bilateral competition and lead to warm relationships between former rivals. Consequently, the dependent variable of this study differs from those of Kupchan, who focuses on lasting peace in which rivals completely transform their relationships into a postconflict friendship, or of Emanuel Adler and Michael Barnett, whose object of inquiry is the development of pluralistic security communities that completely transform the identities of the participants.[23]

Building on George, Miller, Kenneth Boulding, and Arie Kacowicz, though, I am also interested in variations in the postsettlement relations between former rivals.[24] In particular, I explore the factors that lead some peace treaties to remain temporary realpolitik peaces of convenience and others to develop into stable peace settlements that are routinely respected and not challenged by either of the former combatants.

Case Selection

The object of inquiry in this book is peace agreements between regional rivals. To investigate this, I engage in detailed primary and secondary source case studies of highly salient cases of peace settlements (treaties or their functional equivalents) between regional antagonists to determine their causes and the sources of variation in their postagreement stability. Focusing on successful cases only was a deliberate choice, despite the injunction

7

from methodologists not to select on the dependent variable.[25] After all, scholars have noted that in small-N case studies seeking to uncover necessary conditions (or to determine which variables are not necessary or sufficient) or those seeking a heuristic device to discover potential causal paths, selection on the dependent variable is entirely appropriate.[26] Moreover, as scholars in the field of artificial intelligence have observed, with certain types of problems there are distinct learning advantages to single-class concept learning—that is, learning a concept by studying solely positive examples and generalizing from them. In a study of helicopter gearbox failure, for example, Nathalie Japkowicz judged that more can be learned efficiently by studying only the positive class (properly functioning gearboxes) than by studying both positive and negative classes. For, while gearboxes, when they work properly, tend to operate in a similar manner, they may fail in many different ways. Therefore, learning from counterexamples will tell us very little about the entire class of broken gearboxes and should not allow us to make useful generalizations.[27] By the same token, learning from examples of failed economic sanctions or failed peace negotiations may similarly make it difficult to generalize meaningfully about the necessary conditions for sanctions or negotiations to succeed. In this book, therefore, I focus on regional rivals that successfully negotiated peace treaties, based on the expectation that successful treaties may share basic commonalities, whereas failed agreements may fail for a multiplicity of reasons.

Of course, to be certain that this choice does not bias my study, the next phase of my research, which I have already begun to investigate, involves an analysis of near misses: peace negotiations between regional rivals that appeared promising but failed to result in peace treaties. Key cases I am currently investigating include negotiations between Israel and Syria in 1993 and 1999 and between India and Pakistan in 1999, as well as an analysis of the much larger universe of twentieth-century cases of failed negotiations between regional rivals. To include these negative cases in this book would make the book too long and might bias the findings, as these might not be prototypical failures. Therefore, I leave discussion of them for the next step of my research—a comprehensive treatment of failed negotiations—and focus here on a comprehensive treatment of successful twentieth-century peace treaties between regional rivals.

My strategy for case selection was as follows. To begin with, I used research by Paul Diehl and Gary Goertz to identify the universe of enduring rivals in the twentieth century (at least until 1992) and the end dates for those rivalries.[28] I restricted myself to twentieth-century cases for two reasons. First, to categorize peace settlements as successful, I required the treaties to have endured initially for at least ten years without a relapse into conflict.[29] Therefore, the cutoff date for the inclusion of a rivalry as a potential case was rivalry termination before 1999, since I began this research in

2009. Second, I opted not to examine rivalries that terminated before the twentieth century, since much of the data for investigation of bottom-up theories—such as public opinion polls and trade data—is not available for these periods.[30] Similarly, since comparatively few international institutions existed before the twentieth century, these cases would not be fair tests of the constructivist institutionalist approach. I began, therefore, with a list of fifty-five twentieth-century rivalries.

Enduring Rivalries between 1900 and 1992

Those marked with an asterisk (*) are geographically removed dyads; † are dyads with large power discrepancies; ‡ are dyads not properly understood as "regional" rivals—i.e., not participants in a regional security complex; and boldface indicates regional rivalries that terminated in peace treaties in the twentieth century.

USA-Cuba	1959–90†
USA-Ecuador	1952–81†‡
USA-Peru	1955–92
USA-USSR	1946–86*‡
USA-China	1949–72*†‡
USA-N. Korea	1950–85*†‡
Honduras-Nicaragua	1907–29
Ecuador-Peru	**1891–1955**
Chile-Argentina	1952–84
UK-Germany	1887–1921
UK-Russia	1876–1923*‡
UK-USSR	1939–85*†‡
UK-Turkey	1895–1934*‡
UK-Iraq	1958–92*†‡
Belgium-Germany	1914–40
France-Germany	**1911–45**
France-Turkey	1897–1938*‡
Spain-Morocco	1957–80‡
Germany-Italy	1914–45
Italy-Yugoslavia	**1923–43**
Italy-Ethiopia	1923–43‡
Italy-Turkey	1880–1924‡
Bulgaria-Yugoslavia	**1913–52**
Greece-Bulgaria	1914–52
Greece-Turkey	1958–89
Cyprus-Turkey	1965–88†
USSR-Norway	1956–87†
USSR-Iran	1908–87†

Russia-Turkey	**1876–1921**
Russia/USSR-China	1862–1986
Russia/USSR-Japan	1895–1984‡
Congo-Brazzaville-Zaire	1963–87
Uganda-Kenya	1965–89
Ethiopia- Somalia	**1960–85**
Ethiopia-Sudan	1967–88
Morocco-Algeria	1962–84
Iran-Iraq	1953–92
Iraq-Israel	1967–91
Iraq-Kuwait	1961–92†
Egypt-Israel	**1948–79**
Syria-Jordan	1949–91
Syria-Israel	1948–86
Israel-Jordan	**1948–73**
Israel-S. Arabia	1957–81
S. Arabia-N. Yemen	1962–84
Afghanistan-Pakistan	1949–89
China-S. Korea	1950–87†
China-Japan	**1873–1958**
China-India	1950–87
N. Korea-S. Korea	1949–92
S. Korea-Japan	1953–82
India-Pakistan	1947–91
Thailand-Cambodia	1953–87
Thailand-Laos	1960–88
Thailand-N. Vietnam	1961–89

Because my focus here is on regional rivals, I first removed from this list all dyads that are geographically remote from each other (indicated by an asterisk in the above list). For example, while the United States and the Soviet Union during the Cold War could be considered "enduring rivals," by no stretch of the imagination could they be classified as "regional rivals." Next I removed dyads with considerable power disparities (indicated by †), defined in terms of aggregate military and economic capabilities, since my focus is on rivals with roughly equal power capabilities.[31] In unequal rivals, in which one party is substantially more powerful than the other, the likelihood of recurring war is considerably lower, since— barring outside intervention—war would probably lead to complete victory by the stronger state, which would simply be able to impose its preferred terms on its adversary. Moreover, such rivalries are typically not as intense, as the weaker party has every incentive to avoid a direct confrontation.[32] Thus, the rivalry between the United States and Cuba, while persistent, is not as potentially explosive as those between India and Pakistan or between Greece and Turkey, where the rivals are more evenly matched.[33]

I subsequently removed all dyads that, though geographically proximate, are not conventionally understood as belonging to the same region, in that they belong to different geographical entities and do not participate in a common regional security complex (indicated by ‡).[34] Thus, for example, Spain and Morocco, though very close geographically, are not participants in a coherent common region and, instead, are better understood as participants in distinct Western European and North African security complexes, respectively. This reduces the list further to thirty-three rivalries.

Finally, I disqualified all rivalries that were not resolved through treaties or their equivalents that were freely negotiated by the two adversaries before 1999. Given that Diehl and Goertz's list, which I use as my starting point, enumerates enduring rivalries that cease to be contested intensely, many of their cases do not terminate in peace—the phenomenon that I am interested in. (The regional rivalries that terminated in peace are indicated in bold in the list above and are reproduced in the list below.) Between the first list and the second list, therefore, I eliminate all the cases of regional rivalries that did not achieve bilateral peace as indicated by the conclusion of treaties or their equivalents. In other words, I eliminate cases such as: Israel–Saudi Arabia, in which the rivalry de-escalated after a spate of Arab-Israeli wars but did not result in anything approaching peace or even official diplomatic relations; Belgium-Germany, 1940, in which the rivalry terminated with the occupation of one party by the other—hardly what is meant by "peacemaking"; and North Korea–South Korea and India-Pakistan, in which the rivalry de-escalated (at least for a time) but did not approach peace. In addition, because I am interested in treaties freely negotiated by the two rivals, rather than those imposed by the victor on the vanquished in the immediate aftermath of a war, I exclude the Anglo-German case, as that terminated as a result of the 1919 Treaty of Versailles, which was negotiated between the victorious allies in the months after the war and was merely imposed on defeated Germany.[35]

This left a list of nine rivalries (see below). Of these, I selected three particularly salient cases resulting in multiple wars between the antagonists (indicated in italics in the list below): the Franco-German, Egyptian-Israeli, and the Israeli-Jordanian rivalries. These are the cases that I examine in chapter-length depth. In each of these cases, because language skills allowed me access to archival depositories and the ability to conduct interviews with governmental officials involved in peacemaking, I have utilized both primary and secondary sources. To make certain that case selection has not biased my conclusions, I examine each of the six remaining rivalries as mini–case studies in chapter 5. As a result, in this book I explore the entire universe of twentieth-century regional rivalries that terminated with peace settlements.

Enduring Rivalries between 1900 and 1992 that Terminated
with Peace Treaties
This list includes only regional rivals that signed peace treaties before
2000. Detailed case studies are in italics; mini–case studies are in plain text.

Ecuador-Peru	1891–1955
France-Germany	*1911–45*
Bulgaria-Yugoslavia	1913–52
Italy-Yugoslavia	1923–43
Russia-Turkey	1876–1921
Ethiopia-Somalia	1960–85
Egypt-Israel	*1948–79*
Israel-Jordan	*1948–73*
China-Japan	1873–1958

Methodology

To investigate these questions, I engage in three intensive case studies, utilizing the process-tracing method to break open the black box of the state
and find out why the states involved made the decisions they did to reach a
peace treaty and how various pressures and opportunities affected their
calculations.[36] Recognizing that the most reliable means of discovering the
motives and reasoning of foreign policy executives involves unfiltered access to both the decision makers themselves and the decision-making pro-
·cess, I utilize primary sources wherever possible.[37] For the more recent case
of the Israeli-Jordanian peace treaty, where declassified documentary materials are not yet available but many negotiators and decision makers are
still available, I supplement my secondary source research with personal
interviews with Israeli and Jordanian officials involved in negotiating the
treaty, as well as with their published memoirs. In addition, I interviewed
American officials charged with the Middle East peace portfolio to gain additional leverage over the episode. For the Egyptian-Israeli treaty, which is
further back in time, I interviewed the Israeli and US officials involved in
the negotiations who were still alive and available at the time of my research, and supplemented this with a wealth of declassified materials in the
Israel State Archives, the United States National Archives, and the Jimmy
Carter Presidential Library. Unfortunately, my efforts to interview Egyptian
officials were unsuccessful, and the Egyptian archives have a fifty-year de-
classification window for sensitive material such as peace negotiations with
Israel, which prevented me from accessing them. This is an important limi-
tation in that case study. Nonetheless, through secondary sources, published memoirs, and access to American and Israeli officials and documents, I have done my best to uncover the rationale for Egyptian decisions.

Finally, for the Western European settlement, which was concluded six decades ago, I consulted a broad range of documentary materials—some published, some in the Archives Nationales of France, the archives of the Ministère des Affaires Etrangères in Paris, the Public Records Office in London, the US National Archives, the Harry S Truman Presidential Library, and the Dwight D. Eisenhower Presidential Library.

In each case, I address the following sets of questions. First, what led the governments in question to make peace with their former regional rivals? To what extent did they do so because they were compelled by societal pressures, such as broad public pressure to make peace (particularly, if both rivals were democracies or were democratizing, due to a sense that common democratic principles made continued conflict inappropriate) or pressure from economic elites who stood to lose from continued conflict or to gain from a peace dividend? To what extent did they do so because of societal norms generated by membership in common regional institutions? Did territorial changes or population transfers that ameliorated what Miller calls the "state-to-nation imbalance" in the region remove hostility, making peace possible?[38] In contrast, did state-level pressures drive peacemaking? Specifically, did international imperatives, such as more pressing geopolitical threats than the traditional rival posed or pressure from the global hegemon or other interested great powers compel one or both states to negotiate peace? Did either rival face a domestic political or economic crisis that led its leaders to pursue peacemaking as a means of stabilizing their power position? Were either of the states in question new regimes whose leaders preferred to prioritize state building to ensure regime survival?

Second, I ask a series of questions about developments after the peace treaty was signed. To begin with, has there been stable peace between the signatory states since the treaty's signature, an enduring peace, or a relapse into conflict? I treat a treaty as stable if all of the following are true: (1) the two states have refrained from warfare against each other since the peace agreement; (2) neither of the governments has repudiated the treaty; (3) neither of the governments of the states in question has expressed dissatisfaction with the treaty and a desire to revise it; and (4) the bilateral relationship since the treaty has been free of high-level security crises and mutual recriminations. If the two sides have remained at peace and have not repudiated the settlement but have experienced security crises and recriminations or have expressed a desire to revise the settlement, I consider it an enduring settlement but not a stable one. Finally, if either side has repudiated the peace settlement or if the two states have used force against each other since its signature, I consider it a relapse into conflict.

I then examine what explains the stability, or lack thereof, of the settlement. If the agreement remained stable, to what extent was it because the leadership of the two states had statist reasons to maintain the settlement

13

owing to great power pressure, more pressing threats, or regime-survival/ state-building motives? Alternatively, did the states in question engage in mechanisms inspired by bottom-up theories such as democratization, bilateral economic exchange, regional international institutions, or alterations to the state-to-nation balance? To get a sense of whether the bottom-up mechanisms gained any traction, I investigate whether the rival societies embraced the peace settlement and actually overcame their hostility toward the former rival. In the event of a merely enduring settlement or a relapse into conflict, I explore whether socialization mechanisms were employed by the states in question and the degree to which statist pressures favored the continuation of peace.

Overview of the Book

Chapter 1 presents an overview of the different possible paths to peace between regional rivals. It begins with a discussion of the complexity of regional rivalries, complicated as they are by problems of insecurity, geographical proximity, and, frequently, by competing ideologies, religions, and historical grievances. It then discusses a range of liberal and constructivist theories that imply that peacemaking should be most successful as a bottom-up process when key societal actors or society as a whole embrace conflict resolution for economic, political, or normative reasons and press their political leaders to negotiate peace. It also considers Miller's state-to-nation balance theory as an additional bottom-up approach to regional peacemaking, which assumes that the creation of states for stateless nations or the reuniting of dispersed nations is necessary in order to overcome societal antagonism and make meaningful peace possible. All of these bottom-up theories assume that once societal hostility abates, the pressures for war should dissipate; therefore, once a settlement is reached, it should be relatively stable.

It then examines a number of realist and statist theories that suggest that peacemaking should actually begin when states and their leaders recognize that their geostrategic interests or their personal interests in maintaining power and building viable state apparatuses require them to resolve their rivalry, even if society remains hostile. Because societal animosity remains, however, top-down approaches do not expect the settlements to be stable. If statist motivations were to change or if the regimes were to be replaced by one more responsive to society, security competition and war would likely re-emerge.

The chapter then presents my own hypothesis that peacemaking occurs due to statist motivations, both realist and state/regime survival varieties, but that the stability of peace agreements will depend on the degree to which the treaty achieves societal buy-in in the postagreement phase as a result of the use of liberal and constructivist mechanisms. In other words, peacemaking should be top-down, but the sources of stability should depend on mechanisms derived from bottom-up approaches.[39]

To test the competing arguments, chapters 2 through 4 present the in-depth primary-source case studies. Chapter 2 examines the Franco-German settlement after World War II. This chapter begins with a focus on the reasons for the signature of the October 1954 Paris Agreement, which functioned as a peace treaty between the Three Powers (Great Britain, France, and the United States) and the Federal Republic of Germany (FRG), as it replaced the occupation statute and put inter-Allied relations with Germany on a contractual basis. It then evaluates how the agreement has fared since 1954, considering the degree to which societal or statist mechanisms can explain its endurance and the deepening of bilateral relations between France and the FRG, which developed into a stable peace. Overall, this case serves as the paradigmatic case for my argument, with a top-down transition driven by the Soviet threat, US hegemonic engagement, and German and French state/regime survival motives followed by successful economic, institutional, and grievance-reducing strategies to socialize the conflict in the postagreement era.

The Egyptian-Israeli peace treaty of 1979 is the focus of chapter 3. The first part of the chapter examines whether societal or statist strategies and motivations inspired the treaty between these longstanding enemies. The second part examines why the agreement has endured but has not become a stable peace. It concludes that the treaty was motivated by a statist logic, principally the need of both parties to secure US military and economic assistance—as well as to respond to American coaxing and pressure—and Egyptian president Anwar Sadat's urgent need to alleviate domestic economic and political pressures that threatened to topple him from power. Unlike in the Western European case, however, the treaty was never socialized with the help of democratization, international institutions, the generation of extensive bilateral economic interaction, or the elimination of the state-to-nation imbalance. Consequently, while the treaty has endured for statist reasons, it remains fundamentally unstable.

Chapter 4 investigates the Israeli-Jordanian peace treaty of 1994. Once again, the parties engaged in peacemaking because of statist pressures: both Israel and Jordan faced greater regional threats than their traditional rival; Jordan encountered immense pressure to restore its relationship with Washington after it adopted a policy of neutrality during the 1991 Gulf War, and King Hussein needed US economic assistance in order to help him cope with threats to his hold on power. The postagreement phase in this case is similar to that in the Egyptian-Israeli case. Although there was somewhat more bilateral economic exchange between Israel and Jordan than between Egypt and Israel, it was negligible. In this case, too, no serious efforts have been made to entrench the peace treaty through economic, institutional, or grievance-reducing strategies. As a result, this treaty, too, has yielded a peace settlement that is far from stable but endures because the two states continue to have top-down reasons to adhere to it.

To make certain that my findings are not merely an artifact of case selection, in chapter 5 I provide case overviews of all the remaining instances of regional rivalries that terminated in peace treaties during the twentieth century. Specifically, the chapter examines the settlements between Ecuador and Peru (1998); Italy and Yugoslavia (1954); Bulgaria and Yugoslavia (1952); Russia and Turkey (1921); Ethiopia and Somalia (1988); and China and Japan (1978). By and large, these settlements follow the same pattern. In all cases, statist factors were the most significant motivators of peace, whether it was the emergence of greater threats, great power pressures, regime survival/state-building imperatives, or a combination of these. In only one case (China-Japan) were bottom-up pressures—namely, pressure from business communities that expected gains as a result of peace—at all consequential in the transition, but they played only a supporting role, insufficient to motivate a treaty without significant top-down imperatives pointing in the same direction. The postagreement experiences of these six dyads also conformed to the same pattern. Only three of these agreements were cemented with bottom-up strategies to bring the rival societies on board: the Ecuador-Peru settlement, the Italy-Yugoslavia agreement, and the twenty-first century successors to the Bulgaria-Yugoslavia settlement (Bulgaria and Macedonia), which benefitted (in the latter two cases only after the breakup of Yugoslavia) from the development of joint democracy, bilateral economic exchange, and cooperative regional institutions (or at least the early stages thereof). These peace settlements have developed into stable agreements that meet the four criteria for stability outlined above. The remaining agreements, which did not employ societal strategies to any significant extent, either continue to endure in the absence of stability—that is, in the face of mutual recriminations and /or crises—for statist reasons (e.g., the Sino-Japanese treaty) or collapsed when the statist incentives for peace eroded (e.g., the Russo-Turkish settlement).

Finally, the concluding chapter cumulates the case study results and considers their implications. It begins with the observation that realist and statist motives for peacemaking factored into the transition to peace in all nine of the cases examined in this book, whereas bottom-up mechanisms mattered in only one case (the Sino-Japanese settlement) and only in a supporting role. At the same time, because the statist motivations for peacemaking diminished after the treaties were concluded in three of the four stable relationships, top-down logics are unable to explain why the peace settlements that have endured without high-level crises, recriminations, or attempts to revise them enjoyed their stability. Instead, the stable agreements are the only ones that were entrenched societally, with strategies derived from bottom-up approaches. In contrast, the remaining settlements had little or no attempts to socialize the treaties with mechanisms derived from bottom-up theories. Some of these settlements, such as the two Arab-Israeli treaties, continue to hold because the states in question continue to face realist and state survival motives to adhere to them. Others, such as the Russo-Turkish settlement, simply unraveled once the interests of one or more of the signatories changed.

The empirical findings are, therefore, more consistent with my staged approach to regional peacemaking than with either the top-down or bottom-up approaches. The top-down nature of all the transitions to a peace treaty is inconsistent with bottom-up theories. Yet the importance of societal buy-in during the postagreement period is difficult to square with a purely top-down approach. I therefore consider the theoretical implications of these findings, focusing on the utility of multiparadigmatic approaches to international relations. In addition, I discuss how this multistage theory of regional peacemaking presents problems for existing theories of war. After all, if war is caused by international structural dynamics, why is it necessary to resolve societal differences to ensure a stable peace? Alternatively, if war is societal in nature, why must it be resolved with international pressures on states and other statist calculations? To this end, I briefly develop the underlying multistaged theory of war that captures the nature of regional rivalries. This theory begins with the standard realist assumption that war is initially caused by anarchy and insecurity but acknowledges that war can lead to societal hostility that outlasts systemic conditions and develops a dynamic of its own. As a result, without efforts to engage the belligerent societies, changing systemic incentives will have little impact on the underlying rivalry.

Finally, I explore the policy relevance of my findings. In particular, I focus on the importance of well-institutionalized states to promote and institutionalize peace settlements and the consequent difficulty of peacemaking in regions such as sub-Saharan Africa, which lacks strong states; the importance of state autonomy to insulate peacemaking states from societal opposition; the utility of secrecy when negotiating peace, as well as the difficulty of secrecy in the twenty-first century; the importance of selecting opportune moments for promoting peacemaking; and the risks of employing a societal strategy before a peace agreement is reached.

CHAPTER 1

Regional Stabilization in International Relations Theory

Regional conflicts are typically the most intractable of the enduring rivalries.[1] Geographical proximity, which—barring the defeat of one of the parties—ensures that the rivals will continue to interact with each other and will likely be able to project power against each other's core interests, heightens the intensity of the conflict. Consequently, while geographical distance makes recurring conflict between Great Britain and Argentina unlikely, making the Falklands War a unique event, the barriers to war between neighboring Israel and Syria or India and Pakistan are much lower. Furthermore, whereas great power rivalries often involve clashes over interests but not core territory, regional rivalries frequently feature competition over scarce territory that heightens the zero-sum nature of these conflicts. Thus, competition between Great Britain and Russia over colonial territories in the nineteenth century never reached the same degree of hostility as the conflict between France and Germany over the disputed provinces of Alsace and Lorraine. Similarly, the Cold War rivalry between the Soviet Union and the United States never escalated to a hot war, not only because of the deterrent effect of nuclear weapons, but also because the superpowers were located a vast distance from each other and clashed only over territory, such as Cuba, Berlin, or Korea, that was not part of their core national land; in contrast, India and Pakistan waged multiple wars over Kashmir, whose disputed status conspires against efforts to resolve bilateral tensions.

Furthermore, regional rivalries often are exacerbated by incompatible ideological visions for the region or competing aspirations for regional hegemony. This is especially the case when at least one of the rivals is a revolutionary power.[2] Under these circumstances, the consequences of defeat involve compromising deeply cherished ideological or religious values, which increases the stakes exponentially. In this manner, the Shiite revolution in Iran in 1979 intensified the rivalry between Iran and Iraq, as Ayatollah Khomeini's ambition to export Shia Islam throughout the region constituted a mortal peril for the secular Sunni Ba'athist regime in Iraq, transforming the territorial conflict over access to the Persian Gulf into something much more intense.[3] When the states are competing for regional hegemony, such as Brazil and Argentina throughout much of the twentieth century, that similarly increases the stakes of the rivalry.[4]

Because of the nationalist, ideological, and religious nature of many of these conflicts, regional rivalries frequently filter down to the societal level and are deeply personal with high levels of antagonism between the peoples.[5] This problem intensifies as the rivalries persist, especially when they produce great death tolls on the respective populations. Thus, after three bloody wars in seventy-five years, the Franco-German rivalry grew so hostile that the majority of the French public in 1950 did not believe that France should have cordial diplomatic relations with the Federal Republic of Germany.[6] In a similar vein, after decades of intractable Arab-Israeli conflict in the Middle East, more than two-thirds of the Palestinian public in November 2000 approved of suicide bombings against Israeli civilians.[7] Furthermore, because leaders need to enlist public sympathy in order to mobilize societal resources—including manpower, tax revenue, and industrial production—to prosecute wars and maintain a defense posture in peacetime sufficient to deter rival gains, they often stoke public hatred of the adversary.[8]

Given the bitterness of entrenched regional rivalries, conflict resolution is an enormously difficult undertaking. In this chapter, I will consider the approaches to regional conflict resolution suggested by the international relations literature, with a particular emphasis on the levels of analysis at which they operate—namely, whether they expect regional peacemaking to begin with changes in state behavior or with changes in societal attitudes.

Contending Theoretical Approaches to Regional Stabilization

Are societies the engines of regional peacemaking, or are they obstacles to international reconciliation? On the one hand, we might expect peacemaking to require attitudinal change in the rival societies that overcomes entrenched mutual hatred and compels the belligerent states to resolve the bilateral conflict. If so, the way to foster peace would be to engage key societal elites, interest groups, and the public at large over time to generate internal pressure on the states to terminate the conflict. On the other hand, we might expect that societal hatred between enemy states might be so intense, especially if it has been nourished over generations, that it might stand in the way of peacemaking, as leaders who are willing to compromise with the adversary may be treated as traitors. Consequently, it might require forward-thinking state leaders to take the first steps toward peacemaking, perhaps outside the public purview, and bring society on board afterward.

In that case, the path toward peace for belligerent states and interested third parties would lie in contacts between rival governments, bypassing societal actors. To foster peacemaking, therefore, the key would be to create incentives for the states to negotiate with each other in good faith even if domestic attitudes are recalcitrant.

Which of these two approaches is the more useful model of peacemaking between regional rivals? In other words, borrowing from I. William Zartman, does peacemaking require dialogue between hostile societies or negotiations between rival states?[9] This section explores the theoretical underpinnings of these two distinct causal paths in international relations theory, which itself has confronted this levels-of-analysis problem—that is, whether foreign policy choices and international outcomes are the products of external pressures, domestic factors, or some combination of the two—for decades.[10]

BOTTOM-UP APPROACHES

Bottom-up approaches to peacemaking seek to make the societies of the belligerent states the engines of conflict resolution, in the conviction that they can rein in their governments and restrain conflict if they are motivated to do so. To this end, they consist of strategies to create vested interests in the rival societies that favor compromise and conflict resolution, to foster societal norms that eschew conflict, to promote political institutions that facilitate societal control over government, and to resolve underlying societal conflicts by diffusing ethnonationalist grievances. In this regard, they are inspired by liberal theories of cooperation that emphasize interests and institutions and by constructivist theories that highlight the role of societal norms, among others. This section explores four theories that help inform this bottom-up societal approach to regional peacemaking: democratic peace theory, commercial liberalism, constructivist institutionalism, and Benjamin Miller's state-to-nation balance theory.

Democratic Institutions and Norms. An implication of democratic peace theory is that changes to domestic political institutions may inspire regional cooperation. The theory posits that democratic states are unlikely to wage war against other democracies for both institutional and normative reasons.[11] Democratic political institutions allow public scrutiny of and input into decisions of war and peace. Because the people, rather than their leaders, bear the costs of war—in terms of higher taxes to fund the war effort, service in the national military, and privations such as wartime rationing—they are unwilling to accept those costs lightly and, consequently, are reluctant to use force against other democracies, which they perceive both as more legitimate than nondemocracies and as less likely to use force against them. They will, consequently, discourage their governments from waging war against other democracies. Moreover, by requiring leaders to mobilize public and legislative support for war, these institutions slow down the resort to force and create time for the peaceful resolution of disputes. Whereas nondemocracies may abuse this inflexibility to achieve a military advantage through extra preparations or striking first, other democratic states are more likely to use this extra time to resolve the conflict without war.[12]

Democratic states also share political norms encouraging peaceful relations with each other. They are founded on the premise that individuals ought to be free to pursue their self-interests without undue coercion. They consequently reject coercion as a legitimate means of securing consent from other states that allow their people to manifest their will freely (i.e., other democracies). Furthermore, their shared liberal ideology leads democracies to view each other as compatible rather than as rivals. Thus, they consciously refrain from violent conflict with each other.[13]

Democratic peace theory suggests, then, that former rivals should be able to achieve stability and cooperation if they both democratize.[14] Outside actors, such as great powers and international institutions, could best promote regional peacemaking by helping to spread democracy throughout the region, making war less likely between regional participants. Using this logic, President Bill Clinton pursued a national security strategy of enlargement after the Cold War to expand the global zone of peace by spreading democracy to states beyond the democracy-rich regions of North America, Western Europe, and Oceania.[15]

To test whether the logic of public pressure within democracies motivated peacemaking, I address the following sequence of questions in my detailed case studies. First, were both rivals democracies, or did they at least allow significant public input into the policy process at the time of the treaty? To investigate this, I begin by consulting the Polity IV database 0–10 "democracy" score, treating any state with values of 8 or higher as democratic.[16] For states with lower scores, I investigate the nature of the regime and the conduct of foreign policy making within it to make a qualitative judgment about the degree to which the public was consulted on matters of war and peace. Second, I examine whether public opinion in both states favored making peace and expressed willingness to make concessions to reach an agreement. Because public opinion polls are not available for all the states I examine in this book, nor for all time periods, and because the questions asked where they are available are not consistent either within or across cases, I do not evaluate public attitudes with a clear-cut quantitative threshold. Instead, I use whatever public opinion polls exist and are available, together with other indicators of public attitudes—such as protests against the treaty and secondary accounts of public attitudes—to reach a qualitative judgment of the public mood. Third, I explore whether the publics of both states actually compelled their governments to negotiate peace.

This I determine with causal analyses of the states' decisions to make peace. To test whether democratic institutions were used to stabilize the treaty after it was signed, I use the Polity IV democracy scale to determine whether either of the parties democratized in the postsettlement era, as well as indicators of public attitudes toward the former enemy similar to those described above.

Economic Incentives. Commercial liberals suggest an economic path to stabilizing regional conflicts. They argue that high levels of trade and investment between states engender economic interdependence between them. Heavily interdependent states are less likely to resort to force to resolve disputes for two reasons.[17] First, when interdependence is high, states face considerable opportunity costs associated with the use force in terms of trade and investment forgone. After all, they can expect economic relations between belligerents to be drastically curtailed, while other interested states and international investors may reduce their economic exposure to the conflict zone.[18] Second, when trade and investment flow freely across national borders, trade becomes a more efficient means of securing resources from a territory than conquest, which involves the costs of mobilization, war itself, and occupation afterward. Under these circumstances, states will have fewer reasons to use force. The losses associated with war would accrue to business interests in interdependent countries that are most vulnerable to the economic costs of war, which, in turn, makes them pressure their governments for restraint. Therefore, it stands to reason that extending economic relations between military rivals can create a vested transnational interest group that will pressure both sides to resolve their conflicts peacefully.[19] In this regard, a significant component of the Association of Southeast Asian Nations (ASEAN) and Mercado Commun del Cono del Sur (Mercosur) regional trade agreements was the expectation that the economic ties they would engender would help keep the peace among regional members.[20]

Moreover, even the prospects of gains should generate pressures for settlement. After all, if business elites in belligerent countries were to expect significant economic gains as a result of expanded trade and investment opportunities following a peace treaty, they would be motivated to lobby their governments to make peace.[21] It follows, therefore, that third parties could promote regional peacemaking by fostering economic ties between regional rivals, as well as by promising considerable investment in the region as a reward for the signature of a peace treaty.[22]

It is important to note, though, that for economic considerations to be considered "bottom-up" mechanisms, they must filter through the business sector of society. Therefore, not all economic considerations are societal. As we shall see, if the prospect of economic payoffs, such as foreign aid or debt forgiveness, motivates state actors—without significant pressure from business elites—because of their need for economic resources to achieve statist purposes, such as building or strengthening the institutions of the state or maintaining military preparedness, that should properly be considered a statist or "top-down" motivation rather than a societal one. If the business community is the key transmission belt for an economically motivated peace, though, that would be properly classified as a bottom-up imperative.

To test the commercial liberal path to peace, I ask the following sequence of questions. First, is there evidence that the economies of the two rivals were meaningfully interdependent before the peace treaty? This I investigate using International Monetary Fund (IMF) data on bilateral trade and GDP. If at least one country generates 1.5% or more of its GDP in exports to the rival or if both countries produce at least 1% of their GDP through these exports the year that the treaty was concluded, I consider that vested economic interests in peace existed at the time of the treaty. Alternatively, is there evidence that business interests in the rival states anticipated meaningful economic gains as a result of a peace settlement? This I investigate by scouring the primary and secondary sources to explore the nature of the two economies, the prospects for bilateral gains, and the expectations of the business communities, yielding a qualitative judgment. Second, did the business groups lobby their governments to make peace in order to realize these gains or protect their vested economic interests? This, again, I investigate with causal analyses of the states' decisions to make peace. To test whether economic interdependence was used as a strategy to stabilize the settlement after it was reached, I use the IMF data to determine whether the joint "exports exceeding 1% of GDP" or one state exceeding 2% of GDP with bilateral exports was achieved and sustained in the postsettlement era, as well as (for the in-depth case studies) other indicators of the bilateral economic relationship.[23]

Institutional Norms and Identities. The constructivist emphasis on ideas and identities offers another bottom-up approach to regional peacemaking. Constructivists argue that societies are shaped by the ideas and institutions that help forge their identities. To the extent that states and societies become embedded in cooperative international institutions, they begin to view conflict, and each other, differently. In particular, these institutions inspire a collective identity or "we feeling" that permeates the societies of all member states, fostering cooperation and tolerance of the other.[24] The result is a shift from a Hobbesian order, based on conflict and competition, to a Lockean or Kantian order, based on shared rules and values.[25] Consequently, conflictual behavior becomes anathema to society and the leaders they select. Therefore, creating powerful regional institutions with adversarial states as members can stabilize conflict between them.[26] In this regard, Cameron Thies argues that the Economic Community of West African

States (ECOWAS) and its Ceasefire Monitoring Group (ECOMOG) helped forge a Lockean order of negative peace in West Africa.[27]

According to Emanuel Adler and Michael Barnett, institutional paths to peace are most effective if the three societal mechanisms discussed work together—that is, if regional institutions together with democratization and the generation of economic interdependence create a pluralistic security community that ties national identity to membership in the group, making conflict unthinkable.[28] Their conclusion is similar to that of Bruce Russett and John Oneal, who argue that these three liberal mechanisms combine to create a powerful disincentive to the use of force.[29] Others suggest that a smaller degree of overlap may be sufficient. In the case of ASEAN states, for example, Amitav Acharya contends that a security community might be possible without democratization being necessary.[30] Edward Mansfield and Jon Pevehouse argue that preferential trading arrangements, which institutionalize commercial ties, can facilitate peaceful conflict resolution even more than bilateral exchange alone.[31] Consequently, layering bottom-up mechanisms may strengthen their effect as promoters of peace.

To examine whether constructivist institutionalism explains a particular settlement, I ask the following sequence of questions. First, were the two states jointly members of the same cohesive cooperative regional institutions before the treaty was negotiated? This I determine by investigating which, if any, regional institutions these states belonged to, whether there was any overlap in their memberships (i.e., were they both members of any of the same institutions) and whether the international relations literature views those as well institutionalized and cohesive. Second, is there evidence that the two societies developed common identities as a result of these institutions? To this end, I utilize many of the same sources on public attitudes that I use to investigate the democratic peacemaking possibility. Finally, is there evidence that their common identities actually inspired the peace negotiations and the treaty? I investigate this with causal analyses of the states' decisions to make peace to see whether common identities and beliefs that it was illegitimate to wage war against a member of the same regional community affected the decision to make peace. To test whether cooperative regional institutions were used to stabilize the settlement, I examine whether the states joined cohesive regional institutions together in the years after the treaty was signed.

State-to-Nation Congruence. Benjamin Miller offers a fourth possible bottom-up path to regional peace.[32] Miller argues that the sources of regional war and peace are societal. War is likely to occur when a single state contains many nations, which can lead to secessionist conflict, or when a single nation is spread across many states, which can lead to irredentist wars. Therefore, the key to successful peacemaking should be to resolve the state-to-nation imbalance, which will defuse the societal conflict. This can be done by creating new states for stateless groups or with territorial or population transfers to unite dispersed ethnic groups and make state borders congruent with national realities.[33] A similar logic underlay Woodrow Wilson's conviction that applying the principle of national self-determination for all peoples would help to stabilize Europe after World War I.[34] Miller argues, however, that in the absence of a fair state-to-nation balance, it is possible for the great powers to compel incongruent states to reach a cold peace even without resolving the underlying conflict. Therefore, Miller's is not a purely bottom-up approach, although his focus on societal pressures as the underlying cause makes it useful to characterize him in that way.

I ask the following questions to evaluate Miller's explanation of regional peacemaking in my case studies. First, were any new states created, or did significant population transfers or territorial transfers occur that either granted self-determination to a stateless minority or united an ethnic group with its brethren before the peace treaty? This I do with a historical survey of the period leading up to the treaty. Second, did this political or demographic change resolve the state-to-nation imbalance by making state borders congruent with the distribution of the ethnic population? To determine this, I investigate whether significant minorities, particularly those with whom the rival state identifies, remained under the control of one of the belligerents. Third, I study the peacemaking process to determine whether improved societal attitudes resulting from ethnic grievances having been resolved led the states in question to make peace. To determine whether the state-to-nation imbalance was resolved after the treaty was signed, I follow the first two steps described above.

Each of these bottom-up approaches to peacemaking assumes that peace occurs as a result of societal pressure on the state, due to either economic, self-preservation, or moral motives. They work best, therefore, with states that allow societal input into the foreign policy process or less-autonomous states.[35] In these states, regardless of their regime type, leaders cannot enact or implement policy without sufficient domestic consent; thus they must defer to societal wishes—or at least the preferences of politically significant segments of society—at least some of the time. As a result, when society clearly asserts a preference for peacemaking, its demands can be expected to be politically consequential. In contrast, in more autonomous states, which insulate the national security executive from societal pressures, as well as in states that have the capacity to silence opposition through coercion or side payments, societal pressures generated through bottom-up strategies are less likely to restrain states absent a regime change or meaningful changes in the composition of the governing elite.[36]

With regard to the postagreement period, these bottom-up approaches would expect that once societal attitudes are changed and their mutual hostility is overcome the peace settlement is likely to endure. This is especially the case if the states and societies in question continue to reinforce their peace settlement within political institutions, both domestic (i.e., democracies) and regional and with extensive bilateral economic exchange. Under these circumstances, the societies of the former rivals will have resolved their grievances and overcome their animosity. Therefore, they will continue to face powerful incentives to remain at peace.

TOP-DOWN APPROACHES

In contrast, top-down approaches view the state, rather than society, as the engine of peacemaking. In general, classical realists viewed the public (in democracies, but certainly in other regimes, as well) as rather unsophisticated and uninterested in foreign policy.[37] Once they get stirred up in a nationalistic war effort, however, their passions rarely give way to moderation and the spirit of compromise. Consequently, realists such as Walter Lippmann and Reinhold Niebuhr believed that the public was more resentful of the enemy than the state, which is too pragmatic to hold grudges, and that the state is more likely than society to bury the hatchet if its interests require it, often over societal objections.[38] It may do so for several reasons. In accordance with realist theory, states may be compelled to make peace by the great powers or by the need to balance against a more threatening adversary. Alternatively, they may be persuaded by reassurance signaling that the adversary's intentions are not as threatening as initially perceived, although these signals are usually sent only if more compelling threats present themselves. Finally, state leaders might feel compelled to compromise with regional rivals if they believe that continuing conflict could undermine their hold on power domestically. I consider each of these top-down theoretical arguments below.

Balancing against Greater Threats. Realists argue that that in the anarchic realm of international politics, where the slightest misstep can have disastrous consequences for national security, states cannot afford the luxury of either permanent alliances or permanent enmities. Instead, according to both balance-of-power theory and Stephen Walt's balance-of-threat theory, states must be prepared to bury the hatchet and align with their former enemies when they are faced with a greater threat.[39] This dynamic can operate when only one of the rivals faces a more formidable threat that compels it to end the conflict, even at the cost of unsatisfactory concessions, to allow it to concentrate its strategic resources on the more pressing challenge. The likelihood of peacemaking should be greater, though, when rivals face a common threat, which presents both states with an incentive to compromise and creates psychological incentives for them to find common cause.[40] In this vein, states may be compelled toward peacemaking by external "shocks" such as a change in the regional or global distribution of power or a major war that weakens some threatening states while strengthening others.[41]

In a related dynamic, states facing too many threats—even if none of them individually poses a greater threat than the traditional rival—may also conclude that peacemaking with the traditional rival is necessary to foster a more stable security environment. This was part of the British rationale for appeasing Italy and Germany in the 1930s. Faced with threats from Japan in the Pacific, Italy in the Mediterranean, and Germany in Europe and home waters, British defense planners concluded that efforts to reduce the number of enemies the empire faced would be of the utmost importance.[42]

While neither balance-of-power theory nor balance-of-threat theory explicitly identifies any strategy for regional peacemaking, they both imply that the time should be ripe for regional peacemaking when enemy states face a common external threat of greater magnitude than the threat they pose to each other or when one of the rivals is challenged by a considerably more powerful state. In this regard, Saudi Arabia's embrace of the Arab peace initiative toward Israel can be explained in terms of the Saudi regime's growing fear of a regionally ascendant and potentially nuclear Iran, which represents more of an immediate threat to Riyadh than Israel does.[43]

To determine whether a greater-threat logic motivated peacemaking in my case studies, I ask the following sequence of questions. First, did either state (or both) view another state or group of states as a more serious threat to national security than its traditional rival? To reach this judgment, I examined the security environments of the states in question to assess objectively which states might have presented the most serious challenges. Then I read memoir literature, government documents, and secondary sources to determine how state leaders perceived their threat situations subjectively to determine whether they believed they faced greater threats. Second, did that state or states make peace primarily to focus on that greater threat and devote sufficient national resources to containing that threat? Again, I did this through primary and secondary source analysis of the states' motivations for peacemaking.

Hegemonic or Dominant Great Power Influence. Hegemonic stability theory assumes that order and peace derive from an international concentration of power rather than a balance of power. When one state possesses considerably more economic, military, and political power resources than the other states in a system of states, it can use that power to coerce the other states or provide them with selective incentives in order to induce cooperation. In this manner, the dominant state, or hegemon, increases the costs of defection and decreases the risks of cooperation for other states, thereby making peace and stability possible.[44]

To promote regional peacemaking, therefore, a hegemon can motivate states to bury the hatchet with both positive and negative measures. On the positive side of the ledger, the hegemon can provide economic and other incentives for the belligerents to cooperate and issue security guarantees to ensure that neither side is taken advantage of and given the "sucker's pay-off."[45] On the negative side, it can coerce cooperation by providing pressure on regional governments and, where appropriate, by making threats or even using economic coercion or limited force to bring the antagonists to an agreement. In this regard, US president Lyndon Johnson sought to stabilize Greco-Turkish relations in 1964 by threatening to withdraw NATO assistance to Turkey in the event of a Turkish military landing on Cyprus.[46]

In principle, a similar logic could operate in the absence of a hegemon if the great powers are united in offering both incentives and coercion to foster regional peacemaking.[47] Such a scenario is less likely to bring about peacemaking than hegemonic involvement, however, given that the belligerents could hope to play the great powers and their divergent interests off against each other for their own advantage. This may explain why the so-called Middle East Quartet—consisting of the United States, the United Nations, the European Union, and Russia—has had little success in resolving the Arab-Israeli conflict, as each of the states and institutions has its own distinct interests and visions for the shape of the final settlement.[48] If, in the absence of a hegemon, one great power nonetheless has disproportionate power and influence within the region in question, that would be the functional equivalent of hegemony for the purposes of peacemaking. In this regard, Soviet authority over Eastern Europe during the Cold War was tantamount to hegemonic control. The Soviet Union, therefore, should be considered the dominant great power for the region.

While it remains possible under the condition of unipolarity for states to cooperate without the hegemon, the range of issues over which such cooperation is possible is quite small, typically restricted to low-stakes issues—such as the trade in small arms or a convention on child soldiers—where the core interests of the hegemon are not at stake.[49] Therefore, we should expect peacemaking between regional rivals, in which the stakes are high and the need for hegemonic engagement and guarantees is paramount, to be a daunting task without the hegemon's active participation.

To test whether hegemonic or dominant great power pressure was responsible for peacemaking in my case studies, I address the following questions. First, did the United States, as global hegemon, or another great power with disproportionate influence over one or both of the rivals, attempt to encourage peacemaking by applying diplomatic pressure or threats and by offering economic and military incentives to the rivals in an effort to induce compromise? Second, did the states involved seek anticipated hegemonic or great power reactions at least as much as they sought peace with their rival for its own sake? I investigate both of these issues with primary and secondary source analysis of the peacemaking episodes and the primary motivations of the leadership of the rival states. Similarly, regarding the postpeace period, I examine whether the hegemon or a dominant great power employed coercive pressure or political, economic, and military incentives to encourage the parties to respect the settlement.

Reassurance Signaling. Charles Kupchan offers another explanation for peacemaking between former enemies that he identifies as realist.[50] Building on theories of reassurance, he argues that rivalries typically end when one state sends costly signals to its rival that its intentions are benign and that it believes that its adversary (the target) also has nonpredatory intentions.[51] These signals could include "demilitarizing contested areas, destroying fortifications, and making territorial concessions."[52] Indeed, Soviet leader Mikhail S. Gorbachev facilitated the resolution of the Cold War by signaling Moscow's benign intentions toward the United States through his willingness to accept wide-ranging nuclear arms control and his withdrawal from the Soviet Union's Eastern European empire.[53] If these costly unilateral signals are reciprocated by the other party, that can lead to a de-escalation of the conflict, which creates space for greater cooperation and Kupchan's subsequent steps toward stable peace, including reciprocal restraint, societal integration, and narrative generation and identity change.[54]

Although this approach elaborates the path through which balance-of-power pressures can lead to conflict resolution, it does not, in fact, suggest a different causal mechanism. Indeed, Kupchan acknowledges that states typically judge that it is worth taking the risk of giving costly signals when they face competing threats that are more immediate and more compelling than the target of their reassurance attempts. He observes, for example, that "the road to stable peace begins amid peril. A state facing an array of threats against which it has insufficient resources attempts to improve its strategic environment by seeking to befriend one of its adversaries."[55] Consequently, his theory is, in essence, merely a subtype of the greater-threat path to peace outlined above. For this reason, I do not test it as a separate explanation.

State-Preservation Motives. A final statist explanation of regional peacemaking, more consistent with neoclassical realism than with structural realism, would explain peacemaking in terms of other, nonsecurity related, governmental motives. Neoclassical realists contend that domestic political circumstances affect the way in which states respond to the international environment. While states—understood as the foreign policy executive or the president/prime minister/leader and the ministers and officials charged with making foreign policy and grand strategy—conduct national security policy principally with an eye on the constraints and opportunities of the international system, they must frequently temper their responses in order to secure the domestic support necessary to enact policy and mobilize societal resources to implement it.[56] As I argue elsewhere, the likelihood of domestic pressures determining foreign policy increases dramatically when the leadership believes its hold on power is slipping.[57] Under these circumstances, leaders will view national security decisions through the prism of domestic politics and do whatever they deem necessary to maintain power.

Because war frequently leads to the overthrow of the political leadership of a state through an election, revolution, or coup, leaders will be particularly sensitive to this possibility.[58] Thus, the fear of losing power might encourage leaders to make peace with former enemies in much the same way that the diversionary-war theory expects them to wage war to secure their position.[59] In particular, if a protracted, costly state of conflict has undermined the economy of a belligerent to the point that the government risks losing power, that government could be willing to terminate the conflict to engage in domestic reform and ameliorate domestic conditions (even if society favors continuing the conflict).[60] In this regard, consistent with Steven R. David's theory of "omnibalancing," when faced with the prospect of threats to the leadership's hold on power at home, leaders of rival states may settle conflicts with international rivals—even on unfavorable terms—in order to focus their resources on securing their power positions.[61] This is different from a bottom-up logic in which societal groups or the public at large demand that the government terminate the conflict, since in this case domestic opinion may actually support the conflict and oppose its termination; nonetheless, the state leadership calculates that an unpopular peace may still preserve its hold on power through the peace dividend it provides, which it can use to buy off or silence its domestic opponents.[62] The motive force for peacemaking, therefore, comes from the state itself rather than society, which opposes peacemaking.

This logic would suggest that third parties (states and international institutions) could promote peacemaking by imposing costly economic sanctions on regional rivals. Sanctions would increase the domestic economic and political instability in the belligerent countries, which could be alleviated only through peacemaking. In addition, they could sweeten the pot for beleaguered leaders by promising not only to end the sanctions but also to grant lucrative economic incentives that could be used to buy off the regime's domestic opponents once a treaty is signed.[63] As we shall see in chapters 3 and 4, the United States followed this strategy when it offered considerable economic incentives to both Egypt and Jordan in the hope of encouraging these Arab states to conclude peace treaties with Israel.

In a related but distinct logic, the leadership of newly established regimes might conclude that, absent a well-institutionalized state, the new regime may fail to gain traction and be either rejected by society or replaced by a better-organized opposition. As a result, they may prefer to resolve bilateral conflicts with traditional regional rivals in order to focus on state building as a means of entrenching the regime and their hold on power, even if rivalry termination is societally unpopular.[64] The Russian withdrawal from

World War I following the Bolshevik Revolution is an illustration of this dynamic. By implication, the task of peacemaking may be facilitated by political transitions and revolutions that bring new and poorly institutionalized leaderships to power.

To test the regime-survival/state-building explanation of peacemaking, I ask the following questions. First, is there evidence that leaders of at least one of the rivals conducted their foreign policies independently of society? This required me to examine the literature on foreign policy decision making in the rival states, as well as primary and secondary source materials on the nature of the negotiations in question. Second, did these leaders identify threats to their domestic power position that could be overcome by making peace with their rival and concentrating on domestic stability? To investigate this, I examined the nature of the state's economy at the time of the settlement, as well as indicators of public dissent, in terms of large-scale protests against the regime, coup attempts, or very low levels of support in public opinion polls. Alternatively, was either or both of the states governed by new regimes that prioritized building strong state institutions to solidify their regime and/or their power base? I address this by determining whether the states experienced a regime change in the preceding decade, as well as by analyzing primary and secondary sources to determine the leadership's political priorities. Third, is there evidence that these leaders negotiated peace in order to stabilize their regime or engage in state building, rather than for other reasons? This, too, I investigate with primary and secondary source analysis of the leaders' motivations.

All these top-down approaches share the common assumption, which I advance elsewhere, that more autonomous states are more conducive to peacemaking.[65] The more the institutions, decision-making procedures, and procedural norms of the state insulate the foreign policy executive, which is more susceptible than society to realist and statist incentives for peacemaking, from societal pressures, the more likely it is to make the unpopular compromises that are frequently necessary to achieve stable settlements. In contrast, regimes that place extensive societal checks on the foreign policy executive make it more difficult for policy makers to surmount domestic hostility to the adversary.

Of course, not only are the sources of peacemaking different for societal and statist approaches, their expectations for the postagreement environment should also differ markedly. As mentioned, bottom-up theorists would expect that because underlying societal attitudes and identities are transformed before the treaty, eliminating mutual hostility, the settlement should be fairly stable. In this regard, because societal attitudes take longer to change than state interests, an agreement built on a societal foundation should have a longer-term time horizon than one built on a confluence of statist interests.[66] In contrast, for top-down theorists, because peace treaties are products of a window of opportunity provided by a favorable constellation of state interests, and because state interests are not immutable but change over time, peace treaties should endure only as long as states maintain an active interest in preserving them. After all, great powers rise and fall, and their interests in promoting peacemaking wax and wane, threats come and go, fledgling regimes often institutionalize, and unstable regimes usually either stabilize or are overthrown. Therefore, the incentives to preserve a peace agreement should also fluctuate and should not be expected to endure.

MY HYPOTHESIS: A SEQUENCED APPROACH

To this point, I have addressed top-down and bottom-up approaches to regional peacemaking as analytically distinct. Nonetheless, it is at least theoretically possible that mechanisms of both types can together bring about the transition to peaceful cooperation between regional rivals. This is possible in two ways. One possibility is that the two mechanisms work simultaneously, in that liberal and constructivist measures can be utilized to build domestic political support for states responding to top-down imperatives to make peace. This would presume that without at least some degree of societal engagement and support the state would be unable to negotiate and sign a peace treaty. Yet societal traction would be unlikely to bring about a treaty unless there also were strong statist interests in peacemaking.

A second alternative, better represented in the theoretical literature, is that the two mechanisms need to be sequenced and used at different stages of peacemaking. In particular, peacemaking may begin for reasons of state, but once a treaty is reached for top-down reasons, societal engagement might help maintain the peace settlement. Andrew Hurrell, for example, suggests that "the early phases of regional cooperation may be the result of the existence of a common enemy or powerful hegemonic power; but that, having been thrown together, different logics may develop: the functionalist or problem-solving logic stressed by institutionalists, or the logic of community highlighted by the constructivists."[67] Kupchan similarly suggests that peacemaking that began for reasons of state expediency can end with a stable peace if there is attititudinal change in the rival societies and societal integration.[68] And, in a related argument about great power cooperation, Keohane concludes that, while hegemony may be necessary to initiate cooperation, institutions created by the hegemon are able to maintain cooperation even after hegemony has eroded.[69]

Building upon my previous work, my own hypothesis is that peacemaking begins for statist reasons but its stability depends on societal engagement through bottom-up mechanisms. In other words, for the reasons that structural and neoclassical realists advance, the transition from a regional rivalry to a peace treaty should depend on the logic of greater threats, great power pressures, and considerations of state building and regime survival. In the postagreement stage, however, whether or not the agreement will

Table 1.1 Hypothesized sources of enduring and stable peace after a treaty is concluded

	Treaty socialized	Treaty not socialized
Statist motives persist	Stable peace	Enduring peace
Statist motives erode	Stable peace	Temporary peace

become a stable agreement will depend on the ability of the states involved and other actors to socialize the agreement by democratizing the former rivals, fostering economic interdependence between them, embedding the states and their societies in broader cooperative regional institutions, and resolving any outstanding state-to-nation imbalances. If they succeed in changing societal attitudes in this manner, the rivalry will transform into a stable peace that has the potential to endure changes in government, regime, and state interests. Although it is possible for societal attitudes to sour again, they are unlikely to do so absent a war or high-level grievance, which is itself less likely, although not impossible, with a socially accepted peace agreement.

Without such a socialization process, however, the agreement may still endure if the statist logic of the settlement persists. In other words, an enduring agreement that is unstable— one characterized by the absence of war with neither government repudiating the treaty but at least one side wishing to revise the agreement and bilateral relations remaining subject to high-level crises and mutual recriminations—should be the product of a top-down peace that remains top-down in nature without significant societal engagement or societal buy-in. Finally, an agreement that has not been socialized after the fact through mechanisms derived from bottom-up approaches whose statist motivations erode will be only a temporary peace settlement that will relapse into security competition and war. This hypothesis is illustrated in table 1.1, which uses darker shading for deeper forms of peace.

Although there are numerous theories that suggest possible strategies for resolving conflicts between regional rivals, in essence these theories divide along their identification of either the state or society as the engine of peacemaking and the mechanism for preserving the peace settlement after it is concluded. In the next four chapters, I will test these three broad approaches (bottom-up, top-down, and sequenced) and their various theoretical underpinnings against the evidence of every regional rivalry that was terminated by a peace agreement in the twentieth century. After discussing the historical context of the rivalry, I will investigate for each case both the sources of the transition to a peace agreement and the evolution of the peace settlement over time. The next chapter examines the paradigmatic case of peacemaking between regional rivals, peacemaking between France and Germany after World War II.

CHAPTER 2

Franco-German Peacemaking after World War II

For centuries, Europe was a region characterized by great power competition and war. Since the inception of the sovereign-state system ushered in by the Peace of Westphalia, the great powers of Europe waged war rather routinely, with several major wars between the leading states each century. Noteworthy European wars during this period include, among other great power wars: the Anglo-Dutch Wars of 1652–74; the War of the Spanish Succession (1701–14); the War of the Quadruple Alliance (1718–20); the Seven Years' War (1756–63); the Napoleonic Wars (1796–1815); the Crimean War (1853–56); the wars of German unification (1863–71); World War I (1914–18); and World War II (1939–45).[1]

France and Germany, in particular, had an intense militarized rivalry since the wars of German unification in the second half of the nineteenth century.[2] In order to incorporate the Rhenish German states into a united Germany, Prussian chancellor Otto von Bismarck had to dislodge French control over them. The ensuing Franco-Prussian War of 1870–71, in which Prussian troops laid siege to Paris and marched through the French capital in a victory parade, as well as Bismarck's subsequent fateful decisions to require reparations payments from France and to annex the provinces of Alsace and Lorraine, sowed the seeds of a long and bitter rivalry.[3] The rapid growth of Prussian/German power following the war further heightened French insecurity, leading France to forge an anti-German alliance with Russia.[4] Intense Franco-German enmity was a contributing cause of the outbreak of World War I, as German leaders believed Germany was surrounded by hostile states with no defensive barriers to protect them. The German military establishment thus felt compelled to respond to strategic crises with military action on both fronts, west and east, in order to prevent the nightmare of an enemy invasion on both fronts.[5] The utter devastation of northeast France at German hands in World War I, followed by the rapid defeat of France and occupation of Paris by Hitler's army in World War II, only intensified the hostility of France toward its German neighbor.

Despite their long and bitter rivalry, however, in the decades following World War II, "hereditary enemies" France and West Germany, along with the region of Western Europe as a whole, managed to transcend competition and war, building a constructive security community within cooperative economic, political, and military institutions such as the European Economic Community (EEC) and its successors and the North Atlantic Treaty Organization (NATO).[6] The turning point for this relationship was the conclusion of contractual agreements between the Three Powers (the United States, Great Britain, and France) and the Federal Republic of Germany at the London and Paris conferences in September and October 1954 (the Paris Agreements), which officially ended the occupation regime and included the Federal Republic of Germany (FRG) in Western defense arrangements.[7] What explains this relatively sudden and dramatic transition of the Franco-German relationship from the quintessential militarized rivalry to the paradigmatic case of rivalry termination? This chapter will examine the ability of both top-down and bottom-up theoretical approaches to explain the transition to peace in this important case, as well as the stable aftermath of the settlement.

The Path to Transition

In this section, I focus on the causes of the transition to full-scale security cooperation in Western Europe by late 1954, following the signature of the October 1954 Paris Agreements. Although the emerging Cold War prevented a formal peace agreement between the victors of World War II (including the United States, the Soviet Union, and Great Britain) and defeated Germany, the Paris Agreements functioned as a peace treaty between the Western powers (the United States, Great Britain, and France) and the Federal Republic of Germany. Notably, this document replaced the Occupation statute with contractual arrangements, which turned the FRG from a formally occupied state to an independent state—albeit with agreed-on limits on its military apparatus and reserved powers for the Western powers in case of emergency—and initiated regional security cooperation in Western Europe with German participation. Before this agreement, the FRG was prohibited from maintaining national armed forces or participating in Western defense efforts. The Paris Agreements, however, brought West Germany into NATO, making the FRG an almost equal partner in Western European security efforts. This section, therefore, examines whether the Paris Agreements were brought about by bottom-up pressures or whether the agreements came from the top down.

BOTTOM-UP DYNAMICS

Democratic Pressures. The logic of the democratic peace theory suggests a plausible explanation of Franco-German peacemaking after World War II. Since the Three Powers established a liberal democratic regime in West Germany in 1949, both France and the FRG (and, indeed, most of the states of Western Europe) were democratic. Perhaps it was the transition of the principal powers in this troubled region to democracies that caused its pacification and stability.[8] In order to examine this claim, we must determine four things: (1) whether the creation of the FRG preceded the project of Three Power peacemaking with West Germany; (2) whether Western (particularly French) leaders and publics believed that a democratic German regime meant that the Germans no longer posed a military threat to their neighbors; (3) whether the new political regime in West Germany eliminated the chief obstacles to a peace settlement between the former enemies; and (4) whether the peacemaking process was driven by public pressure.

It is unclear whether the establishment of the FRG truly preceded Three Power efforts to rehabilitate West Germany and bring it into the Western orbit. The first steps toward rebuilding Germany clearly took place before 1949. The American and British decisions to promote German economic recovery were taken as early as 1946, amid growing distrust of Soviet intentions and rising occupation costs. By 1947, even French leaders accepted that, in order to participate in the Marshall Plan and foster French economic recovery, they had to permit a rapid German recovery.[9] Nevertheless, the most significant steps to cement regional peace—that is, the Schuman Plan for the European Coal and Steel Community (ECSC) and the Paris Agreements of 1954—were taken only after the FRG was established as a democracy. Thus, while some elements of the postwar regional order predated the Bonn regime, there is some basis for concluding that the democratization of West Germany preceded Franco-German peacemaking.

Furthermore, many Western leaders clearly believed that German democratization could inspire long-term peace and stability in the region. From the early days of the postwar occupation, the US deputy military governor in Germany, General Lucius D. Clay, believed that "his primary mission was the establishment of a democratic German government at the earliest possible moment," as he viewed this as a prerequisite for peace in Europe.[10] British foreign secretary Ernest Bevin, likewise argued that Great Britain had a fundamental interest in "the reconstruction of a stable, peaceful and democratic Germany," which would stabilize the Continent.[11] The US high commissioner in Germany, John J. McCloy, agreed that democratizing Germany could facilitate peace and stability in Western Europe. In 1950, he advised President Truman: "For the longer range, Germany must be viewed in light of our ultimate purpose: security from the threat of German aggression. Our means to this goal have been basically two: (1) to deprive Germany of the power of aggression; and (2) to develop in Germany a peaceful democracy without the desire for aggression."[12] Secretary of State Dean Acheson accepted the logic of McCloy's position, advising Truman in June 1950 that it would be unwise to allow German rearmament before democratic values and traditions were firmly entrenched in the FRG.[13] There is, therefore, evidence that influential Western leaders believed that democracy was a precondition for peace.

From the all-important point of view of French leaders and French public opinion, however, democracy was not a sufficient basis for peace and security. Even after a democratic regime was established in West Germany, French public opinion and key French leaders continued to distrust the FRG. Significantly, French military planning continued to treat Germany as a potential enemy.[14] Furthermore, the French government refused to allow the new German democracy to participate in Western defense efforts without extensive safeguards against German militarism, including British and US military guarantees and a prohibition against a German national army or general staff.[15] Even in 1953, after four successful years of German democracy, French president Vincent Auriol continued to voice his "fear of Germany," especially his concern that German nationalism and militarism would drag the West into another war, perhaps over East Germany.[16] Clearly, French leaders did not view democracy as a reliable basis for peace.

The French public also remained suspicious of West Germany, despite the new democratic regime. A 1950 Gallup poll, for example, indicated that a majority (55%) of decided French voters did not think that France should have even "cordial relations" with the FRG.[17] After the outbreak of the Korean War, despite intense fears of a Soviet invasion of Western Europe, the French public continued to oppose FRG participation in a European army.[18] As late as July 1954, after five years of German democracy, a public opinion poll conducted by L'institut français d'opinion publique (IFOP) reported that 66 percent of decided French respondents judged German rearmament to be a danger in any form, while 28 percent believed it could be benign only with extensive safeguards.[19]

The French public's distrust of German democracy should not come as much of a surprise, given Germany's abortive experience with democracy after 1919.[20] Far from guaranteeing peace between France and Germany, the Weimar democracy lasted only fourteen years before collapsing into authoritarianism during Adolf Hitler's chancellorship. Moreover, the consequences of Weimar's descent into authoritarianism had been catastrophic for France, as the Nazis had occupied Paris and most of France.[21] Thus, the French were not inclined to give West Germany the benefit of the doubt merely because of its transition to democracy, nor would it be correct to say that public pressure for reconciliation drove the French government's willingness to make peace with West Germany.

Nor was the West German transition to democracy the key element that motivated France to conclude the Paris Agreements with the FRG and cooperate with the FRG on European defense, a core element of the October 1954 settlement. While the French National Assembly rejected German participation in Western defense with its August 1954 defeat of the European Defense Community (EDC) treaty, despite Bonn's five years of democracy, it approved German rearmament within NATO only four months later, after Washington and London guaranteed that they would not withdraw their troops from the Continent unilaterally.[22] If the transition to democracy drove peacemaking, these guarantees would have been unnecessary.

The establishment of the FRG as a democracy in 1949, therefore, was insufficient to overcome French distrust of Germany, nor did it lead to a speedy resolution of bilateral differences and inspire a rapid peace settlement and security cooperation between the now democratic former rivals. Indeed, the French were largely unconvinced that the new German democracy would last and were skeptical that even a democratic Germany could remain at peace without extensive safeguards.[23] Consequently, while we may still inquire whether the democratic character of the Western European states affected the longevity and nature of the Franco-German peace after its conclusion, there is no evidence that it was responsible for peacemaking in the decade after World War II.

Business Interests. On the surface, commercial liberalism also suggests a plausible explanation of Franco-German peacemaking after World War II. Perhaps the growth of economic ties within the region—and, in particular, between France and the FRG—transformed the character of bilateral relations by engendering economic interdependence and making the use of force irrational.[24] For this explanation to be correct, we would need evidence that (1) either (a) the national economies of the region were meaningfully interdependent prior to the security decisions of 1954, which created vested interests in peacemaking, or (b) business interests in the rival states anticipated great economic gains as a result of peacemaking; and that (2) business groups drove the peace process. The evidence, however, does not support this hypothesis.

To begin with, economic exchange in the region took off only *after* a regional security framework was established. Although the Marshall Plan encouraged Franco-German economic cooperation, bilateral trade and investment between these two war-ravaged economies in the late 1940s and early 1950s was nowhere near the extensive economic interdependence between them before World War I.[25] To be sure, the ECSC envisioned a much-deeper economic integration of the region. The treaty enacting it, however, was not signed until 1951 and was not ratified by the parliaments of all signatories until June 1952. Given that the institution's first five-year period of operation was merely a transitional period, the ECSC did not dramatically alter regional economic patterns until after the key arrangements for Western European security had been made and an effective peace agreement, the 1954 Paris Agreements, had been enacted.[26] Only in 1955 did the two countries sign an important bilateral commercial treaty that would begin to make each the other's principal economic partner.[27] More specifically, the extensive economic integration brought about by the European Economic Community did not materialize until after the 1957 Treaty of Rome. In this regard, bilateral Franco-German exports accounted for only about 0.6 percent of each country's GDP in 1954. It more than quadrupled in the next decade and more than doubled as a percentage of each country's GDP, exceeding the 1 percent of GDP threshold for both countries only years after the peace settlement was reached.[28]

There is reason to believe that French and German business groups anticipated that economic gains would result from a peace treaty that had economic integration as a centerpiece. To begin with, there was a clear complementarity between the two economies. Significantly, France required German coal and coke to rebuild its steel industry and restore dynamism to its economy after the devastation of World War II. The Germans required a lucrative market for their mineral and energy resources to help rebuild German infrastructure and jump-start Germany's war-ravaged economy. Both countries would clearly reap large economic gains through economic cooperation.[29] Thus German industrialists decided early on after the war that reconstructing historical economic links with France would be an essential prerequisite for German re-entry into the international economy, even if they did so less on purely economic grounds than because failure to do so might lead to continued industrial dismantling and punishment of German industry by the occupying powers.[30] From the French point of view, once Washington and London moved to restrict German coke exports in order to rebuild German industry as a means of improving the postwar German standard of living, French industrialists were dependent on some means of securing adequate supplies of German coke. Schuman was convinced, therefore, that integration of the region's coal and steel production would ensure French industry access to this vital resource.[31]

There is no evidence, however, that economic interests drove the decision-making process that led to regional peacemaking. As we shall see shortly, the Western impetus for peacemaking came from a strategic rationale and not an economic one. In particular, it would be difficult to explain French reluctance to allow a complete German economic recovery if it were making decisions on the basis of economic calculations and a desire to satisfy the business community.

Following the war, General Clay sought to promote German economic recovery in the Western administered occupation zones as a means of encouraging the Germans to resist communism and build their future in the West.[32] The French government, however, refused to administer the French zone jointly with the Anglo-American bizone and continued to limit German economic recovery within it as a means of preventing a renewed German economic and military menace. They also plundered the zone of coal, timber, industrial equipment, and electricity both as a form of reparations and as a means of weakening Germany.[33] Indeed, French reluctance to allow for a broader West German economic recovery eventually led a frustrated Washington to use the Marshall Plan, which made a US-assisted French recovery dependent on a broader European, including German, recovery.[34] Only after the announcement of the Marshall Plan did the French agree to merge the three Western zones and allow for the establishment of the Federal Republic of Germany in June 1948.[35]

Even after the Marshall Plan, however, the French government continued to cling desperately to the industrial dismantling provisions of the Three Power Prohibited and Limited Industries Agreement that placed strict limits on German industries that produced goods that could contribute to the defense establishment and dismantled plant capacity in excess of those limits, despite US pressure to stop the practice. Clearly, the economic gains of cooperation with Germany were not foremost on the minds of French leaders.

Only when the strategic rationale changed for France did the government begin to pursue meaningful economic (as well as political and military) cooperation with Germany. The exigencies of the Cold War and US pressure to stop industrial dismantling and harness German productive capacity in support of Western defense efforts presented French leaders with a serious dilemma: How could they stimulate German industry without risking a return of German militarism and the attendant threat to France? Schuman's solution was to pursue economic integration within the ECSC to allow German industrial growth but simultaneously restrain it within a multilateral European framework.[36]

In this regard, the Schuman Plan and Jean Monnet's blueprint for Franco-German economic cooperation, on which it was based, were not designed as economic enterprises primarily to elicit economic gains. Instead, both Schuman and Monnet were seeking a way to control German industry, and hence the possibility of German militarism, without stifling German production, which the Americans opposed.[37] Moreover, Schuman and his colleagues feared that, if they were unable to take the lead in rebuilding the European economy in a manner that satisfied Washington's security objectives in Europe, the Truman administration might bypass France and make the more compliant FRG chancellor Konrad Adenauer their principal ally on the Continent.[38] Monnet also shared the American concern that an arrangement that was too punitive to the Germans might drive them into Soviet arms, which would be disastrous for French security.[39] Thus great power politics and security concerns drove economic cooperation rather than economic considerations motivating peacemaking.

If business leaders motivated by the expected gains of peacemaking and cooperation had driven French decision making during this period, the French government would not have dragged its feet on German economic recovery and would not have persisted in its efforts to implement the Prohibited and Limited Industries Agreement to its fullest. Instead, as will be elaborated on later, French leaders pursued a strategic rationale throughout the period, opting for economic cooperation to maximize their strategic objectives rather than pursuing strategic objectives to advance the economic interests of the French business community. As it turns out, the French plan to internationalize Ruhr coal and steel production was agreed on by government, labor, and intellectual opinion in France and was seen as a way to prevent both French and German industrial interests from re-forming prewar cartels.[40] In other words, rather than being inspired by French industrialists, the plan was a tool to control French industrialists. Indeed, French heavy industry was actually hostile to the Schuman Plan and Monnet's negotiations to build the ECSC, fearing that cooperation with Germany would force French firms to compete with their more efficient German counterparts on unfair terms.[41]

From the German perspective, Chancellor Adenauer embraced the Schuman Plan, not because German industry pushed him to, but because it offered the occupied, stigmatized FRG a chance to recover its sovereignty and equality within the confines of limitations to be imposed on all member states, not simply the FRG. To be sure, German business interests supported the plan—even though they believed the French would use it to their advantage, e.g., by requiring Ruhr industries to purchase lower-grade French iron ore—but primarily because it allowed them to escape the shackles of the Prohibited and Limited Industries Agreement and not because they expected to realize the greatest gains through economic cooperation.[42] Thus, while Andrew Moravcsik may correctly stress that economic considerations and Franco-German business interests motivated the deepening of the ECSC as part of the 1957 Treaty of Rome, which established the European Economic Community, that was only after the ECSC was established and the Paris Agreements were concluded.[43] These crucial first steps toward peace and economic integration were driven by a realpolitik logic, not an economic one.[44]

Commercial liberalism cannot be considered a cause of peace in Western Europe, then, given that neither of its causal processes—either vested interests in peace that fear the disruption of lucrative economic ties or business interests anticipating great gains due to peace and economic cooperation—drove the decision-making processes that led to rivalry termination.

Institutional Norms. A constructivist institutional explanation of Franco-German peacemaking would suggest that the Western European regional institutions that were constructed in the early Cold War era caused the transition from a zone of war to a zone of peace by generating cooperative regional norms and changing the mind-set of French and German leaders and peoples. In particular, they may have fostered mutual trust and a sense of "we-ness" among the states of the region, including France and the FRG, which eliminated the security dilemma between them.[45] If a constructivist institutional explanation is correct, we would expect to find that (1) France and the FRG embedded themselves within cooperative regional institutions prior to the de facto peace treaty and high-level regional security cooperation; (2) before the Paris Agreements, these institutions led the French and German peoples to view themselves as a security community and evinced a sense of we-ness characteristic of Kantian orders;[46] and (3) these changed societal attitudes made it incumbent on the leadership of the rival states cum institutional members to make peace with each other.

There is little support for the claim that regional institutions existed before peacemaking and security cooperation. The key institution that sparked a united Europe, the EEC, was not established until the late 1950s, a few years after the Paris Agreements. Furthermore, while most of the regional participants were members of NATO, a military alliance established in 1949 linking North American and western and southern European states against the Soviet threat, the FRG was not invited to join NATO until 1955, as a result of the Paris Agreements. The same is true of the Brussels Treaty Organization—eventually renamed the Western European Union, following the inclusion of the FRG and Italy after the 1954 Paris Agreements—a security, economic and cultural organization established in 1948 by France, the United Kingdom, Belgium, the Netherlands, and Luxembourg. The only significant institution to which France and Germany both belonged prior to the peace agreement was the ECSC, which was established by the Treaty of Paris in April 1951 and commenced operations in early 1953, about a year and a half before the Paris Agreements. It is conceivable that the ECSC helped pave the way for peacemaking, although that is a very short time in which to forge a common identity between nations that fought three wars in seventy-five years.

There is also some indication that key Western officials believed that regional political institutions could transform and pacify the region. High Commissioner McCloy, for example, wrote to Truman in September 1950:

> For the long-run, our ultimate assurance against future German aggression must lie, in my opinion, in the closest integration of Germany into Western Europe, and not in an imposed system of controls. Thus our aim should be to promote in every way the creation and development of European institutions, (like the Schuman Plan, the Council of Europe and the proposed

European Defense Force) which will tie together France and Germany into a common political and economic community and defensive system and make each dependent on the other.[47]

Foreign Secretary Bevin similarly told the British cabinet on numerous occasions that associating the FRG with European political and economic institutions could foster "a peaceful and constructive spirit" in both Germany and Western Europe.[48]

As we have already seen, however, the French public and French leaders showed no evidence by 1954 that they felt a common identity with the Germans and did not act as if they constituted a pluralistic security community together with Germany. Instead, they continued to fear Germany, distrusted Germans, and were suspicious of German rearmament even with stringent safeguards in place. For this reason, as we shall see, even though the French secured virtually all of the changes to the EDC treaty they required prior to its signature in May 1952, and secured many more concessions from the British and Americans to guarantee against renewed German militarism, the National Assembly defeated the treaty in an August 1954 ratification vote because the French people and their representatives still feared a rearmed Germany.[49] It is implausible, therefore, that peacemaking in Western Europe resulted from changed societal attitudes owing to membership in common regional institutions. The most significant European institutions were created after the Paris Agreements, and French attitudes did not reflect a changed identity at the time of the agreement.

State-to-Nation Congruence. The case for restoring the state-to-nation balance as a cause of Franco-German peacemaking would revolve around the territorial and population changes that occurred as a result of World War II and in its aftermath. Indeed, Benjamin Miller argues that the pacification of Europe was ultimately brought about by the resolution of the German problem that had dogged the Continent since the nineteenth century. He maintains that this problem was resolved both by agreement and by force. In the West, the restoration of Alsace-Lorraine to French control and the Saar plebiscite, which returned the region to German control, eliminated irredentist claims that could lead to war. In the east, the establishment of the Oder-Neisse eastern border and the forcible expulsion of ethnic Germans from Poland and Czechoslovakia and their repatriation in East Germany effectively terminated the basis for German claims in Eastern Europe.[50] He concludes that "the end of the dispute over the Saar region completed the process that created a balance between the German nation and the political boundaries of the two German states, thus creating a greater state-to-nation balance in Europe. . . . Only after reducing the state-to-nation imbalance could the two states [France and Germany] reach high-level warm peace, starting from the late 1950s."[51]

43

For Miller's argument to be correct, we would need to see first that the changes he identifies truly resolved the state-to-nation imbalance that existed in Europe as a result of the German problem. Second, we would need to see that the restored state-to-nation balance provided an impetus for peacemaking.

While it is true that border changes and population transfers did affect the state-to-nation balance in the region, Miller's account of Western European pacification is difficult to square with the evidence. To begin with, although the Franco-German dispute over the Saar was politically significant, historians agree that it was largely peripheral to, and of secondary importance to, the security and sovereignty aspects of bilateral relations. Jacques Freymond, for example, judges that "though [the Saar dispute] complicated Franco-German relations for some years, it never assumed a very serious character."[52] Consequently, though it was at times an obstacle to progress toward a settlement, it was hardly the central issue whose resolution led to the Paris Agreements. Moreover, neither the French public nor the French political leadership believed that the territorial dispositions of Alsace-Lorraine and the Saar or the population transfers in the east were a sufficient basis for security cooperation with Germany. As indicated, they continued to view Germany as a medium- to long-term threat that could only be overcome with extensive safeguards and an American security guarantee. Thus the Saar dispute was not as critical to the peace treaty as Miller suggests.

Furthermore, as Jonathan Rynhold observes, the eastern territorial settlement and population transfer did not truly resolve the German question or bring about peace. He argues that, until the 1970s, the FRG viewed the Oder-Neisse border as illegitimate, and "population transfer alone was insufficient to resolve matters. In fact, it created a strong sense of injustice in Germany that could have underwritten a revisionist policy."[53] To assume that the population transfers pacified relations between Germany and its neighbors is therefore problematic.

At core, however, Miller's bottom-up argument is unsatisfactory because the construction of what he calls a "warm peace" between France and Germany preceded the resolution of the state-to-nation imbalance in Europe. Before 1990, Germany was divided into two separate German states: the FRG and the German Democratic Republic. In addition, because the 1938 Anschluss of Austria and Germany was undone after World War II, Austria constituted a third state populated by ethnically German people. Yet the dispersal of the German nation across these three states did not serve as an obstacle to the creation of a pluralistic security community in Europe. Instead, it was precisely because the character of regional relations and bilateral relations between France and the FRG had been transformed between 1954 and 1990 that German reunification became possible.[54] The French public and the French leadership were willing to entertain the prospect of a large, reunited Germany only on the under-standing that it would be democratic and embedded within cooperative European institutions, and only because it expected that the new German state would remain a part of the stable European security community that had functioned well with West German participation for decades. In other words, it was the peace settlement that eventually facilitated the amelioration of the state-to-nation imbalance, rather than the other way around.

Assessment of Bottom-Up Explanations. Based on the foregoing, bottom-up mechanisms cannot explain why France and the FRG made peace in the decade after World War II. Democratization did not generate popular pres-sures for peacemaking, nor did French political leaders view it as a suffi-cient basis for peace. Economic interests did not drive the peacemaking process to realize expected gains or protect vested interests. Regional insti-tutions did not foster a common identity that impelled leaders to negotiate peace. Nor did the postwar territorial and population transfers spur peace-making by resolving the state-to-nation imbalance in Europe. The next sec-tion will therefore consider whether top-down theories of peace provide better guides for this case.

TOP-DOWN DYNAMICS

More Pressing Threats. Balance-of-power and balance-of-threat theory could explain Franco-German reconciliation as a direct result of the advent of a far more serious Soviet threat to both states in the postwar era. An im-portant consequence of the war was the weakening of the great powers of Western Europe. Great Britain had exhausted itself economically in the war against Nazi Germany. France had been defeated and occupied early on. Germany was defeated and in the postwar era remained occupied and divided. At the same time, the Soviet Union ended the war in control of half of the Continent, with by far the most powerful armed forces in Eu-rope. By 1947, the Soviets had reduced their armed forces, based within striking distance of Western and Central Europe, to 2.8 million troops; the United States had reduced its worldwide military forces to only half that amount, 1.4 million, with only 400,000 left in Europe to protect the badly weakened Western European allies.[55] This tremendous disparity between Soviet and Western conventional forces was significant in and of itself in power-political terms. It was all the more menacing in light of Western perceptions that Stalin harbored aggressive intentions for ideological rea-sons. Consequently, realists would have expected the Western European states to align together in the hope of resisting Soviet power. This would mean that France and the FRG, too, had to make peace and cooperate if they were to survive.[56]

In order to confirm this explanation of Franco-German peacemaking, we would need evidence that (1) either French or German leaders, or both, actually perceived the Soviet Union to be a greater threat than their traditional rival; and (2) this more pressing threat led them to pursue a peace settlement and security cooperation.

The evidence for this hypothesis is strong. Initially, after having been defeated by Germany for the third time in seventy-five years, the French began the postwar era intent on declawing Germany politically, economically, and militarily. According to the French policy toward Germany drafted by the president of the provisional government of the French Fourth Republic, General Charles de Gaulle, French security and recovery required a decentralized German confederation; removal from Germany of the industrial Ruhr, which would be occupied and internationalized; removal from Germany of the left bank of the Rhine, which was to be divided into two or three separate states and occupied; French administration for the Saar; and high German reparations payments in order to weaken German industry and fuel the French economic recovery.[57] Even de Gaulle, who initiated this policy, however, "made it clear to the Americans in November 1945 that he considered the Russian threat more important than the German problem and that he understood that France had to cooperate with America if she 'wished to survive.' "[58] By 1948, however, a more active Soviet Union and more imminent Soviet threat made French leaders aware of the need to soften this punitive policy and associate Germany with the Western powers.[59]

Before 1948, the French government, though wary of Soviet power and intentions, tried to cooperate with both Moscow and the Western allies and to coordinate allied policy toward Germany with Stalin. By mid-1948, however, the Soviet Union began to grow more menacing for the French. To begin with, the Soviet-sponsored coup d'état in Czechoslovakia shook French foreign minister Georges Bidault and the French foreign ministry to the core and "touched off panic in Paris."[60] The foreign minister noted that the Soviets had eliminated "an intermediate, autonomous zone of Europe" by subverting all of the Eastern bloc and feared that they would soon turn their attention to Austria, Italy, and Germany—all politically unstable countries. He therefore implored the Americans to help construct a military "bulwark of freedom against this onslaught" to prevent Moscow from steamrolling though the Continent.[61] He went so far as to tell his American interlocutors that, without a serious US commitment to save France, "it would be easy for the Russian armies to overrun France, and we shudder to think of what would happen to our beautiful country. We are defenseless, as you well know."[62] Clearly, the French fear of the USSR was considerable, and the French believed that the Soviet threat was more immediate than their British or American counterparts expected.[63]

French fear grew as the Soviet Union took a more menacing stance toward France and began to intervene overtly in the fragile French polity by fomenting strikes, protests, and industrial sabotage of French coalfields in late 1948.[64] In addition, the Berlin blockade—Stalin's attempt to use his strategically superior position in East Germany to surround West Berlin and compel the West to abandon the city—persuaded many French leaders that the Soviet Union was eager to use its immense power "to expand across Europe and towards the Middle East."[65] As a result, the French judged that they had little alternative but to align more closely with the West and create stability in West Germany in order to check Moscow's expansion. Indeed, Bidault informed Marshall that although French politicians needed to talk publicly of security against Germany for domestic political reasons, "by now everyone knew who was the real enemy" (i.e., the Soviet Union).[66] It is significant, in this regard, that even Monnet, the originator of economic cooperation with Germany, was inspired in the wake of the Berlin blockade principally by the fear that the Soviet Union, now in possession of an atomic bomb, might wage a European war for which Germany would be the prize rather than the aggressor.[67]

The strongest support for this argument comes from French attitudes toward German rearmament in the early 1950s. After World War II, the French were firmly committed to disarming Germany permanently and forbidding the Germans from possessing an army and a general staff.[68] Yet, after the 1948–49 Berlin crisis, French military leaders joined their British and American counterparts in concluding that a Western defense against a Soviet attack would be extremely difficult, if not impossible, without a German military contribution.[69] Moreover, they deemed it necessary for the Germans to share the economic burden of rearmament lest keeping the FRG disarmed threaten both Western European defenses and the French economy, which was already overtaxed by the war in Indochina.[70] While their political masters initially maintained their staunch opposition to German rearmament, the outbreak of the Korean War in June 1950 changed their minds, too. Thus, after the Soviet-supported invasion of South Korea, the political leaders of all three Western allies—including France—judged that the USSR posed a far greater and more immediate military threat than even a rearmed FRG could for the foreseeable future.[71]

For French leaders, moreover, in the wake of the 1949 Soviet nuclear test, the Korean War underscored that "suddenly American atomic superiority was of less importance, and the imbalance in conventional forces in Europe loomed ominously."[72] As French prime minister René Pleven explained to Truman in 1951, the French government believed that the only reason the Soviet Union had not exploited its conventional advantage in Europe was that US atomic superiority prevented it. The French feared what would happen, however, once the Soviet atomic arsenal caught up, which led them to the conclusion that every effort must be made to beef up Western defenses by any means necessary.[73] For these reasons, the French government reluctantly acknowledged the need to equip German units to participate in the Western defense effort to help counter the Soviet conventional threat. While agreement over the modalities of German rearmament would take five years to negotiate owing to French domestic political opposition, it is clear that France would not have approved of rearming its mortal enemy without the imperative of the Soviet threat.[74]

From the West German perspective, the Soviet Union and its proxy forces in East Germany constituted by far the most pressing threat that the FRG had to contend with. The 1948 Berlin blockade convinced the Germans that Stalin was willing to exploit his military advantage to overturn the status quo in Germany.[75] Especially after the outbreak of the Korean War, the fear that the Soviet Union would initiate a similar attack against West Germany in short order created something akin to a mass hysteria in the FRG. As David Clay Large has described:

> The outbreak of war in the Far East generated something close to panic in the FRG. McCloy's office was besieged by requests for air tickets to America. Thinking they see red handwriting already on the wall, a number of Ruhr industrialists placed advertisements in Communist newspapers. Police in North Rhine-Westphalia stopped arresting Communists for fear of being subjected to later retribution.
>
> Other Germans, however, loudly declared their determination to fight to the death against a Communist attack. Charles Thayer, McCloy's aide, recalled that a dozen bureaucrats stormed into his office demanding weapons to shoot invading Communists or, if worst came to worst, themselves. A member of parliament complained that he could not obtain a single grain of cyanide because his colleagues had bought it all up. Kurt Georg Kiesinger, the future chancellor, wanted to establish a "defensive wall" in France, to store weapons and food for a final heroic stand. Adenauer himself requested two hundred automatic pistols to defend the Palais Schaumburg in the event of a "Communist uprising."[76]

Adenauer, in particular, was very fearful of the Soviet Union, a point he emphasized regularly in his conversations with McCloy and in his public statements and media interviews.[77] From early on, he concluded that "the aim of the Russians was unambiguous. Soviet Russia had, like Tsarist Russia, an urge to acquire or subdue new territories in Europe." He judged that it was Moscow's ambition "to include the whole of Germany in their sphere of influence," by force, if necessary.[78] Thus, Western unity was essential for the FRG if the Soviet threat was to be effectively contained.[79] As the chancellor explained, "I believe that the incentive to make war is greater for Soviet Russia than is generally assumed. In these circumstances, peace can only be secured if the Soviet leaders are convinced of the hopelessness of conquering Europe."[80] After the outbreak of the Korean War, Adenauer believed the threat was considerable and imminent: "The Federal Republic was in a very dangerous situation indeed. We were totally unarmed, we

encourage the occupying Western powers to devolve as much independence as possible to the FRG over time.[106] Peacemaking with France, even on terms that were more favorable to France, would be an important way for Adenauer to demonstrate the responsibility of the new West German democracy and, therefore, that it deserved to have its sovereignty and equality restored.[107] Indeed, it was this calculation that led Adenauer to accept the residual Allied emergency powers in Germany, key limitations on the German military establishment, and a German renouncement of the right to produce nuclear weapons on German soil.[108] Thus the settlement can be attributed, at least in part, to the unique circumstances of the West German state after World War II.

The French government, to some extent, also had regime-survival motives for peacemaking with Germany. In the aftermath of World War II, the French Communist Party (PCF) was the largest single party in the National Assembly, winning 28 percent of the vote in November 1946, a strong plurality in a fragmented multiparty system.[109] From within the governing coalition, the PCF sought to extend its influence on French economic political institutions and French society. When, for this reason and under pressure from the United States to do so, socialist premier Paul Ramadier expelled the PCF from the government in May 1947, the Communists escalated their assault, paralyzing the French economy with a series of debilitating strikes in which nearly 5 million people took part.[110] Societal and labor unrest intensified a European-wide economic crisis in 1946–47 that hit France—a country that had never really recovered from the world economic crisis of the early 1930s—particularly hard, with skyrocketing inflation, large trade deficits (reaching over $2 billion in current dollars in 1946), and large-scale capital flight.[111] This was potentially disastrous for an economy suffering from persistent labor shortages owing to the large proportion of working-age men killed during the war and the magnitude of the postwar reconstruction program.[112] It also drastically reduced the production of coal and industrial goods that were essential to the French economic plan.[113]

Because, as mentioned earlier, the United States conditioned French recovery within the Marshall Plan on German reconstruction, the French government was compelled to begin the process of German political and economic rehabilitation in order to stabilize a chaotic domestic political and economic environment that could easily have toppled the French Fourth Republic. This logic was reinforced by the dire French need for Ruhr coal to stave off disaster.[114] Thus, regime-survival considerations of different kinds affected the willingness of both French and German leaders to make concessions for peace in the postwar era.

At least to some extent, then, state-preservation and state-building considerations encouraged German and French leaders to terminate the rivalry in 1954.

Assessment of Top-Down Explanations. Franco-German peacemaking and security cooperation in 1954, therefore, had little to do with bottom-up mechanisms and societal pressures. As John Young noted, the French embraced Franco-German reconciliation and the Atlantic alliance because "the threat presented by the Red Army and the need for US financial assistance made such an arrangement seem vital."[115] These concerns dovetailed with the need to promote French economic recovery in order to stabilize a fragile and turbulent postwar French domestic environment. Because West Germany was occupied by the Three Powers, Adenauer, too, was compelled to make peace with France on terms favorable to Paris in order to engage in state building to secure as much sovereignty and independence as he could negotiate from the occupying powers. Moreover, faced with what he perceived as an imminent threat from a vastly superior Soviet military force, Adenauer judged it essential to do whatever was necessary in order to secure a credible Western defense effort. Thus, the transition to peace in this important case was driven by statist motivations.

The Post-Transition Era

The transition to peace between France and Germany in 1950s was very successful, and Franco-German relations underwent a remarkable transformation in the decades thereafter. While the French initially viewed the FRG with distrust and suspicion, over time the two countries began to view each other as partners rather than rivals. This shift began with de Gaulle's accession to the presidency of the new Fifth Republic in 1958. Eager to construct a French-led Western Europe independent of the superpowers, de Gaulle found Bonn to be his natural ally. Unlike Great Britain, which was unrelentingly Atlanticist and resisted French leadership—de Gaulle viewed London as "an American Trojan Horse,"[116] and unlike Italy and the Benelux countries, which were too weak economically and politically to serve as France's principal partners, the Federal Republic was clearly a sufficiently powerful European entity.[117] Moreover, Adenauer's Germany was frequently willing to defer to French leadership to prove that it had permanently abandoned its Nazi past and was now a changed liberal state.[118] Consequently, in the five years from de Gaulle's warm September 1958 meeting with Adenauer in Colombey-les-Deux-Églises to the signature of the Franco-German cooperation treaty in January 1963, the FRG made the transition from hated enemy to France's primary strategic partner.[119] Even when, in the mid-1960s, the "empty chair crisis" and the French position on the EEC's Common Agricultural Policy strained de Gaulle's relations with Adenauer's immediate successors (Ludwig Erhard and Kurt Georg Kiesinger) Paris's relations with the FRG were still on a better footing than with any of its other great power allies.[120] In the late

1970s, under the stewardship of Valéry Giscard d'Estaing and Helmut Schmidt, bilateral cooperation intensified, as "Europe's two big Siamese twins" carved out the European Monetary System and dominated the European Community's political revival.[121] When François Mitterrand and Helmut Kohl took the reins of power in their respective countries in the 1980s, they extended Franco-German cooperation in the security and defense theater by initiating joint military exercises, and deepened economic and political cooperation by jointly spurring on the Single European Act to strengthen the EC by 1992.[122] Clearly, French leaders treated the FRG as a close partner rather than a potential adversary.[123]

This is not to say that French leaders completely overcame their fears of a revived Germany. Throughout the Cold War, even while Franco-German cooperation was deepening, the nightmare of renewed German militarism remained a central focus of French grand strategy. Thus, for example, Georges Pompidou, French president from 1969 to 1974, was deeply concerned about German chancellor Willy Brandt's Ostpolitik strategy, which he feared would bring about a reunified and neutral Germany.[124] In the 1980s, Mitterrand worried about two disturbing trends in the FRG. On the one hand, he feared growing German economic power, which threatened to dominate the EC. On the other hand, he was concerned about growing pacifism and neutralism in West Germany, which could threaten German participation in NATO—a core element of the institutional arrangement to entrench Germany within liberal Europe.[125] Throughout the Cold War, therefore, French political elites vacillated between two broad strategies to contain German power: a realist strategy premised on finding a great power counterweight to Germany (either the United States, Great Britain or, after Mikhail Gorbachev's accession to power, the Soviet Union) and a liberal strategy premised on enmeshing the FRG further within European economic and political institutions.[126] As we shall see, these nagging doubts continued to trouble French leaders when the end of the Cold War raised the specter of German reunification.

Nor was the Franco-German partnership without its share of discord.[127] In June 1965, for example, France under de Gaulle clashed with Germany and other EEC members over European Commission plans to increase the autonomy of the EEC from member governments, threatening the national sovereignty that de Gaulle cherished. That precipitated the empty chair crisis, in which France withdrew its representative to the European Council, grinding EEC business to a halt.[128] The two countries similarly clashed over de Gaulle's 1966 withdrawal from NATO.[129] They also had lower-level but still politically significant disputes over other matters, such as the large French trade imbalance in the early 1980s and the stringent European Monetary Union conversion criteria and fiscal discipline that Germany proposed in the 1990s, much to France's chagrin.[130]

Many of these disagreements stemmed from divergent Franco-German strategic priorities stemming from their peculiar postwar circumstances.[131] Having declined precipitously following the two world wars, France prioritized restoration of its great power status by promoting French leadership of Europe as an independent force between the superpowers and, by doing so, to project French military independence of Washington. In stark contrast, German leaders preferred multilateral cooperation and wanted Washington to continue playing a central role in European military affairs.[132] Disagreements of this sort, however, are normal between Western liberal allies, whose interests overlap considerably but are not identical. In this regard, relations between the United States and Japan have gone through difficult periods, such as the trade disputes of the 1980s.[133] The close Canadian-American partnership has also undergone strains, such as during the years when Pierre Trudeau was prime minister of Canada.[134] Even the special relationship between the United States and Great Britain has gone through both good times and bad.[135] Franco-German disagreements, therefore, are not inconsistent with a close partnership. Indeed, as the FRG remained France's closest ally throughout the remainder of the Cold War, and France and united Germany have retained this close degree of coordination since the end of the Cold War, we can reasonably conclude that, at least at the level of political elites, the Franco-German relationship has been transformed into a relatively stable partnership between liberal states. Consequently, according to the criteria set out in the introduction to this book, the peace treaty is a stable one: neither France nor the FRG has repudiated the peace settlement, nor have the two countries resorted to the use of force against each other since 1954; moreover, neither party has expressed a desire to revise the settlement, and the bilateral relationship has been free of significant recriminations or high-level security crises.

What accounts for the stability and deepening of Franco-German peace and cooperation in the postwar era? Although top-down factors brought about peace between the two rivals in the early to mid-1950s, there are reasons to doubt that statist calculations are sufficient to explain the development of the relationship after 1954. Indeed, if the Soviet threat to both countries was the catalyst for the transition to peace, the absence of regional conflict since the Soviet Union's collapse presents a considerable puzzle. Why didn't Franco-German cooperation evaporate after the motivation provided by the Soviet threat disappeared, as Sebastian Rosato would have expected?[136] Furthermore, the deepening of Western European cooperation and the Franco-German partnership during the era of détente and the Gorbachev years indicates that the perception of a powerful and imminent Soviet threat was not a prerequisite for the maintenance of regional peace. For, while the Soviet threat to Western Europe was viewed as substantial in the early 1950s and perhaps even as late as the 1961 Berlin Crisis, after the 1962 Cuban Missile Crisis the Europeans felt far more secure. This was the case, not only because most Western European states had rebuilt their armed forces and Great Britain and France had developed nuclear deterrent capabilities, but also because the Soviets moderated their risk-taking behavior in the era of détente. As a result of these strategic changes, even the 1968 Soviet invasion of Czechoslovakia failed to increase the level of threat perception in Western Europe, as that was seen not as evidence of Soviet expansionism but as an internal matter in the Soviet bloc.[137]

The other statist reasons for the peace agreement also faded as the Cold War progressed. Although John Mearsheimer credits American offshore balancing with pacifying Europe throughout the Cold War, US hegemonic engagement subsided somewhat during the latter stages of the Cold War.[138] After all, what made the United States so important to the Europeans as a catalyst for defense arrangements in the 1950s was its tremendous conventional military strength, coupled with its monopoly on nuclear weapons within the Western alliance. By the late 1960s, however, the Europeans had rebuilt their own conventional forces, and the British and French had developed their own nuclear arsenals. Meanwhile, the United States scaled back the number of active US troops both worldwide and in Europe throughout the 1960s and 1970s. Active US ground-force strength dropped from about 1.8 million in 1953 to fewer than 1 million in 1980. During the same interval, the United States reduced its complement of active ground forces in Europe from five divisions to four.[139] In contrast, Western European countries ratcheted up their defense spending from 21.4 percent of US military spending in 1952 to over 75 percent in 1979, as Washington faced increasing economic pressures and the Europeans increased their contribution to Western defenses.[140] Clearly, the Europeans had reduced their dependence on the United States in the defense theater, even if US military power was still important to them. Beyond these numbers, the Europeans perceived that the American political commitment to Europe was flagging amid Congressional pressure, starting in the late 1960s, to reduce the US troop commitment to Europe and increasing governmental demands for European "burden sharing" to alleviate Washington's political and financial burden.[141] Even in economic terms, where the US share of gross world product was declining and financial pressures led President Nixon to close the gold window, American hegemony vis-à-vis Europe was less than it was in its heyday.[142]

Finally, regime-survival pressures for bilateral cooperation also receded. The French economic crisis of the late 1940s eventually gave way to a broader European recovery under the auspices of the Marshall Plan and the European Economic Community. Notably, French GDP doubled between 1950 and 1965 and quadrupled between 1950 and 1985, while real income per capita doubled between 1960 and 1985, a tremendous rate of growth.[143] Overall, between 1955 and 1975, France posted annual growth rates averaging over 5 percent.[144] Postwar growth in France was so strong that the period from 1946 to 1975 is referred to as the "thirty glorious years."[145] Consequently, the fear that the Communists would take power through election or revolution had long since faded as the Franco-German relationship flourished. After de Gaulle established the French Fifth Republic, with a strong executive insulated from the National Assembly, the political regime in France had also stabilized greatly.[146] Having established an independent West German state and placed its relationship with the West on a contractual, rather than an occupation, basis, the FRG also found its need for state building reduced after the 1954 settlement. Thus, with a dramatically weaker Soviet threat in the latter part of the Cold War, a reduced US hegemonic commitment to Europe, and reduced regime-survival and state-building imperatives for Franco-German cooperation, it would be difficult to attribute the endurance and deepening of Franco-German peace and security cooperation in the decades following the October 1954 defense arrangements to top-down considerations.

Instead, bottom-up mechanisms helped entrench Franco-German relations after the 1954 agreement. To begin with, the democratic nature of the FRG endured throughout the period and experienced many peaceful governmental changes. As a result, the French public had every reason to believe that, unlike the Weimar regime, this new German democracy was not just a flash in the pan.

Franco-German economic exchange also increased exponentially after the Treaty of Rome. Thus, for example, while French exports to West Germany in 1954 amounted to only about $350 million or about 0.6 percent of total French GDP, by 1964 that number had more than quadrupled to over $1.5 billion or nearly 1.4 percent of French GDP. These numbers increased steadily on an annual basis such that by 1990 French exports to Germany had skyrocketed to over $38 billion, accounting for close to 4 percent of French GDP. In the same time frame, German exports to France had grown steadily, from under $350 million in 1954 (almost 0.6% of German GDP) to $1.8 billion in 1964 (1.4% of German GDP) to over $48 billion in 1990 (about 3.6% of German GDP).[147] Even discounting inflation, this growth and level of economic interdependence is remarkable and greatly exceeds the 1 percent threshold. In general, the two economies have had a high degree of complementarity, with a French advantage in agriculture and a German advantage in heavy industry and manufactured goods.[148] As a consequence, although bilateral economic exchange has not always been free from tension—particularly the French fear of being dominated by a superior German economy—the two countries have created a significant economic partnership with a high degree of bilateral exchange and a significant number of joint ventures, most notably the European Aeronautic Defence and Space Company/Airbus, television channel ARTE, and the Alle-TGV fast train.[149]

As noted, France and Germany progressively embedded themselves within cooperative regional military, economic, and political institutions during the postagreement era. France and the FRG were already members of the ECSC, but this institution eventually spawned the EEC, a very successful customs union and common market, and the European Atomic Energy Community (EURATOM), responsible for developing and distributing nuclear power among its members. In time, the EEC was subsumed in the European Union, which was more of a political institution, with police and judicial cooperation and efforts to develop a common foreign policy. Within these European institutions, the states participated in the European Parliament and the European Court of Justice. France and the FRG also gave up their national currencies, the franc and the deutsche mark, in favor of the euro, a multinational European currency.[150] In addition, the 1954 agreement brought the FRG into NATO, which coordinated the military operations of its members within an integrated military structure. Thus, the two countries cemented their bilateral ties within a dense web of institutions, which deepened their mutual trust and their cooperation. For this reason, Haig Simonian concluded that "co-operation between Bonn and Paris within the framework of the European Communities has played a vital part in cementing, and even accelerating, the restoration of good bilateral relations."[151]

As a result of these socialization mechanisms, in the decades following the settlement, public attitudes in France toward Germany and Germans underwent a dramatic transformation, as indicated by IFOP public opinion polls. In the 1950s, for example, French respondents who held negative opinions of the FRG outnumbered those with positive opinions by almost three to one.[152] It is no surprise, therefore, that the French public exhibited little or no confidence in West Germany as an ally.[153] Within a decade, however, the French view of Germany began to shift. In 1964, an overwhelming majority of French respondents told IFOP that they had a good opinion of the FRG.[154] By October 1967, more French respondents judged that German reunification was in the French national interest (52% of decided respondents) than opposed it (48%).[155] A series of public opinion polls taken from December 1968 to January 1971 consistently showed that, aside from Belgium, with whom the French shared a common language, the French public viewed the FRG as France's best friend in Europe.[156] By March 1972, a whopping 86 percent of decided French respondents expressed the view that Germany no longer represented a danger for France.[157] This is a remarkable turnaround in attitudes. Consequently, when widespread political changes were sweeping Europe in October 1989, 80 percent of decided French people surveyed by the French periodical *Libération* reported that they supported German reunification.[158] This is profound evidence of a change in French attitudes toward Germany.

There is evidence that at least some of these bottom-up changes affected state calculations over time, helping the former rivals to navigate challenges and stabilizing the peace between them. Most notably, French attitudes in 1989, when the Soviet empire in Eastern Europe collapsed and the prospect of German reunification seemed imminent, indicate the importance of German democratization and participation in European institutions in transforming bilateral relations.

With the disappearance of the Soviet threat—the top-down raison d'être for Franco-German cooperation—French leaders still worried that a united Germany could destabilize Europe and threaten French interests. They expressed these fears by imposing preconditions for reunification, including a joint FRG–German Democratic Republic declaration recognizing the Oder-Neisse border with Poland; a guarantee that the future German regime would never develop nuclear weapons; and a commitment that united Germany would respect international treaties signed by the FRG.[159] French defense minister Jean-Pierre Chevenement explained the conditional French policy: "The German people, like all people, have a right to self-determination so long as it is in accord with their neighbors and in the interest of peace in Europe."[160] To ensure that adequate institutional safeguards were in place for a united Germany, the French government initially sought Gorbachev's support in an attempt to delay German reunification.[161]

Despite these concerns, however, French policy evinced a basic trust in Germany provided that it would be entrenched within Western liberal institutions and would continue to be democratic. Less than a week before the Berlin Wall was toppled, Mitterrand declared that "I do not fear German reunification" as long as it would occur peacefully and that the new state would remain democratic, within European institutions.[162] Throughout the following year, his government continued to endorse German unity provided that the new German state would be Western and democratic.[163] In this regard, when they negotiated the Two Plus Four agreement in February 1990 to set the parameters for German reunification with the Soviet Union and the two German states, France and its Western allies insisted that a united Germany could not be neutral and must be embedded within a NATO–European Community framework to ensure that Germany would not again threaten the peace of Europe.[164] As a consequence, in March 1990, when it appeared that reunification would occur more quickly than the French government had originally anticipated, Mitterrand declared that accelerating the process of European integration was the only way to surmount the problems it posed.[165] Thus, democratization and the development of cooperative international institutions in the region—two of the bottom-up mechanisms identified by liberals and constructivists—enabled the settlement to endure challenges despite the disappearance of its top-down founding conditions.[166] Bilateral trade was also quite high and constituted a significant percentage of both countries' GDP. After the Cold War ended, the state-to-nation imbalance improved further with the reunification of East and West Germany into a single German state, embedded as it is within European institutions and democratic traditions, which may lend additional stability to the transformed region.

This most important case of peacemaking between regional rivals indicates that the causes of peace do not necessarily determine the level of postagreement stability. As table 2.1 indicates, statist factors—including a common Soviet threat, US economic and military incentives, and regime-survival and state-building motives—brought about Franco-German cooperation and peace. The most important causal factors for each (shaded in gray) were the Soviet threat and US involvement for French leaders, which compelled them to cooperate with Germany in order to rebuild the French economy and allow an effective defense against the USSR, and the need for the FRG to establish itself as an independent regime, which necessitated compromise with its occupying powers. In contrast, there is no evidence of public pressures for peacemaking, significant pressure from business interests, or that a common identity created by participation in powerful regional institutions compelled peacemaking in 1954. There was an improvement in the state-to-nation balance prior to the agreement (in the form of territorial and population transfers in both the east and west); nonetheless, a significant imbalance remained, as ethnic Germans were spread out across three states (the FRG, the German Democratic Republic, and Austria). At best, therefore, we can consider this only weak support for Miller's argument.

Although the transition was top down, the stability of the Franco-German settlement cannot be explained by top-down dynamics. Although the Soviet threat ultimately disappeared, American hegemonic engagement in Europe scaled back, and Franco-German regime instability was overcome, bilateral relations continued to improve. Instead, postagreement stability was attained because the settlement was socialized with liberal and constructivist mechanisms after its signature. In particular, the entrenchment of German democracy within a network of economic interdependence and the institutions of the EC/EU as well as NATO helped abate societal

Table 2.1 Causes of the Franco-German transition to peace

	Public opinion	Business pressures	Institutions	Improved state-to-nation balance	Greater threats	Great power pressures	Regime survival/ state building
France-Germany	—	—	—	weak	√	√	√

Table 2.2 Developments in the postagreement phase

	Democra-tization	Economic exchange	Regional institutions	Improved state-to-nation balance	Greater threats	Hegemonic pressure	Regime survival
France-Germany	√	√	√	weak	—	—	—

antagonism and build a solid foundation for a stable peace. Table 2.2, which uses dark shading to indicate that the agreement became a stable peace (subsequent chapters use light shading for enduring agreements and no shading for temporary settlements), illustrates this extensive use of bottom-up mechanisms to stabilize the treaty, whereas statist pressures did not contribute to its stability or endurance.

The next chapter will investigate a peace settlement that has not achieved the stability of the Franco-German settlement: the Egyptian-Israeli treaty of 1979.

CHAPTER 3

The Egyptian-Israeli Peace Treaty

The rivalry between Egypt and Israel began in 1948 with Israeli leader David Ben-Gurion's declaration of independence.[1] Together with the other Arab states in the region, Egypt rejected what it deemed an alien European presence in land it considered Arab territory and declared war on the nascent Jewish state. Although the fledgling Israel Defense Forces managed to defeat the Arab coalition of Egypt, Syria, Jordan, Iraq, Lebanon, and Saudi Arabia (with a small Yemeni contingent), the postwar armistices did not resolve the underlying conflict.

Under Gemal Abdel Nasser's revolutionary leadership, Egypt continued the conflict by allowing Palestinian *fedayeen* to stage cross-border raids on Israel from Egyptian territory and by interfering with Israeli shipping through the Suez Canal. Nasser's actions led to two wars against Israel. The Sinai War of 1956—in which Israel attacked the Sinai in cooperation with the British and French, who wanted to keep the canal open following Nasser's decision to nationalize it—served only to deepen the rivalry.[2] The Six-Day War of 1967, however, had an important transformative effect on the nature of the conflict. During this war, which began when the Egyptian military buildup in the Sinai, its blockade of the Straits of Tiran, and its request to the UN Secretary-General to remove UN peacekeepers from the Sinai compelled Israel to attack Egypt and Syria pre-emptively, Israeli armed forces captured the strategically important Sinai Peninsula, as well as the Gaza Strip, from Egypt. As a result, Egypt's primary goal in the conflict after 1967 changed from eliminating the Jewish state to regaining the Sinai, which it viewed as core Egyptian territory.[3]

Nasser's successor, Anwar Sadat, had to confront the fallout from the 1967 war, which led him ultimately to take steps that de-escalated the conflict for three reasons. To begin with, the military conflicts with Israel, which compelled the government to devote over half the national budget to defense spending, had left the Egyptian economy in tatters. By 1974, national growth declined to an anemic 1 percent, with the government heavily indebted to foreign creditors and the country dangerously short of foreign currency. Moreover, because the government slashed subsidies to comply with International Monetary Fund requirements, inflation soared to as much as 50 percent a year in the mid-1970s. The domestic political consequences were monumental, as the average Egyptian's buying power plummeted and the prices of foreign food rose dramatically. Egyptians took to the streets in large numbers to protest rising prices, a situation that was exacerbated by Sadat's failed *infitah* economic liberalization program.[4] From Sadat's perspective, any measure that could help him stabilize the Egyptian economy would be welcome.

Second, after suffering a humiliating military defeat in 1967 and losing the Sinai, the Egyptian people were restive. Egyptians expected their new president to recover their lost territory in its entirety, and failure to do so and reverse the sting of defeat could threaten his hold on power.[5] Since three wars against Israel all ended badly for Egypt, however, Sadat did not believe that the prospect of recovering the Sinai through military means was high, especially in light of the third motivating factor: Sadat's growing skepticism about his Soviet benefactors.

Sadat reached the conclusion that the Soviet Union, Egypt's great power ally, was either unwilling or unable to assist Egypt in regaining the Sinai, his overriding strategic objective. Indeed, Moscow seemed reluctant to provide Egypt with the state-of-the-art weaponry it requested and appeared eager to stabilize the Arab-Israeli conflict as a stalemate in the context of détente with the West.[6] If Egypt was to regain the Sinai, it might have to do so without a significant Soviet contribution. In light of these considerations, Sadat began to re-evaluate Egyptian foreign policy in a manner that would reshape the Egyptian-Israeli rivalry and eventually lead to peace negotiations.

His reasoning was that, regardless of Moscow's motives, Egypt—and the Arabs in general—had bet on the wrong superpower to advance its claims vis-à-vis Israel. Since 1948, alignment with the Soviet Union had failed to tip the Arab-Israeli balance of power in favor of the Arab states and secure victory in war. As Sadat's spokesman, Saad Zaglul Nasser, told Israeli foreign minister Moshe Dayan's press secretary, Naphtali Lau-Lavie, Moscow "had proved unable to assist in reaching any resolution of the problems in the region."[7] Therefore, the Arabs were unlikely to eliminate the State of Israel, or even regain the territory they lost in 1967, with Soviet diplomatic or military support, while Israel enjoyed military superiority and US support. Persisting in futile attempts to defeat Israel, with or without Soviet assistance, would only ruin the Egyptian economy and undermine domestic stability in the country. Consequently, a Soviet-aligned military option could threaten regime survival without providing any likely material gain. Conversely, improving Egypt's relationship with the United States held out the prospect of a diplomatic victory where no military victory was possible. To begin with, the United States had considerable leverage over Israel that it could use to persuade Israel to return the Sinai to Egypt.[8] Furthermore, Washington had considerable economic resources that could be used to bail out the flailing Egyptian economy as a reward for peacemaking.[9] This logic was reinforced by Sadat's calculation that the Soviet Union was unlikely to win the Cold War against the United States, making it imperative to side with the United States, the likely winner.[10]

With this objective in mind, Sadat adopted a more flexible position toward Israel than his predecessor soon after taking power following Nasser's death in September 1970. In his first year in office, his "year of decision," he endorsed UN envoy Gunnar Jarring's report on the Middle East, which implied that, if Israel were to return all the Arab territories it occupied in 1967, Egypt would make peace with Israel.[11] In 1972, Sadat expelled Soviet military advisers from Egypt, a move designed both to facilitate an opening to Washington and to enable Egyptian military planners to prepare a secret attack against Israel. Such an attack was designed to serve two purposes. First, it would act to dispel domestic pressure in Egypt for concrete action to regain the Sinai and reverse the humiliation of the 1967 defeat. Moreover, a successful Egyptian advance could restore the Israeli sense of vulnerability that, Sadat believed, Israeli leaders had lost after their resounding 1967 victory. Absent Israeli insecurity, Sadat feared that it might be difficult to negotiate with Israel, which might prefer to hold on to the conquered territories—a fear underscored by the apparent Israeli lack of interest in Sadat's willingness to entertain a land-for-peace formula. A successful Arab surprise attack, therefore, could compel Israeli leaders to the bargaining table.[12]

Although the resulting 1973 Yom Kippur War, which began as a joint Egyptian-Syrian surprise attack, turned into another disastrous military defeat for Egypt, Sadat did make progress on both of his objectives. Even though they were reversed, the initial Syrian advance in the Golan Heights and the limited Egyptian progress in the Sinai delivered a psychological blow to Israel that shook Israeli leaders from their complacency. The war, therefore, underscored that Israel was still vulnerable to an Arab attack and that a peace treaty taking one or more Arab states out of the conflict would be worth making limited concessions for.[13] Sadat also gained limited domestic breathing room from his initial military successes in the Sinai. The Egyptian public rewarded Sadat's bravado and embraced Sadat as "the hero of the crossing." This public embrace did not initially erode in the aftermath of the eventual military defeat. Consequently, it released the public pressure on him to retake the Sinai by force.

Over time, however, the war accelerated Egypt's economic turmoil, which in turn fueled domestic discontent. Sadat's moves to correct the country's economic distortions through deregulation and the elimination of price controls enraged ordinary Egyptians, whose buying power was decimated by the double-digit inflation that resulted from 1974 to 1979.[14]

Particularly irksome was the doubling of the price of bread—a key staple of the Egyptian diet. In frustration, the impoverished masses took to the streets in the January 1977 bread riots, which resulted in hundreds of deaths, hundreds of injuries, and thousands of arrests.[15] The credit Sadat received from the 1973 war had clearly evaporated, as the masses turned against him with the chant, "Hero of the Crossing, where is our breakfast?"[16] Consequently, Sadat feared for his regime and his personal safety.[17] Because member states of the Arab League were not willing to offer Egypt a sufficient aid package to help Sadat alleviate his domestic difficulties, he became all the more eager to reach a peace treaty with Israel, which could yield a peace dividend and lucrative American economic assistance.[18]

Initially, Sadat hoped to pursue negotiations jointly with other Arab states as part of the proposed Geneva conference (envisaged by the recently passed UN Security Council Resolution 338) in an effort to reach a comprehensive peace settlement that obliged Israel to withdraw from all the territories it occupied in 1967 in accordance with UN Security Council Resolution 242.[19] In this manner, Egypt would not be out of step with the rest of the Arab world, which would minimize the domestic and regional consequences Sadat might face if he made peace with Israel. Moreover, combining Arab power would help offset Egypt's bargaining disadvantage vis-à-vis Israel, a point Sadat's foreign ministry was adamant about.[20] It quickly emerged, however, that Israeli leaders were uneasy about a comprehensive settlement that would require them to surrender all of the territorial buffer they had captured in the Six-Day War. Of potentially greater significance, in the months before the Geneva conference, Syrian leader Hafez al-Assad showed himself to be unwilling to give any quarter in pursuit of a peace treaty. Given the importance Sadat placed on a peace settlement, he concluded that "linking the settlement process on all three fronts would have given Syria and radical Palestinian groups a veto power over Egypt's policy regarding its own territory, and it would have promised no settlement at all."[21] Consequently, he made the strategic decision to relieve himself of "the burden of Arab consensus" and to negotiate a separate peace between Egypt and Israel.[22]

To demonstrate his willingness to make peace, he broke a longstanding Arab taboo and traveled to Jerusalem in November 1977 to address the Knesset (the Israeli legislature). This dramatic gesture helped generate sufficient trust to allow the new Israeli government, led by the right-wing Likud Party and its leader Menachem Begin, to entertain territorial concessions in return for a peace treaty. After difficult and intense negotiations and a summit hosted by the United States in Camp David, Maryland, they signed a peace treaty in 1979 that provided both countries with what they desired most: Egypt received all of the Sinai—Sadat's sine qua non—while Israel received diplomatic recognition from, and a peace treaty with, the leading Arab state. Beyond the core territorial and security arrangements, the two countries signed between fifty-five to sixty normalization agreements that sought to enrich the content of peace with bilateral economic cooperation, cultural and educational exchanges, cooperation in distributing scarce water resources, and tourism. The agreement also granted autonomy to the Palestinians in the West Bank and Gaza for a five-year interim period, until more permanent arrangements could be reached.[23] In the years since, although the normalization agreements did not survive Sadat's October 1981 assassination, and the autonomy provisions fell by the wayside, the security framework has held despite regional tensions.[24]

The Path to Transition

What explains the relatively rapid turnaround in Egyptian-Israeli relations after 1973? Why did these formerly implacable enemies negotiate a peace treaty after four bitter wars in twenty-five years? In this section, I will investigate whether the path to peacemaking ran through Egyptian-Israeli societies or whether it was driven by state-level calculations.

BOTTOM-UP DYNAMICS

Democratic Pressures. To conclude that the logic of democratic peace brought about the peace treaty between Egypt and Israel, we would need evidence that (1) at the time of the settlement, both states were democracies or at least allowed the public to influence foreign policy; (2) the public in both states favored a peace treaty, as well as the concessions their leaders would have to make to reach an agreement; and (3) the public in both countries actually acted on their peaceful preferences and pressured the two states to embark on peacemaking. The proposition fails on all three counts.

First and foremost, whereas Polity IV classifies Israel as a democracy from 1977 to 1979 with a +9 on its Polity scale, it classifies Egypt as a nondemocratic state with a score of –6.[25] Although Egypt was a presidential republic holding parliamentary elections, the president, who wielded an enormous amount of political power, was unelected. Instead of contested presidential elections, the regime at the time held presidential plebiscites in 1970 and 1976 in which Sadat was the only candidate and the public had the choice either to support him or to oppose him.[26] This falls well below the standard of democracy. Furthermore, in the post-Nasser era, the Egyptian president was able to bolster his power and suppress opposition using the emergency law, which declared a continuous state of emergency in the country following the 1967 war. This state of emergency, which was valid for three years at a time and renewed routinely under Sadat, made it possible for the unelected president to insulate himself from criticism and dominate the parliament.[27]

Although Sadat touted a political liberalization program in Egypt that fostered the creation of political parties in the parliamentary assembly, he used both the emergency powers and the powers he retained under the 1971 constitution to control the assembly and the country. To begin with, after assuming the presidency, Sadat purged his main opposition by dismissing Vice President Ali Sabri and compelling Sabri's supporters to resign and be replaced by Sadat loyalists.[28] Sadat also regularly suppressed popular political opposition in the country, a situation that escalated in January 1977 when "new laws provided harsh punishments for all forms of public protest."[29] Consequently, far from being a democracy, the Egyptian political system during this period can best be described as "a semi-institutionalized authoritarian-bureaucratic polity" dominated by Sadat.[30] For this reason, analysts of Egyptian foreign policy during this period typically have viewed Sadat as its sole author because of the authoritarian nature of the country's political system.[31] Consequently, there were no democratic domestic or foreign policy institutions in Egypt to serve as a basis for a democratic peace, and the Egyptian public had little input into foreign policy.

Second, until after the agreement with Egypt was reached, public opinion in Israel opposed the extent of the concessions made to Egypt (i.e., giving back all of the Sinai, including the oil fields and strategic positions, and evacuating settlements), which suggests that the government was ahead of the public. Significantly, a confidential report on the state of Israeli public opinion commissioned by the Carter administration revealed that "by 78–15% a big majority oppose 'returning the entire Sinai Desert to Egypt.' "[32] Even after Sadat's unprecedented November 1977 visit to Israel helped soften Israeli attitudes to the point where, if pressed, "a majority would favor returning much of the Sinai" as part of an agreement, the Israeli public still "sees no connection between gaining peace and yielding territory" and was still unwilling to return all of the Sinai, as its leaders would eventually do.[33]

Certainly, there were elements about which the Israeli public was more conciliatory than its leaders after Sadat's visit. Most notably, public opinion opposed the construction of settlements in the West Bank while negotiations with Egypt were ongoing.[34] And the public heartily welcomed the treaty once it was signed, as did the majority of the Knesset, which approved the treaty by an 84 to 19 margin, with 17 abstentions.[35] On the core outlines of a potential settlement, however, Israeli leaders were willing to entertain more far-reaching compromises. And the Israeli public's willingness to compromise commenced only after the negotiations were in progress. Furthermore, though the Israeli public endorsed the treaty, as US secretary of state Cyrus Vance informed Carter, Begin faced "heavy criticism that he gave away too much at Camp David."[36] Even the dovish opposition leader, Shimon Peres, criticized the Camp David agreement as conceding far too much to Egypt, including the Sinai airfields, evacuation of the Sinai settlements, an autonomy plan for the West Bank and Gaza that Peres feared would lead to a Palestinian state, and a defensible border.[37] Clearly then, although the public embraced the treaty after it was concluded, Israeli democratic pressures did not drive the peace process.[38]

On the Egyptian side, the public also did not appear to drive peacemaking. Instead, Egyptian public attitudes toward Israel were quite hostile. Indeed, in July 1977, Sadat reportedly told Carter that "if we resurrected Jesus Christ and Prophet Mohammed together, they would not be able to persuade Moslem or Christian Arabs to open the borders with Israel after 29 years of hatred, four wars, rivers of blood and massacres."[39] Thus, while the Egyptian public may have been willing to entertain a peace treaty with Israel that returned all Arab land captured in 1967 to the various Arab states, they were hostile to the idea of a separate peace for Egypt and Egyptian concessions to Israel as part of a settlement.[40] Moreover, in November 1977, Egyptian public opinion was opposed to Sadat's visit to Israel. According to a White House top secret memorandum, "Sadat's unprecedented intention to visit Israel has stunned the Egyptian public," who "fear that he is giving everything away and is unlikely to receive anything in return."[41] For this reason, the Egyptians were eager to keep the content of meetings between Israeli defense minister Ezer Weizman and Egyptian war minister Mohammed Abd al Ghani al-Gamasy in Egypt, as well as the fact that such meetings were taking place, completely secret.[42] When Weizman met with Sadat in Egypt in March 1978, he noted that, owing to Sadat's peace policy, "opposition within his country was growing more vociferous." Students had attempted to hold rallies denouncing Sadat, the Progressive National Unity Party had publicly denounced the peace initiative, and, even within the regime, opposition was growing in the Egyptian foreign ministry.[43]

Furthermore, Sadat faced domestic pressure to suspend the negotiations. In May 1978, the Egyptian parliament was pushing the government to expel from Egypt the Israeli military representatives who arrived after the Sadat visit to Jerusalem to negotiate peace. By expelling them on the pretext of a lack of progress, the parliamentarians hoped that the Egyptian government would be able to "return to Arab solidarity" by scuttling the prospects of a peace treaty.[44]

Once the settlement was reached, very few Egyptian officials attended the signing ceremony. Most refused to go because they disliked the concessions Sadat made and believed the treaty would be unpopular in Egypt.[45] After its signature, the treaty was never really embraced by the Egyptian population. Initially, because Sadat and Prime Minister Mustapha Khalil misled the Egyptian public about the extent of Israeli withdrawals required by the treaty—stating that the document "called for an Israeli withdrawal from the territories occupied in 1967, including East Jerusalem, the West

Bank and Gaza" and that "Israel's borders are those which existed prior to June 1967"—most of Egyptian society approved of the settlement.[46] When it became clear that the treaty would not compel Begin to meet Arab demands regarding the West Bank and Gaza, and when the Egyptian economy failed to experience a significant peace dividend, the public grew hostile to the treaty and Sadat.[47] Societal antipathy to the treaty is evidenced by Sadat's assassination and the fact that, after his death, his successor, Hosni Mubarak, was unable to follow through with all the economic, social, and cultural protocols to the agreement that were negotiated.

Because public attitudes in the two states were more hostile to compromise than the leaders were, there is no basis to conclude that public opinion caused the two states to bury the hatchet.

Business Interests. If peacemaking was inspired by business groups and economic interests in pursuit of economic gains, we would need evidence that (1) either (a) the rival states were meaningfully interdependent prior to the peace treaties, *or* (b) key economic interests in both countries expected to benefit from a peace dividend; *and* (2) these economic interests pressured their governments to reach an agreement in order to realize or preserve economic gains. As it turns out, economic interdependence and pressures from business communities that had vested interests at stake also cannot explain Egyptian-Israeli peacemaking. The Arab boycott of Israel meant that there was very little economic exchange between Israel and Egypt prior to the peace treaty.[48] In fact, according to IMF Direction of Trade Statistics, as reported by Gleditsch, bilateral trade between Egypt and Israel was 0 as late as 1980.[49] Thus, there could not have been significant vested economic interests to drive the peace process.

Nor is there any evidence that economic interest groups drove Egyptian or Israeli decision making in anticipation of economic gains. Indeed, the Egyptian business community was rather cool to the idea of a peace treaty with Israel, which accounts for the economic provisions of the treaty never being implemented.[50] Overall, Egyptian society did not expect economic gains from bilateral economic cooperation with Israel and did not want normalization on political grounds.[51] Galia Press-Barnathan thus observes that the "group of private businessmen [in Egypt] who were interested in promoting cooperation with Israel was small," and "the political clout of private business was limited."[52] Consequently, it was clear even to the most optimistic observers of Egyptian-Israeli relations that "for a long time to come the volume and composition of trade and other economic transactions between Egypt and Israel will undoubtedly be influenced to an important degree by political considerations." As Arad, Hirsch, and Tovias noted, " it is inconceivable that the two governments will allow economic and other transactions between their citizens to be determined solely by economic considerations."[53] Thus, few expected significant bilateral exchange for the foreseeable future, especially while Egyptians were isolated in the Arab world and did not want to embrace full economic normalization with Israel.[54] Moreover, Egyptian leaders themselves—even Sadat—made clear from the beginning, in conversations with the Carter administration in Washington and during Sadat's groundbreaking November 1977 trip to Jerusalem, that they wanted a peace agreement involving the return of captured territory but without economic and political normalization.[55] As we shall see, Sadat and the military were extremely interested in economic gains in the form of economic aid from the United States, but this was more of a statist concern, as Sadat wanted these gains to stabilize the Egyptian economy in order to preserve his power position.[56]

On the Israeli side, Israeli leaders anticipated that, at least in the short term, peace with Egypt would actually impose costs on Israel, especially those associated with the return of the Sinai oil fields to Egypt, the costs of redeployment, and the economic toll associated with dismantling the Sinai settlements.[57] To be sure, the government did anticipate longer-term economic gains as a result of the peace treaty, in the form of a peace dividend from de-escalation on the southern border and the prospects of trade with Egypt.[58] Israelis also hoped for broader economic exchange with Egypt with the full panoply of trade, investment, and movement of goods and services.[59] Nonetheless, as we shall see, the overriding purpose of peacemaking from the Israeli point of view was about security rather than economics. In this regard, Begin's press secretary, Dan Pattir, emphasized that, although Israeli leaders anticipated a peace dividend in terms of not having a recurrence of war and the consequent potential to attract foreign investment, there was "no question that economic incentives were not pivotal in terms of the other incentives" that motivated Israel to make peace with Egypt.[60] Similarly, while former Israeli defense minister Ezer Weizman acknowledged that American economic incentives as part of the Camp David process were important, "the real reason for a peace agreement was that all three [Israel, Egypt, and the United States] wanted peace."[61]

Because the two sides had little economic interaction, and in neither state did the impetus for peacemaking come from business interests that anticipated large economic gains, commercial liberalism cannot explain the Egyptian-Israeli settlement.

Institutional Norms. For institutionalism to be an appropriate explanation of Egyptian-Israeli peacemaking, we would need to see that (1) Egypt and Israel were jointly embedded within cooperative regional institutions prior to the signature of the treaties; (2) these institutions created common interests and identities in the rival societies; *and* (3) these common interests and identities compelled their societies and their leaderships to make peace.

It would be difficult to explain the Camp David process as the product of cooperative international institutions. Prior to the treaty, there were no regional institutions that included both Arab states and Israel as members. Even after the signing of the treaty that remains largely true. While the Arab states are part of the Arab League (a rather weak institution) and the Arab Monetary Fund, the lack of Israeli membership makes it impossible to create a sense of common identity or we-ness that could inspire reconciliation.[62] Moreover, these institutions' steadfast opposition to the Egyptian-Israeli treaty, which culminated in the expulsion of Egypt from the Arab League following its signature, makes it clear that regional institutions and their cooperative norms did not inspire peacemaking. Consequently, there would appear to be no basis to explain the settlement in terms of the impact of regional institutions.

State-to-Nation Congruence. If Benjamin Miller's state-to-nation incongruence theory is a useful guide to explain the Egypt-Israeli settlement, we would have to see a change to resolve the state-to-nation imbalance in one of three forms preceding the peace agreement: (1) the creation of a new state to allow national determination to a stateless national minority; (2) population transfers to unite a dispersed nationality within one state and/or eliminate a source of irredentism; *or* (3) a territorial transfer that places a national minority within a state dominated by its compatriots. Then we would need to see that this change actually resolved the state-to-nation balance and provided an impetus for peacemaking.

There is some evidence that ameliorating the state-to-nation imbalance between Israel and Egypt helped pave the way for a peace treaty. In particular, Sadat made it clear that a prerequisite for an agreement was the return of the entire Sinai Peninsula, which Israel captured from Egypt in 1967.[63] Since this involved the restoration of the Sinai's Arab population to Egypt, it ameliorated the state-to-nation imbalance. Furthermore, by pushing the cause of the Arabs on the West Bank and Gaza, and by securing a pledge from Begin for an interim autonomy plan for the West Bank prior to some more definitive arrangement, Sadat was further trying to redress the state-to-nation imbalance as part of a peace settlement.

Nonetheless, because a state-to-nation imbalance remained, with a large Arab population with whom the Egyptians identified still under Israeli control in the West Bank, Gaza, and the Golan Heights, it would be difficult to say that the return of the Sinai actually resolved the state-to-nation imbalance. Consequently, the settlement was reached without restoring the congruence between states and nations in the region. Moreover, the Sinai was returned only *after* a settlement was reached, as a result of the treaty. It could hardly explain the move toward negotiations and peacemaking during a period of heightened state-to-nation incongruence.

Assessment of Bottom-Up Explanations. Overall, bottom-up theories provide us with little leverage over peacemaking between Egypt and Israel.
There is no basis whatsoever for claims that democratic pressures, economic interests, or institutional norms compelled leaders to conclude an
agreement. In addition, although the state-to-nation balance was somewhat
ameliorated by the anticipated return of the Sinai, the treaty does not appear to have been spurred on by improved state-to-nation congruence. In
the next section, we consider whether top-down theories provide a better
guide for Egyptian-Israeli peacemaking.

TOP-DOWN DYNAMICS

More Pressing Threats. If the peace treaty was driven by a desire to focus
on greater threats, we would have to see that (1) either Egypt or Israel (or
both) actually perceived another state to be a greater threat than its traditional rival; and (2) this greater threat led that state to make peace in order
to concentrate scarce resources on balancing against the more serious
threat.

Balance-of-power and balance-of-threat theory do not provide much
leverage over the Egyptian-Israeli peace settlement. To be sure, the Israeli
calculation was that removing Egypt from the Arab-Israeli conflict would
allow Jerusalem to concentrate its strategic efforts on the other leading
Arab antagonists (principally Syria).[64] Nonetheless, this is hardly a case of
Israel terminating the conflict with Egypt because of more pressing, more
powerful challenges. At the time, Egypt was the most powerful Arab state.
Indeed, Israeli leaders believed that without Egypt, it might not be possible
for the other Arab states to contemplate war with Israel. As Israeli foreign
minister Moshe Dayan explained to US National Security Council (NSC)
office director for Middle Eastern affairs, William Quandt, "if you take one
wheel off of a car, it cannot drive. Egypt is the biggest wheel amongst the
Arab states."[65] Israeli leaders even believed that if Egypt were to sign a
peace treaty with Israel, the other Arab states, denied the possibility of war
as a result, might eventually be compelled to negotiate peace, as well.[66]
Consequently, the balance-of-threat frame does not really fit, given that
Israeli leaders viewed Egypt as the primary threat.

Nor was Egypt making peace in order to concentrate its resources on a
more threatening rival. Although Egypt had a rivalry with neighboring
Libya, which led to border fighting in July 1977, and Sadat told Carter that
"further conflict with Libya is in the cards," and although Egypt had other
security concerns emanating from Sudan, Somalia, and North and South
Yemen, Egypt was still the dominant Arab state in the late 1970s, with as
yet no apparent challengers.[67] As we shall see, the main threats that Sadat
confronted were internal, rather than external, making a balance-of-power
approach focusing on more pressing external threats inappropriate.

Hegemonic or Dominant Great Power Influence. If hegemonic pressure brought about the Egyptian-Israeli settlement, we should see that (1) active US political, economic, and military engagement—in the form of inducements and pressure—preceded the peace treaty; and (2) the rivals were seeking anticipated American reactions at least as much as they were seeking gains from their peace partner.

American hegemonic leadership played a central role in the Egyptian-Israeli treaty. Having realized after the 1973 Yom Kippur War that Soviet arms and influence were unable to secure the return of the Sinai Peninsula, Sadat concluded that the United States was the only actor with the power and influence over Israel able to help him.[68] When Secretary of State Kissinger and President Carter proved willing to broker a deal, provided that it included a formal recognition of Israel and a peace treaty as the price for the Sinai, Sadat was willing to acquiesce to gain US leverage. Kenneth Stein, therefore, observes, "In short, Sadat did not *want* to make peace with Israel; rather, he *needed* to make an arrangement with Israel in order to enhance the likelihood of a positive relationship with the United States."[69] In this regard, in 1974, long before the Camp David negotiations, Sadat told Egyptian Chief of Staff Gamasy, "We are planning for peace *with the Americans* [i.e., not the Israelis]."[70]

Sadat also was eager to secure economic assistance from the United States at a time when its Arab benefactors were less forthcoming. In this regard, Sadat's journalist friend Mohammed Heikal wrote that, in Sadat's mind, "the top priority was to find the right political key to unlock Washington's generosity . . . perhaps the right one was peace with Israel."[71] Thus, as Janice Stein observed, "the support of the United States was essential for Egypt to achieve its domestic and security objectives; the strategy of economic liberalization depended critically on American aid, investment, and technology transfer, and resolution of the crisis with Israel depended on the active participation and commitment of the United States."[72]

Moreover, the United States prodded Sadat along during the process by promising him food aid, military assistance, and equipment as part of a peace treaty with Israel.[73] The Carter administration also provided Sadat with "one of the largest aid programs in [US] history" prior to the treaty in the hope of reducing the domestic friction Sadat faced as he made peace.[74] Following the treaty's signature, Carter sent a supplemental appropriations request to Congress, asking for a two-part aid package for Egypt totaling $1.8 billion to supplement existing aid facilities to the country. The first part consisted of $1.5 billion in military sales credit financing. The second consisted of $300 million of special economic aid loans for development projects and to "help satisfy the expectations of the Egyptian people for a better life."[75] It is noteworthy that, after receiving $1 billion in economic assistance from the United States in 1979, the year of the treaty, Egypt had become "the single largest recipient of US economic assistance in the world."[76] Moreover, in the years following 1982, US aid to Egypt took the form of grants rather than loans.[77] Carter also promised other economic sweeteners to Sadat. As the president noted in his diary in March 1979, "I promised Sadat that I would have at the White House after the peace treaty was signed a large number of American business leaders, the names to be worked out between Vance and Ghorbal, to encourage them to make investments in Egypt. And that I would also pursue our joint Israeli-Egyptian effort for economic development."[78]

From the Israeli point of view, the attitude of the United States was also of great significance. As Dayan made clear in a meeting with the Israeli foreign office staff before Camp David, he was overwhelmed by the historic importance of the summit. Never before had a US president called a summit meeting with an Israeli prime minister, nor had there ever before been a meeting between an Arab president, the US president, and the Israeli prime minister to discuss a peace treaty between Israel and an Arab state. The acceptance and legitimacy this conveyed to Israel, a young state that many states did not recognize, by the greatest power in the international system was of paramount importance and required Israeli representatives to behave responsibly.[79] Moreover, although some Israeli leaders were wary of trading a secure territorial buffer for what they felt was a risky treaty with an Arab state, they believed that a peace treaty involving territorial concessions would cement their relations with the United States, an important objective for an insecure state.[80]

The United States also put quite a bit of pressure on Israel—Dayan's spokesman, Naphtali Lau-Lavie, writes that "Carter used a steamroller"—to make territorial concessions to Egypt, accommodate Egyptian demands for concessions to the Palestinians, and stop settlement activities during the peace negotiations.[81] Indeed, although Carter promised that he would not directly hold economic or military aid to Israel hostage in order to extract Israeli concessions, there is ample evidence that the overall US strategy in negotiations with Israel was to keep up public and private pressure on Begin to compromise, or generate enough domestic opposition to topple his government and replace it with Shimon Peres's Labor Party.[82] On several occasions, Carter noted in his personal diary that peacemaking required the United States to "put as much pressure as we can on the different parties to accept the solution that we think is fair."[83] In a telling pre–Camp David memorandum to National Security Advisor Zbigniew Brzezinski, for example, Gary Sick noted, "The test now is how we can bring influence to bear over the next month to get Begin to modify his views or get a change in Israel."[84] At Camp David, US pressure came in the form of ultimatums that if Israel did not accept its bridging proposals, US officials would publicly blame Israel for being the obstacle to peace. Of perhaps greater concern, Carter intimated that Begin risked harming the special relationship between the United States and Israel—the cornerstone of Israeli security policy—if he refused to compromise or to live up to concessions made.[85] The Israeli cabinet felt immense pressure from Washington to make conces- sions, and, although they resented that pressure, because of the importance of the United States as an ally, they simply could not ignore it.[86] In fact, the constant pressure Carter applied on Israel ultimately soured the relation- ship between Begin and Carter.[87]

In addition, there are suggestions that despite Carter's prior commit- ment the Carter administration was stalling on new arms and military fi- nancing requests from Israel before and during the negotiations to pressure Begin into making concessions on the West Bank.[88] Secretary of State Vance also included linkage pressure in his strategy toolbox, telling Carter in November 1978, "We also need to decide how we manage our response to Israel's request for additional economic assistance so as to achieve our ob- jectives."[89] He continued, "On the question of aid . . . when we are satisfied that Israel is working in good faith for implementation of the Camp David general framework, we could begin listening to the Israeli presentation on the subject, but we would hold off a response until sometime next year when we are satisfied with the progress in the negotiations."[90] Nonetheless, he advised the president to deny publicly that he was providing aid "as in any way payment to one side or the other for concluding this Treaty."[91]

Washington also softened the blow of Israeli concessions by providing military assistance and hardware and by covering the costs of airport and base relocations from the Sinai to the Negev Desert. Consequently, Carter requested a larger aid package for Israel than for Egypt after the treaty, mainly consisting of $800 million in grants for the airport and base reloca- tions and $2.2 billion in foreign military sales credits to "finance other Is- raeli relocation costs and some upgrading of force structure consistent with the new territorial arrangements."[92] In addition, as part of the Sinai II com- mitments, Washington agreed that if, as a result of relinquishing the Sinai oil fields, Israel were to be unable to meet its oil needs through normal ar- rangements, the United States would, if possible, "promptly make oil avail- able for purchase by Israel." In addition, "the US will include in its annual aid to Israel some funds to help offset the costs of oil imports and to build oil stocks."[93] Following the signature of the treaty, the United States also concluded a memorandum of understanding between Israel and the United States that "committed America to support the implementation of the peace treaty, to take steps against violations, and to give Israel military and eco- nomic aid."[94] Moreover, it appears that Carter may have been willing to offer more extensive inducements to Israel as part of his Camp David strat- egy. In his handwritten notes for the conference, Carter listed possible "in- ducements to Israel (per Saunders): US technology transfers; Increased FMS [foreign military sales] transfers; Military sales policy equal to NATO; Mutual defense pact; Support for Is[raeli] military action if treaty broken."[95] Although some of these inducements never materialized, the United States did provide economic and military assistance to Israel as part of the treaty process and did sign a protocol with Israel that promised US support if Egypt were to violate the terms of the peace treaty.[96] It is clear, therefore, that the US strategy for peacemaking involved both lucrative carrots and intimidating sticks. Moreover, there are clear indications that the Israeli government was afraid of souring relations with the United States, Israel's principal ally and great power benefactor, which led Begin to concessions that he would ordinarily not have entertained.[97] Begin also deliberately linked the peace treaty to requests for aid from Washington.[98]

To be sure, the United States recognized that too much pressure on Israel could be counterproductive, as it might allow Begin to rally the Israeli public around him due to unwanted American interference.[99] Furthermore, US pressure was not always successful, as it failed in 1977 to keep Egypt and Israel committed to a multilateral settlement of the entire Arab-Israeli conflict rather than a bilateral agreement affecting only the Egyptian-Israeli dispute.[100] Nonetheless, within careful limits, the United States played an important role throughout the negotiations, pushing and prodding both Israel and Egypt to make concessions, engaging in "hard bargaining" and playing power politics.[101] Indeed, one of the main reasons for the Camp David process was the Carter administration's preference for summits, which reduced Egyptian and Israeli domestic input in the negotiations and allowed the United States to place maximal pressure on both sides to compromise.[102] Overall, then, active US leadership was an important component, without which a peace treaty would have been difficult, if not impossible, to obtain.

State-Preservation/State-Building Motives. If other rationalist/statist motives drove this peace treaty, we should see that (1) state leaders of at least one state conducted their policies rather independently of society; (2a) these leaders identified threats to their power position that could be ameliorated by making peace with their regional rival, or (2b) they were preoccupied by a desire to build strong state institutions to institutionalize their regime and/or their power base; and (3) these leaders embarked on peacemaking to secure their power positions or concentrate on state building.

At least on the Egyptian side, there is strong evidence that Sadat conducted Egyptian negotiations independently of Egyptian society and that he did so with an eye on the stability of his regime and his power position, which could be strengthened through the fruits of peace. Regarding the first issue, there can be no doubt that Sadat was the principal actor negotiating the settlement. I have already noted that compromise with Israel was unpopular among the Egyptian public. But even Sadat's advisers opposed the extent of Sadat's concessions. When he consulted with his aides before his November 9 speech to the Egyptian People's Assembly, declaring his willingness to visit Jerusalem, they were all shocked and pleaded

77

with Sadat to reconsider.[103] Two foreign ministers, Ismail Fahmy and Muhammad Riyad, resigned in protest over Sadat's peace initiative to Jerusalem, and a third, Muhammad Kamil, resigned over Sadat's concessions at Camp David.[104] Moreover, Sadat's decision-making style was to reach decisions on his own and keep his ministers and negotiators in the dark.[105] He also frequently overruled his negotiators publicly, to their great humiliation.[106] Sadat, rather than Egyptian society or even the Egyptian political elite, was clearly driving Egyptian peacemaking policy.[107]

State-preservation motives were of paramount importance for Sadat when he entered into the negotiations. Sadat faced an economic shambles at home and growing unrest over the *infitah* market reforms that were impoverishing the masses. Indeed, the January 1977 bread riots, in which thousands of protesters around the country burned police stations and attacked government property, threatened both Sadat's political power and even his life, as rioters sought to ambush him in his palace in Alexandria, from which he escaped by helicopter.[108] In August 1977, the US military attaché in Cairo reported that "the Egyptian officer corps is very pessimistic about chances of regaining Egyptian territory from Israel and is contemplating a government takeover if it becomes clear that Sadat's policies are not bearing fruit."[109] Moreover, while the bulk of the military establishment—without whose support Sadat could not remain in power—supported Sadat's peace initiative, many officers suffered from the same economic deprivations as the broader Egyptian public and were, therefore, growing discontented with the government.[110] The prospect of foreign interference only magnified these concerns. After Egyptian-Israeli negotiations commenced, for example, Sadat told Weizman of his fears that the Soviet Union, which he had ousted from the country, and Libya would sponsor coups in Egypt to unseat him if popular opposition persisted.[111] These domestic difficulties, which threatened Sadat's hold on power, led him to seek a way to stabilize his power position and cushion the blows of his reforms. Although the public and most of the Arab world opposed recognition of Israel and were horrified by his 1977 visit to Jerusalem, Sadat calculated that the economic benefits of regaining the Sinai (including its oil wells) and demobilization on the Egyptian-Israeli front, together with US food aid and Western foreign investment and technology, would pay both short-term and long-term dividends that would strengthen his hold on power.[112] Consequently, he concluded that he should abandon the conflict with Israel to help him combat a far-greater domestic threat to his regime.[113]

It is significant in this regard that, while discussing the peace negotiations with US representatives, Sadat and his representatives frequently made requests for American aid, which at least informally linked the two issues. In October 1978, after concluding the Camp David Accords, Egypt asked the United States for an additional 500,000 tons of wheat to help meet domestic demand.[114] In the wake of significant Egyptian concessions at

Camp David and afterward over Begin's autonomy plan for the West Bank, the timing of the Israeli withdrawal from the Sinai, and other key issues, the Egyptian minister of economy Haled al-Sayed met with US representatives in February 1979 to discuss the dismal state of the Egyptian economy and request additional American assistance. He noted that:

> . . . in his judgment, the infrastructure of Egypt has 'collapsed.'
>
> (a) at least $1,200,000,000 is urgently needed in the housing field alone.
> (b) The forward system was almost not functioning.
> (c) Water supply-sewer systems were in urgent need of repair.
> (d) Transportation.
> (e) City planning.
> (f) Food security.
>
> President Sadat needs a crash program on all these programs.[115]

Finally, when Carter traveled to Egypt in March 1979 to make the final push for Egyptian and Israeli concessions to secure a peace treaty, he noted in his diary that Sadat was preoccupied with economic considerations after the treaty and wished US assistance.[116]

The Americans were certainly convinced that Sadat was under pressure to provide the Egyptian people with a peace dividend and that his regime could fall without economic assistance. As Quandt observed soon after Carter's presidency began, "Sadat's effectiveness relies to a considerable extent on his ability to demonstrate tangible gains (or at least the absence of significant losses) as the result of his break with the USSR and his shift toward the West. It is in Israel's interest above all to ensure that Sadat's shift to moderation does not result in his downfall."[117] In a similar vein, Secretary of State Vance firmly believed that if Sadat was unable to "divert resources presently being spent for defense to the economic and social sectors," he would "be kicked out of office."[118] Thus, a memorandum by Herman Eilts, the US ambassador to Cairo, to Vance on the political situation in Egypt concluded: "The political and economic situation in Egypt is such that Sadat has every reason to seek a comprehensive peace settlement. He, more than anyone else, recognizes the need to devote his country's energy to solving its domestic difficulties."[119] Thus, there is good reason to conclude that Sadat's decision to make peace with Israel was inspired in large measure by his need to stabilize his regime by stabilizing his economy.

Assessment of Top-Down Explanations. An analysis of the path to the Egyptian-Israeli treaty, then, clearly indicates that it was a statist top-down settlement. In Israel, where public support for peacemaking did exist, the political leadership was far more willing to make concessions for a viable peace treaty than the public was in order to achieve high-level state interests, such as taking the leading Arab state out of the conflict and keeping its US ally on board. On the Egyptian side, peace-making was entirely a statist endeavor, with Sadat pursuing the settlement single-handedly, alienating many of the Egyptian elite and much of the Egyptian public in the process. His motives were clearly statist, as well. Indeed, President Carter, analyzing these motives retrospectively, enumerated: "What Sadat wanted was very clear. He wanted good relations with the United States, which Begin also wanted. He wanted his sovereign territory returned. That was something on which he would not deviate at all. He wanted peace with Israel for many reasons so that he could deal with other challenges to his own regime."[120] These motives put the Egyptian leadership at odds with Egyptian society. Indeed, as Ewan Stein observes, "from the mid-1970s, [Egyptian] official and intellectual society diverged: the state pursued a policy of peace; society a policy of war."[121] Finally, the American mediators also consciously pursued a peace treaty with states, recognizing that societal reconciliation would take more time. As Quandt responded to my queries: "Top-down is the way we initiated and pursued it, with Carter realizing more than the rest of us that normalization would break down the barriers over the long-run for a more comprehensive peace."[122]

The Post-Transition Era

How stable has this treaty been since it was signed? In this section, I assess whether the treaty has been the basis of a stable peace between the two countries, whether it has merely endured since its signature, or whether it provided merely a temporary lull in the conflict. I then consider what explains that level of stability.

Since the conclusion of the peace treaty, Israel and Egypt have refrained from using force against each other for over thirty years, and neither side has repudiated the treaty. Nonetheless, although the treaty envisioned a full normalization of relations between the two countries, only the security aspects of the agreement have been adhered to.[123] Consequently, the Israeli government has been dissatisfied with the implementation of all but the security and territorial aspect of the treaty.[124] For its part, the Egyptian government has charged that Israel did not fulfill the aspects of the agreement relating to Palestinian autonomy, given that the five-year interim period lapsed and no autonomy statute was concluded.[125] Despite the Oslo Accords of 1993 and 1995, progress toward Palestinian statehood has been halted. In this climate, the two sides have had a few diplomatic crises since 1979, most notably when Egypt withdrew its ambassador from Tel Aviv for extended periods from 1982 to 1988 to protest Israel's actions in Lebanon and from 2000 to 2005 in reaction to the Israeli response to the Second Intifada.[126] Moreover, although the treaty has held, the specter of war has not completely disappeared from the Egyptian-Israeli relationship. Indeed, Hillel Frisch comments that "almost all of Egypt's capabilities, equipment, and deployment of forces are concentrated on one front, to engage one opponent only: the Israel Defense Force. The Egyptians have made this explicit since the Badr-96 exercises in 1996, in which they specifically named Israel as the training target."[127] Thus, given that the two states have refrained from warfare and neither side has repudiated the treaty yet there have been crises and continual mutual recriminations and both sides have expressed dissatisfaction with elements of the treaty and its implementation, this can be classified as an enduring, but not a stable, peace.

How can we explain the endurance of this agreement, as well as its lack of stability? We will now consider the degree to which the statist motives for peacemaking persisted in the post-transition period, as well as the degree to which bottom-up mechanisms were employed to socialize the agreement. As it turns out, Egyptian-Israeli relations continue to be characterized by a top-down peace without societal buy-in.

The top-down conditions that facilitated the peace treaty largely persisted in the decades following its signature and continued to encourage both Egypt and Israel to abide by its security provisions. On the Israeli side, Egypt continued to be the only neighboring Arab state with which it had a peace treaty and diplomatic relations until the mid-1990s. It remained essential, therefore, for Jerusalem to cultivate the relationship and keep the largest Arab state out of a future war, especially as, over time, Jerusalem began to face greater threats from Iraq and Iran.[128] From the Egyptian point of view, with the nation still suffering from the economic costs of defeat in three wars in two decades as well from the stagflation of the 1980s, which hit the Egyptian economy quite hard, a peace treaty that kept the country out of another costly war retained immense value for the regime.[129] Moreover, both states faced common cause at different times in containing threats from revolutionary Iran and regional Islamist groups such as Hamas and the Muslim Brotherhood.

Furthermore, American hegemonic involvement continued to encourage both sides to respect the treaty. After Sadat's assassination, the United States pressed Mubarak, his successor, to continue to adhere to the security settlement as the cornerstone of his policy. Indeed, the importance of US support for Egypt was a paramount consideration for Mubarak, who emphasized repeatedly that, although he was personally uncomfortable with the treaty he inherited from his predecessor, it was essential to adhere to it to maintain Egypt's indispensible relationship with Washington.[130] For these reasons, although there were numerous bilateral irritations that could have led to a diplomatic rupture—especially the lack of movement on Palestinian autonomy, the application of Israeli law to the Golan Heights in 1981, the 1982 Israeli invasion of Lebanon, and the Israeli government's continued settlement activity—the security elements of the peace treaty remained in force throughout the Mubarak era.[131]

At the same time, the societal measures taken in Western Europe to cement the peace treaty were never implemented. Although a range of economic, cultural, educational, and social protocols were concluded between the two countries shortly after the treaty's signature as part of the settlement, only the security framework was ever implemented.[132] Egyptian society remained steadfastly opposed to the normalization of relations with Israel, especially as the Arab world as a whole opposed the treaty. Consequently, after Sadat's death, the Mubarak government had little interest in meaningful economic exchange or other forms of interaction with Israelis.[133] As a result, even by the most optimistic assessments, bilateral trade remains quite low and is not a significant source of revenue for either country, accounting for far below the 1 percent of GDP threshold.[134] While a few Egyptian businessmen, particularly those in the field of agrotechnology, saw an advantage in joint ventures with Israeli firms, they represented a tiny minority of the Egyptian business community. Overall, no significant economic interaction has taken place between Egypt and Israel since the peace treaty.[135] Indeed, instead of seeing a peace dividend from peacemaking with Israel, the economic embargo that the other Arab regimes imposed on Egypt for breaking with Arab solidarity and concluding a separate peace with Israel meant that Arab businesses and society viewed peace as costly in economic terms.[136] And, although in 2005 Egyptian businessmen finally endorsed a qualified industrial zones (QIZ) program similar to the one in Jordan, which allowed exports to the United States on favorable terms, provided goods were produced in the zone with a minimum of Israeli and Egyptian input, the QIZ did not promise much economic cooperation between the two countries, given domestic opposition and the lack of complementarity between the two economies.[137] Nor did Egyptian society, or even most of the business elite, truly embrace the QIZ. As Press-Barnathan comments, "the QIZ with Egypt was clearly a top-down, state-led initiative."[138]

Furthermore, in the three decades since Camp David, no cooperative Middle Eastern regional institutions of note have been created that include both Israel and Egypt as members. The only regional institution that includes both countries is the Union for the Mediterranean, established in July 2008, comprising the members of the European Union together with Balkan, Middle Eastern, and North African countries. This is a rather weak institution of limited political significance, whose second biennial summit, originally scheduled for November 2010, has been repeatedly postponed owing to a lack of progress in Israeli-Palestinian negotiations, and whose secretary-general (Ahmad Masa'deh) resigned after only a year in office.[139] Moreover, its appearance on the Middle Eastern scene so recently means that it cannot have been responsible for three decades of peace between Egypt and Israel.

Nor has there been any basis for building a democratic peace between the former rivals. Until his ouster in February 2011, Mubarak dominated the Egyptian political system, refusing to allow free and fair elections and restricting the operation of opposition groups, which were routine targets of government coercion.[140] Although in 2012 the country held presidential and parliamentary elections in which the Muslim Brotherhood emerged victorious, the subsequent reassertion of military rule and arrest of the elected government casts doubt on whether democracy will take hold in the country. Furthermore, the victory of Islamists in the 2012 election also raised doubts about the nature of a potential Egyptian democracy and whether Islamist democracy would be able to produce the pacifying effects of liberal democracy. As yet, there is no basis for concluding that Egypt has been transformed into a stable liberal democracy.[141] Under these circumstances, there has never been any prospect for common democratic norms or democratic institutions to crystallize peace between Egypt and Israel.

Finally, the state-to-nation balance has not been restored since the Camp David treaty. Although the interim autonomy provisions agreed on for the Palestinians on the West Bank held open the prospect of a return of the West Bank and Gaza to Arab rule within five years, this did not materialize.[142] Instead, negotiations and recriminations over the plight of the Palestinians dragged on for years until the 1993 Oslo I Accord between Israel and the Palestine Liberation Organization provided for Palestinian administration of Gaza and much of the West Bank. Nonetheless, Oslo, too, failed to resolve the issue, since Israel and the Palestinian Authority, created by the Oslo agreement, have been unable to conclude final-status negotiations. With a large Palestinian population under Israeli control in Gaza and the West Bank, as well as almost 1.5 million Arabs living in Israel, there remains little congruence between states and nations in the region.[143] Overall, then, none of the societal mechanisms derived from bottom-up approaches have been employed to socialize the Egyptian-Israeli peace settlement.

More than three decades after the peace treaty, therefore, Egyptian and Israeli societies remain, at best, suspicious of each other, if not downright hostile. As Kenneth Stein observes, "neither Sadat's visit to Jerusalem, nor Begin's response with autonomy for the Palestinians, nor the signing of the Camp David Accords, nor the Egyptian-Israeli Peace Treaty changed the long-term objectives or perceptions in either Cairo or Jerusalem."[144]

For Egyptians, Israelis have remained an enemy nation. In the years after the treaty, the Egyptian press frequently ran anti-Semitic and anti-Israel articles, indicating that societal hostility remained entrenched.[145] Egyptian society also shunned cultural and societal contact with Israel. Consequently, Israeli prime minister Yitzhak Shamir was able to complain in 1991 that "normalization [with Egypt] . . . has sunk into oblivion; there is no normalization now. So many years after signing the peace treaty, there are no normal trade relations with Israel; there is no cultural cooperation; there is no Egyptian tourism to Israel. It is as if Israel and Egypt were not living in peace but were two absolute alien and estranged countries."[146]

Under these circumstances, the peace treaty remained in force for statist reasons despite continued bilateral tensions and Egyptian societal antipathy. In 1983, for example, under pressure from the Arab world and Egyptian society to consider canceling the Egyptian-Israeli treaty in response to the 1982 Israeli invasion of Lebanon and the subsequent murder of civilians in Palestinian refugee camps by Christian Phalangists under the Israeli watch, Mubarak explained:

> What is the meaning of the annulment of the Camp David agreement? . . . Shall I return Sinai to Israel? . . . It means the declaration of a state of war with Israel. If I want to declare a state of war, it is imperative for me to be militarily prepared. In other words, I should halt development and focus on the evolution of services. I should concentrate all my efforts on war. Who will foot the bill for war? The Arabs? I do not know.[147]

Because the peace treaty has never been socialized and remained a top-down settlement, Mubarak's fall and the prospect of a democratic regime in Egypt were the military ever to release its hold on power—especially one led by the Muslim Brotherhood or a successor Islamist party—might not augur well for Egyptian-Israeli relations. During the 2011–12 parliamentary election campaign, and after the Muslim Brotherhood emerged as the largest faction within that short-lived parliament, prominent Egyptian politicians served notice that they might cancel the treaty with Israel.[148] While it remains conceivable that any new government in Egypt might recognize the pragmatic utility of remaining at peace with Israel, if the military were to relinquish its role as a restraining influence, it is possible that the peace treaty could end up as the most important long-term casualty of the 2011 revolution in Egypt.

Overall, the experience of the Egyptian-Israeli peace settlement is consistent with the logic of the Western European settlement in that it too was initiated for statist reasons over societal objections. As table 3.1 indicates by its shading and the absence of check marks on the left-hand side, the transition was top down, driven by American hegemonic pressure and incentives and Sadat's desire to resolve an economic crisis that could topple him from power. Rather than driving the treaty, society was at best a laggard and at worst downright hostile to it. At the time of the treaty's signature, the Egyptian public and business community were hostile to Israel, and most Israelis did not wish to make extensive concessions to secure a treaty. The two countries did not jointly belong to the same regional institutions, and, while the return of the Sinai did constitute an amelioration of the state-to-nation imbalance, a more significant state-to-nation incongruence remained with the large Arab population in Gaza and the West Bank under Israeli control.

As table 3.2 illustrates, where the Egyptian-Israeli experience differs from the Franco-German settlement is in the postagreement phase, in that the former treaty remains only an enduring peace—thus the table is partly shaded, in accordance with the convention used in this book—as the two countries were not able to overcome crises and mutual recriminations. As the table indicates, this can be explained by the fact that the treaty was never socialized through economic and cultural exchanges or through the creation of common identities within cooperative regional institutions or the bonds of joint democracy. Consequently, it remains a statist peace with little societal buy-in. Indeed, US negotiator Harold Saunders, in a retrospective analysis of Camp David, stressed that "the one major failure on the part of everybody at Camp David . . . was the fact that to this day there has not been success in somehow conveying the essence of this evolving process and changing relationships to the grass roots. The people in many instances did not come along." He concluded that the lesson of the Egyptian-Israeli peace treaty is that after peacemaking, leaders must confront "the need to engage people in the policy."[149]

Despite Egyptian-Israeli peacemaking not being driven by a restoration of the state-to-nation balance, this case is also consistent with Benjamin Miller's theory of regional transition. Progress toward a peace treaty was facilitated to some extent by a territorial and population transfer, as a result of the return of the Sinai to Egypt, as well as a commitment to resolve the

Table 3.1 Causes of the Egyptian-Israeli transition to peace

	Public opinion	Business pressures	Institutions	Improved state-to-nation balance	Greater threats	Hegemonic pressures	Regime survival
Egypt-Israel	—	—	—	Weak	—	√	√

Table 3.2 Developments in the postagreement phase

	Democratization	Economic exchange	Regional institutions	Improved state-to-nation balance	Greater threats	Hegemonic pressure	Regime survival
Egypt-Israel	—	—	—	—	√	√	—

plight of Palestinian Arabs under Israeli control. Furthermore, since Miller does not predict more than a cold peace in the event that the state-to-nation imbalance is not completely corrected, his theory is not damaged by the fact that peace treaty was signed while a large Arab population remained under Israeli control. Instead, he would explain the lack of socialization of the treaty as an artifact of the continued state-to-nation incongruence.

Given that Egyptian society never was socialized to accept the treaty, there are reasons to fear that Egyptian-Israeli peace is more precarious in post-Mubarak Egypt. After all, the peace treaty remained a statist peace, which served the regime's interests. If the Egyptian military were to relinquish power, to the extent that Egypt undergoes a democratization process, the possibility exists that a government hostile to the treaty could rise to power and no longer view peace as consistent with Egypt's state interests. If that happens, the government will face no deep-seated societal objections to terminating the treaty.

CHAPTER 4

The Israeli-Jordanian Treaty

The Israeli-Jordanian rivalry was never quite as intense as the one between Egypt and Israel. Whereas Egypt had consistently maintained its implacable opposition to a Jewish state in the Middle East, the Jordanian relationship with Israel was more complex. Alone among Arab countries, Transjordan (after 1949 the Hashemite Kingdom of Jordan) had a history of bilateral relations with the Jewish Yishuv (settlement) in mandated Palestine dating back to 1921.[1] Significantly, King Abdullah I of Transjordan was the only Arab leader to accept the 1937 Peel Commission report that called for the establishment of a Jewish state on part of mandated Palestine, in the hope that he could annex the Arab part of Palestine to Transjordan.[2] He also held secret partition talks with the Yishuv prior to the State of Israel's declaration of independence in May 1948.[3] In this regard, as three of the Jordanian negotiators of the 1994 treaty observe, "had the atmosphere and political and economic conditions been favorable, Jordan would have negotiated a peace treaty with Israel in 1948."[4]

When the Arab states declared war on the nascent Jewish state, Abdullah felt compelled to play a leading role in the Arab coalition, serving as the supreme commander of the Arab forces. After Israel defeated the Arab armies, however, he entered into secret negotiations with the Israeli military governor of West Jerusalem, Moshe Dayan, to replace the postwar armistice with a comprehensive peace treaty between Israel and Transjordan, which would allow Abdullah to focus his efforts on his true goals: establishing Hashemite control over greater Syria and recapturing his ancestral Hejaz from Saudi Arabia.[5] Although he eventually broke these talks off when the other Arab states got wind of them, the Arab world viewed Abdullah's "secret dealings with the Jews" as treachery to the Arab cause. Consequently, when suspicions grew in 1951 that Abdullah was again negotiating secretly with Israel, the king was assassinated at the al-Aqsa Mosque in Jerusalem.[6]

In 1967, King Abdullah's grandson and successor, King Hussein, fought against Israel alongside Egypt and Syria in the Six-Day War and lost control of the West Bank, which Abdullah had annexed to Jordan in 1950. Yet, in subsequent years, Hussein met secretly with Israeli leaders on several occasions to coordinate on matters of mutual interest, such as containing Syria and keeping bridges over the Jordan open to commerce between West Bank Palestinians and Jordan.[7] During the 1970 civil war in Jordan, the Israeli government came to Hussein's assistance by mobilizing the Israel Defense Forces along the border to protect the Hashemite regime when Syrian troops crossed into northern Jordan to intervene on behalf of the Palestinian rebels.[8] To return the favor, Hussein warned Israeli prime minister Golda Meir in September 1973 of an impending Syrian surprise attack against Israel in co-ordination with Egypt.[9] In addition to this very significant security cooperation, the two countries also collaborated covertly in the fields of agriculture, irrigation, and health.[10]

In spite of this unusual covert cooperation, Israel and Jordan remained enemies from 1948 until 1994. Notably, Jordan actively participated in three Arab wars against Israel: the 1948 war following Israel's declaration of independence, the Six-Day War of 1967, and the Yom Kippur War of 1973. Jordan was also the staunchest Arab opponent of Israeli settlement policies and its actions to counteract the Palestinian Intifada in the West Bank. The result of this bifurcated public and private relationship has been what Ian Lustick has termed an "adversarial partnership" between the two countries with elements of remarkable cooperation within the context of a longstanding rivalry.[11]

Important elements of bilateral cooperation had been possible between Israel and Jordan, despite the Arab-Israeli conflict, because the two countries shared several high-level common interests. To begin with, they shared a fear of Palestinian nationalism and, in particular, the Palestinian Liberation Organization. For Israel, Palestinian nationalism represented an attempt to delegitimize the Jewish state, with its claim that all of the land comprising mandated Palestine belonged to Palestinian Arabs, thereby threatening the very existence of the Jewish state. At a minimum, the Palestinian movement threatened Israeli control over the West Bank and Gaza, which Israel had captured in the 1967 war, by making these territories ungovernable—especially during the 1986–93 Intifada, during which the Palestinians used violent protests and civil disobedience to resist Israeli administration.[12] Moreover, the PLO engaged in terrorist attacks against Israeli civilians both in Israel and abroad as a means of advancing its nationalist agenda.[13] Palestinian nationalism also represented an existential threat for the Hashemite monarchy in Jordan, the majority of whose population consists of Palestinian refugees from the 1948 and 1967 Arab-Israeli wars. Under these circumstances, the eternally unstable Hashemite regime must always be fearful of becoming "the next victim of PLO irredentism."[14] Consequently, both Israel and Jordan shared a fundamental interest in defusing and containing Palestinian nationalism.

The two rivals also had a common interest in ensuring the survival and preserving the territorial integrity of the Hashemite regime in Jordan. For King Hussein, this interest is self-evident. For Jerusalem, the monarchy's collapse would represent a grave security threat, as it would likely replace a moderate Arab government with one of three more dangerous alternatives: a hostile Palestinian governing coalition, radical Islamists, or, as in the case of Lebanon, a Syrian puppet regime. In addition, a Jordanian collapse would bring instability to Israel's longest border, removing an important strategic buffer separating Israel and an implacably hostile Iraq. The two states also shared a mutual interest in border security. Israel needed to prevent the infiltration of terrorists and militant Palestinian nationalists from Jordan into the West Bank and Israel proper. For its part, Jordan was eager to stem the influx of additional Palestinian refugees, which threatened the regime's precarious stability, and radical elements that could mobilize Palestinians in Jordan against the monarchy.

Last, but hardly least, Israel and Jordan depended on each other for access to, and the safety of, their water supply in the arid Middle East. From the Israeli perspective, the security of Israel's water supply from the Jordan and Yarmouk Rivers depended on Jordan not diverting the water from these rivers, as they had sought to do prior to 1967. The Jordanians were eager to restore water levels that were drastically reduced after the 1967 war, when Israel captured the Golan Heights and the West Bank, putting Jerusalem in possession of the Sea of Galilee and the Upper Jordan. Furthermore, King Hussein wanted to get Israeli permission to build a diversion on the Upper Jordan to enable Jordan to utilize the share of water they had been allocated from that river. The two sides, faced with perpetual shortage, also would need to cooperate with each other if they were to be able to expand their water supply.[15] Thus, the two rivals had many interests in common.[16]

Despite these common interests, the Israeli-Palestinian conflict kept the official relationship between Israel and Jordan hostile. King Hussein's July 1988 decision to cut its legal and administrative ties to and renounce its claims to the West Bank perpetuated this status quo, ensuring that Jordan could not reach a bilateral agreement with Israel without involving the PLO. Furthermore, because Palestinian refugees constituted such a large percentage of the Jordanian population, the king was wary of making public concessions to Israel before the Israeli government resolved its conflict with the Palestinians to the satisfaction of the Palestinian majority in the kingdom. Doing so would risk another civil war if he appeared to abandon the Palestinian cause. The 1993 Oslo Accord between Israel and the PLO, however, opened up a strategic window for a peace treaty between Amman and Jerusalem.[17]

As a result, thirteen months after the Oslo signing ceremony, Israel and Jordan concluded a peace treaty codifying the Western border of Jordan;

restoring 340 square kilometers of West Bank land to Jordan but leasing that land to Israel for agricultural purposes; committing both parties to fighting terrorism and avoiding coalitions and alliances that threaten the other; allocating fifty cubic meters of water to Jordan from the Jordan and Yarmouk Rivers; establishing full bilateral diplomatic relations; and paving the way for bilateral cooperation in a host of economic fields, including trade, transportation, tourism, communications, energy, navigation, health, and agriculture.[18]

This chapter will investigate the sources of the Israeli-Jordanian peace treaty, as well as the evolution of the Israeli-Jordanian relationship since it was signed.

The Path to Transition

BOTTOM-UP DYNAMICS

Democratic Pressures. If democratic pressures were responsible for peacemaking between Israel and Jordan, we would need evidence that (1) both countries were democracies, or at least allowed significant public input into the policy process, when they made peace; (2) public opinion in both states wanted to make peace and were willing to make concessions to reach an agreement; and (3) the Israeli and Jordanian publics actually pushed their governments to negotiate peace.

The Israeli-Jordanian treaty cannot be attributed to democratic pressures for several reasons. To begin with, although Israel in 1994 was democratic, Jordan was not. Indeed, the Polity IV data set gave Israel a ranking of +9 on its Polity scale (making it a democracy), whereas it gave Jordan only a +2 (making it an anocracy).[19] Jordan's poor score reflects the unelected king's overwhelming dominance over Jordanian society and politics. Although Jordan ostensibly possesses the trappings of a parliamentary democracy, in practice the king completely dominates the Jordanian legislature, and political participation is heavily constricted. Under the terms of the 1952 Jordanian constitution, the Jordanian legislature is subordinate to the monarch. While the cabinet was drawn from and nominally responsible to parliament, the king was entitled to dismiss the legislature at will if he so chose. Moreover, the parliament itself disproportionately represented the sparsely populated East Bank and its Hashemite families loyal to the king while diluting the influence of Palestinians, who were concentrated in urban areas such as Amman, and Islamists.[20] In the conduct of foreign policy especially, parliament has little to no role.[21] Despite the controlled liberalization that the monarchy allowed beginning in 1989, the king retained all the levers of political power, keeping political parties under the scrutiny of the security services, prohibiting them from running on a party policy platform, and severely curtailing, regulating, and scrutinizing civil-society organizations.[22] Thus, the Jordanian regime fell well short of a democracy and did not allow public input into the foreign policy process.

Beyond these broader institutional classifications, the causal mechanisms suggested by democratic peace theory did not manifest themselves in this settlement. Although it has been surprisingly difficult to get public opinion data on Israeli attitudes toward peace with Jordan, there is every reason to believe that it supported the project. Avi Shlaim observes, for example, that "the treaty enjoyed wide popular support in Israel and elevated Rabin's prestige to new heights."[23] Furthermore, the Israeli Knesset also ratified the treaty immediately (actually the day before the treaty's signature, on October 25, 1995) by an overwhelmingly large margin (105 in favor to 3 opposed).[24] Nonetheless, there is no indication that the public actually compelled Israeli leaders to make peace. Indeed, at the time of the peace treaty, the Israeli public's attention—and even the peace movement's—was focused on the more pressing issue of the Oslo Accord with the PLO and Israeli negotiations with Syria. There is no evidence that, before the treaty, the public viewed a peace treaty with Jordan as a priority or pressed the government to negotiate such a pact.[25]

The logic of a publicly driven peace process is particularly difficult to square with the Jordanian experience, given that the Jordanian public was far less conciliatory than Jordanian leaders. Broad-based public opinion polls from Jordan and elsewhere in the Arab Middle East are difficult to obtain, since "intrusive internal security systems, traditional reticence with strangers, and so forth" interferes both with the polling agency and the average citizen's willingness to respond.[26] We do have limited polling data and other indicators, which can be used, albeit with caution, to determine the public's mood. Overall, we can conclude that, while Jordanian professionals supported the idea of peace negotiations with Israel after the fact, much of Jordanian public opinion remained hostile to the treaty, which was widely regarded as "the king's peace," after its signature.[27] This hostility stems, in large part, from the demographic composition of Jordan, where, in 1993, Palestinians constituted almost 50 percent of the official population and close to 60 percent of the total number of people in Jordan.[28] As a group, these Palestinians rejected the existence of the State of Israel, which they accused of usurping their land.[29] Palestinian opinion in Jordan was, therefore, upset by the prospect of peace with Israel.[30] Indeed, in a poll of the attitudes of Arab professionals toward peace with Israel in 1993 prior to the peace treaty, only 26 percent of Palestinian professionals living in Amman supported negotiations with Israel, whereas 51 percent opposed such talks.[31] Furthermore, Islamist forces, including the Muslim Brotherhood—the single largest bloc in the Jordanian parliament, although they did not constitute a majority—opposed peacemaking with Israel.[32] Consequently, support for the treaty was largely confined to a small circle around the king.[33] Thus, although the Jordanian parliament did ratify the treaty by a margin of 55 to 23, that is misleading, because the king completely dominated parliament.[34] Furthermore, to ensure he could overcome domestic hostility to peace with Israel, the king rolled back the controlled liberalization he had initiated in the late 1980s. Significantly, he enacted a new electoral law in 1993 that further reduced the representation of the Palestinian majority and the Islamists in parliament, thereby further concentrating power in the hands of his East Bank supporters, and he put additional restrictions on the right to protest.[35] Thus, as Nigel Ashton comments, "peacemaking took him in a more authoritarian direction."[36]

The king appealed to the public to support "his" peace, on the grounds that it was good for Jordan and part of a broader movement toward peace with Israel in the Arab world, represented by the Egyptian-Israeli treaty, the Oslo Accord between Israel and the PLO, and ongoing negotiations between Israel and Syria.[37] Nonetheless, despite the clear implication that opposition to the treaty meant opposition to the king himself, public manifestations of opposition were apparent. In the days leading up to the treaty, numerous groups protested, prompting a governmental ban on demonstrations in the aftermath of its signature.[38] Indeed, according to the British Broadcasting Corporation, the protest movement included "the secretaries-general of the Jordanian opposition parties, trade unions, popular organizations, women and youth groups and a number of House of Representatives members."[39] Thus, although the *Jordan Times* reported that public opinion polls indicated that 80 percent of Jordanians favored peace, there is reason to suspect that the government's English-language mouthpiece might have exaggerated support levels.[40]

Moreover, Jordanian labor unions banned all Jordanian workers from working on Israeli projects. In addition, the Jordanian professional associations, which certified most of the country's professionals, banned their members from traveling to Israel or working with Israelis at the risk of blacklisting and having their membership revoked, which threatened their ability to work, receive pensions, and access unemployment and health benefits.[41] That these organizations could oppose the king so openly indicated the degree to which the treaty was unpopular, which made the government unwilling to crack down on its opposition.[42] It is clear, then, that the Jordanian government was more conciliatory than its public was. The treaty, therefore, did not result from democratic pressures.

BUSINESS INTERESTS

To reach the conclusion that economic interests drove the peace process, we would need to see evidence that (1) either (a) the Israeli and Jordanian economies were meaningfully interdependent before 1994, *or* (b) key Jordanian and Israeli business interests anticipated meaningful economic gains as a result of a peace settlement; *and* (2) business groups lobbied their governments to make peace in order to realize these gains or protect their vested economic interests.

As in the case of the Egyptian-Israeli treaty, it would be difficult to explain the Israeli-Jordanian peace treaty in terms of economic interdependence and pressures from business communities that had vested interests at stake. Because of the Arab boycott of Israel, there was very little economic exchange between Israel and Jordan before the peace treaty.[43] Indeed, as late as 1995, the IMF's Direction of Trade Statistics reported zero trade between Israel and Jordan, reflecting its insignificant character.[44] Thus, there were no significant vested economic interests prior to the treaty to drive the peace process.

Nor is there evidence to suggest that anticipated gains by the Israeli and Jordanian business communities motivated them to pressure their governments to make peace. Although the Israeli-Jordanian peace treaty officially called for the development of economic cooperation between the two countries, neither country expected too much in that theater.[45] From the Israeli perspective, the two economies lacked complementarity, especially since Jordan lacked sufficient infrastructure to make Israeli investment and bilateral joint ventures lucrative and the Jordanian market is rather small.[46] Moreover, unlike other Middle Eastern states, Jordan was not endowed with oil reserves or any rentable raw materials to speak of, with the exception of far-less-lucrative materials at the time, such as phosphates and potash.[47] Whereas the Israelis could have profited by using Jordan as a market for Israeli goods, they correctly anticipated that the kingdom would not wish to be dominated economically by Israel in this manner.[48] Consequently, there was little reason for the Israeli business community to anticipate significant bilateral gains from a peace treaty with Jordan.

For Jordan's part, although the king attempted to sell the treaty to the Jordanian public in terms of the economic boon it would be to the country because of the anticipated inflow of foreign investment and foreign aid, the Jordanian business community was largely uninterested in normalization with Israel.[49] It is significant in this regard that the Jordanian professional organizations banned all contact with Israel and Israeli businesses after the treaty's signature, which indicates their opposition to peace with Israel and their rejection of its economic benefits.[50]

Some degree of bilateral economic cooperation did emerge as part of the US-sponsored QIZ, which allowed duty-free exports to the United States from defined industrial areas in Jordan provided they contained a minimum of 8 percent of Israeli inputs as a percentage of total cost (only 7% for high-tech goods).[51] In particular, these provided important gains to participating Jordanian businesses in terms of investment from third parties and easier access to the lucrative US market. Nonetheless, this was an American initiative that commenced four years following the peace treaty as a means of cementing the agreement, and it had not been envisioned at the time of its signature.[52] It could not, therefore, have motivated business interests on either side of the border to pursue peacemaking. Nor, as will be discussed in the section of this chapter on the postagreement period, did it ever amount to a very significant payoff for either country. Consequently, there is little evidence that either vested economic interests or anticipated gains by business elites drove peacemaking between Israel and Jordan.

Institutional Norms. To explain this settlement in terms of constructivist institutionalism, we would need evidence that (1) Israel and Jordan were jointly members of the same cooperative regional institutions before the treaty was negotiated; (2) Israeli and Jordanian societies developed common identities as a result of these institutions; *and* (3) their common identities actually inspired the peace negotiations.

As in the Egyptian case, there is no basis to conclude that regional institutions generated cooperative norms and a "we-ness" that fostered conflict resolution between Israel and Jordan. The two rivals simply did not belong to common regional institutions. They did participate in joint bilateral consultations over the distribution of Jordan River water resources and the management of other cross-border issues.[53] These, however, fell well below the level of a cooperative regional institution, were not well publicized to Israeli and Jordanian societies, and consequently did not result in the generation of a new, more cooperative identity. As a result, as indicated earlier, Jordanian society, as a whole, remained quite hostile to the project of peacemaking. An institutionalist explanation of Israeli-Jordanian peace, therefore, holds no water.

State-to-Nation Congruence. To attribute Israeli-Jordanian peace to a rectification of the state-to-nation imbalance, we would need to see evidence of either the creation of a new state, population transfers, or territorial transfers that eliminated separatist or irredentist pressures among Israeli and Jordanian societies. Furthermore, we would need to see that this change restored the state-to-nation balance and jump-started the peace process.

It would be difficult to explain the Israeli-Jordanian peace treaty in terms of an alleviation of the state-to-nation imbalance in the Middle East. To begin with, the peace treaty involved no significant territorial transfers nor transfers of population, nor did it create new states that could facilitate the self-determination of stateless nationalities. The extent of the territorial settlement was the return of Wadi Arava and an area near the confluence of the Yarmuk and Jordan Rivers to Jordanian sovereignty, although Jordan agreed to lease this land to Israel indefinitely for agricultural purposes, so this did not have any meaningful effect on life on the ground.[54] Moreover, although the Oslo Accord had begun to envision a process that could lead to the resolution of the Israeli-Palestinian conflict, two considerable challenges to regional state-to-nation congruence persisted: (1) a large Palestinian Arab minority under Israeli control in Israel, the West Bank, and Gaza; and (2) the Palestinian majority in the Hashemite Kingdom of Jordan. Consequently, peacemaking proceeded without any reasonable expectation of the restoration of a regional state-to-nation balance.

Assessment of Bottom-Up Explanations. Overall, then, the evidence in support the claim that the Israeli-Jordanian peace settlement was a bottom-up peace driven by societal pressures is quite weak. There were no democratic pressures for peacemaking: neither the Jordanian nor the Israeli business communities anticipated large economic gains; no cooperative institutional norms were fostered; and a large state-to-nation imbalance remained. In the next section, therefore, we will turn our attention to top-down approaches to see if this is more properly understood as a state-driven peace process.

TOP-DOWN DYNAMICS

More Pressing Threats. If peacemaking between Israel and Jordan followed a balance-of-power or balance-of-threat logic, we would have to see that (1) either state (or both) viewed another state or group of states as a more serious threat to national security than its traditional rival; and (2) peacemaking was designed primarily to focus on that greater threat and devote sufficient national resources to containing that threat.

Balance-of-power considerations do appear to have played an important role in the Israeli-Jordanian peace settlement. As far as Israel was concerned, Jordan was a relatively minor player in the Arab-Israeli conflict. It was considerably weaker than other Arab and regional antagonists, such as Iraq, Iran, and Syria, and far less threatening, given the Hashemite Kingdom's desire for good relations with the United States. It made sense, therefore, to terminate the conflict with Jordan—especially since an agreement would cost Israel quite little—thereby securing Israel's longest land border in order to concentrate on more pressing threats.[55] It would deny Iraq, which though defeated in the 1991 Gulf War was still the most unpredictable Arab state and the one with the largest army, its natural axis of attack.[56] The treaty provision preventing Jordan from allowing foreign forces to be stationed on Jordanian territory thus meant that Jordan had become a critical buffer against an attack against Israel from the east, which, in effect, meant both the Iraqi and Syrian fronts.[57] Rabin also calculated that a strong and viable Hashemite regime in Jordan, which had an interest in restraining the Palestinians, would be a critical plank of Israeli security strategy in the postagreement environment.[58]

Furthermore, Rabin viewed Iran as the greatest long-term strategic threat, the containment of which required Israel to maintain peace with more moderate Arab states. His strategic vision was fixated on his greatest fear: "a situation where two states—Iraq and Iran—were on the verge of nuclear weapon capability without having abandoned the Arab dream of 'throwing Israel into the sea.'"[59] Of these two, after the 1991 Gulf War in which Iraqi power had been severely curtailed, Iran was by far the greater concern given that it represented the twin threats of Islamic extremism and the potential to acquire weapons of mass destruction.[60] Under these circumstances, carrying on a pointless rivalry with a state such as Jordan, with which Israel had so many overlapping interests, would be counterproductive.[61] For all these reasons, "Rabin felt that peace with Jordan improved Israel's strategic situation."[62]

Jordan, as a country that possessed no natural barriers to separate it from its more powerful neighbors, also faced more compelling potential threats in the region.[63] The 1990 Iraqi invasion of Kuwait and the threat Iraq posed to Saudi Arabia made moderates in the Arab world (and even less moderate states, such as Syria) fear Saddam Hussein more than they feared Israel, which they judged to be the only regional power capable of containing Iraq. Although Jordan had hedged its bets by staying neutral in the Gulf War and maintaining good ties with Iraq despite the postwar sanctions, the Jordanian leadership also feared Iraq more than it did Israel.[64] After all, by coming to King Hussein's assistance during Black September in 1970, when Syria prepared to invade Jordan in support of the PLO, the Israelis had demonstrated that they viewed an independent, secure Jordan as an essential Israeli national-security requirement.

In addition to Iraq, the Jordanian regime also had reason to fear Syria, which had threatened to destabilize the country in 1970 and also had its tethers in another of its weaker neighbors (Lebanon). Former US ambassador to Israel and member of Clinton's Middle East peace team, Martin Indyk, therefore, suggested that one of King Hussein's primary motivations in making peace with Israel was to secure US support in the event of a Syrian threat to Jordan.[65] Furthermore, Hussein harbored important suspicions about the emerging PLO-led Palestinian entity on the West Bank, which could foment unrest among Palestinians in Jordan, as Yasser Arafat did in 1970, and seek to replace the Hashemite monarchy with a Palestinian state on both banks of the Jordan.[66] Indeed, according to some, this was the overriding reason why Jordan believed it had to negotiate a treaty with Israel once Israel and the PLO signed the 1993 Oslo Accord. Since it was apparent that Oslo would put a Palestinian political entity on the king's western border, it was essential for Jordan to have some say over the security arrangements in order to limit the potential damage that entity could cause Jordan.[67]

The treaty would, therefore, help Jordan focus its attention on a variety of more pressing regional threats. In this regard, King Hussein's remark on requesting extensive US military assistance following the signature of the peace treaty with Israel is telling: "Our problem is not one of a particular frontier . . . but all of them."[68] Because resolving the destructive conflict with Israel within the context of the Israeli-Palestinian peace process that was underway following the 1993 Oslo Accord would also help mend fences with Washington, it might further help to secure Jordan from all its regional threats.

Hegemonic or Dominant Great Power Influence. If hegemonic or dominant great power pressure caused Israeli-Jordanian peacemaking, we should see evidence that (1) the United States, as global hegemon and the most interested great power, attempted to encourage peacemaking by applying diplomatic pressure or threats and by offering economic and military incentives to the rivals in an effort induce compromise; and (2) the Israeli and Jordanian leaders were seeking anticipated American reactions at least as much as they were seeking peace with their rival for its own sake.

There is strong evidence in support of this proposition, as the United States loomed large in King Hussein's calculations. To begin with, in order to encourage the king to make peace with Israel, the United States offered him significant economic, military, and political payoffs. In the economic sphere, President Bill Clinton promised to cancel all Jordanian debts to the United States, which amounted to a one-time grant of about $700 million, on signature of the treaty and committed to making an appeal to the Paris Club countries to forgive Jordanian debts to them (about $4.3 billion), as well.[69] King Hussein also requested additional economic incentives from the United States, including the termination of maritime inspections on shipping in the Gulf of Aqaba to prevent Iraqi sanctions evasions via Jordanian waters, and US support for Israeli-Jordanian joint-development projects.[70] In light of widespread disgust in the United States regarding the Jordanian position during the Gulf War, Clinton and Secretary of State Warren Christopher made it clear to the king that securing debt forgiveness from Congress would be difficult and would only be possible if Jordan were to sign a formal peace treaty with Israel.[71] King Hussein himself acknowledged this in his publicly broadcast address to the Jordanian legislature on July 9, 1994, in which he justified his direct negotiations with Israeli prime minister Yitzhak Rabin: "The US Administration has a sure desire to support this country in the material and military fields. However, the effects of the Gulf crisis continue to dominate the thought of many people in the US legislative authority. The United States is prepared to ask the legislative authority to cancel all the debts and lift restrictions on Jordanian armaments. . . . However, this is linked to Jordan's continuing in the peace process."[72] Finally, Clinton promised to recommend that Congress pass a large foreign aid package to Jordan if it were to sign a peace treaty.[73]

King Hussein also requested military incentives from the United States, most notably the resumption of US military assistance to Jordan, which had been suspended in retaliation for Jordanian nonparticipation in the Gulf War coalition.[74] The loss of US military assistance was a serious concern to

Jordan and hampered its national security effort, which began to suffer from a lack of up-to-date equipment and the shortage of critical spare parts.[75] After the treaty's signature, the United States would classify Jordan as a major US non-NATO ally, effectively the same status as Israel and Egypt. Moreover, Jordan was also included in the Excess Defense Articles program, which provides surplus US military equipment virtually free of charge to selected countries.[76] Although it is not clear whether these measures were promised explicitly in advance of the treaty, they represent considerable security payoffs for Amman.

Politically, a peace treaty with Israel allowed King Hussein to solidify his status as a moderate, pro-Western Arab leader. This would have direct material implications in that it would help secure US support in the event of war with Iraq, US military assistance and advanced hardware (such as F-16 aircraft), and US economic support. Almost as important, however, was the less tangible payoff of helping get Jordan back in the American good book after being the only Arab state not to support the Gulf War coalition.[77] Finally, the Clinton administration warned Jordan that if it did not make peace with Israel, it risked being excluded from the new Middle East resulting from the Oslo Accord. In light of these considerations, it is clear that, in making peace with Israel, King Hussein was more concerned about Washington's reaction than he was about Jerusalem's. US hegemonic leadership, therefore, was of paramount importance in the transition to peace.

The circumstances of the early 1990s were also ideal for the prospect of US hegemonic leadership in the Middle East. After the collapse of the Soviet Union in the late 1980s, Arab states had lost the only great power competitor to the United States that held out the prospect of advancing their interests vis-à-vis the American strategic conception, which favored Israel. Of comparable significance, the dramatic US-led victory in the Gulf War against Iraq, by far the most powerful Arab state in 1991, demonstrated American dominance over the region and its active interest in the Middle East. Under these circumstances, Jordan had little alternative but to comply with American regional plans or risk isolation.[78]

The United States did not pressure Israel to make peace with Jordan directly, nor did it provide an economic payoff for doing so, but it did play a significant role in Rabin's strategic calculations, which compelled him to make peace with Israel's Arab neighbors after the Cold War. Rabin believed that US political and economic support for Israel was of paramount importance, especially in the wake of the Cold War, when the United States had secured global primacy. Yet he feared an erosion of that support as the Cold War imperative for the United States in the Middle East disappeared. The spat between Israel and the George H. W. Bush administration over loan guarantees to resettle Russian Jews because of American dissatisfaction with Prime Minister Shamir's policy toward the Palestinians further convinced him of the utility of pursuing a policy that would help maintain US support.[79] Making peace with the Palestinians and with Jordan, thereby stabilizing American interests in the Middle East, could help Israel achieve that goal.

There is strong evidence, therefore, that Jordan was motivated to make peace in large part by American pressure and incentives. There is also reason to believe that Israel may have been taking Washington's expected reactions into consideration, as well.

State-Preservation/State-Building Motives. If this peace treaty had its origins in attempts at state building or regime survival, we should see evidence that (1) leaders of at least one of the rivals conducted their foreign policies independently of society; and these leaders either (2a) identified threats to their domestic power position that could be overcome by making peace with their rival and concentrating on domestic stability, or (2b) prioritized building strong state institutions to solidify their regime and/or their power base; and (3) they negotiated peace in order to stabilize their regime or engage in state building.

At least on the Jordanian side, the peace treaty was, indeed, negotiated by the leader with little societal input. As already indicated, the king dominated the Jordanian government in general and retained special authority over matters of foreign policy. He took a special interest in the peace negotiations, however, which he orchestrated personally, frequently reining in negotiators who overstepped the brief he gave them or risked a diplomatic rupture by being uncompromising.[80] Indeed, as Dennis Ross told me, "the king drove the [peace] process; the level of enthusiasm was not the same among his ministers."[81]

As it turns out, regime survival was very much on King Hussein's mind when he negotiated peace with Israel. A primary consideration for him was that negotiating peace with Israel held out the prospect of alleviating a severe economic crisis in Jordan that could undermine the regime's authority in a perpetually unstable state.[82] The kingdom had suffered immensely due to the stagflation of the 1980s. These pressures were heavily compounded by international sanctions on Iraq, which was Jordan's leading trading partner and leading source of foreign aid, following the 1991 Gulf War and the oil-producing Arab states' decision to reduce aid to Jordan because of its support of Saddam Hussein.[83] In this global context, Jordanian GDP had fallen considerably, with a 9.1 percent drop in 1989 and an additional 2.3 percent decline in 1990. These economic pressures, coupled with the influx of Palestinians and Jordanian citizens expelled from Kuwait and the Gulf states after the Iraqi invasion of Kuwait, led to extremely high unemployment in Jordan, which reached 18.8 percent in 1991.[84] Although the Jordanian government had managed to stanch the most serious bleeding with an economic-liberalization plan—encompassing the devaluation of the dinar; the introduction of fiscal austerity; liberalization of the Jordanian foreign-exchange market; and structural reforms to the trade, agricultural, and public sectors—the Jordanian financial system was highly unstable, and public debt remained extremely high. Moreover, these steps, together with measures to raise prices as part of an IMF recovery plan, had added to domestic instability, as evidenced by violent riots in 1989, which suggested that poor economic performance could lead to the regime's downfall.[85]

These problems were compounded by the country's economic and political isolation after the Gulf War.[86] As the leading Jordanian treaty negotiators commented:

> For Jordan, the success of the peace process was crucial. . . . It needed to redeem its international image, which had suffered during the Iraqi occupation of Kuwait. Aqaba, its only seaport, was under siege by the US Navy since the boycott of Iraq in 1990 and that caused a big problem for Jordan's trade. Commercial airlines had avoided Jordan since the Gulf War, and the Royal Jordanian airline was the only carrier that serviced the country. Indeed, some analysts thought that, with the economic hardships it was facing and the damage to its international reputation, Jordan was doomed, and it was only a matter of time before it would fall apart.[87]

To the extent that peace could provide American economic incentives and end Jordanian isolation, it could ease the Jordanian economic crisis and take pressure off the regime. To this end, the Jordanian leadership explicitly linked peacemaking with Israel to US efforts to secure forgiveness of Jordanian debt as well as money and equipment to modernize the Jordanian armed forces.[88] In this regard, King Hussein justified his willingness to negotiate peace directly with Israeli leaders to the Jordanian parliament in terms of "our suffering" and the "critical and difficult circumstances" Jordan faced, which required Washington's assistance to surmount.[89]

Another key consideration related to the king's traditionally delicate domestic and regional balancing act. Hussein had been much closer to Israel than other Arab leaders were, especially after the 1970 Black September uprising, when at the king's (indirect) request Israel mobilized its armed forces to deter the Syrian army from joining the PLO assault on the Hashemite regime.[90] Hussein realized at this point that, as a moderate Arab leader, he could count on Israeli support to secure himself from potentially aggressive Arab neighbors and a radical Palestinian majority.[91] A peace treaty with Israel, therefore, could solidify the friendship with a neighbor that could help King Hussein hold on to his throne. Given the Palestinian majority in Jordan and Jordan's relative weakness in the Arab world, however, open cooperation and a formal peace treaty were never possible until the Oslo Accord gave him diplomatic cover.[92]

Clearly, then, the king's delicate power position favored friendlier rela-tions with Israel. He was also alarmed by the Israeli Likud Party's insis-tence that Jordan was the Palestinian state.[93] If Jordan were to become the de facto Palestinian state, that would make it very unlikely that the Hash-emite regime would survive. For this reason, one of Hussein's most im-portant demands in the negotiations was a guarantee that Israel would no longer claim that Jordan was the Palestinian homeland.[94]

A final consideration for the king was that the Oslo Accord itself threat-ened the king's position if he were to remain on the outside. To begin with, the king feared that Israel and the PLO could detrimentally affect Jordanian security interests by making decisions on security in the West Bank—and especially on the movement of Palestinians to and from the West Bank—without including Jordan.[95] If Jordan were to be left out of decisions on policing and border crossings, that could make it difficult for him to keep hostile elements from infiltrating into Jordan. That would especially be the case if the PLO, which had always had an uneasy relationship with the Hashemite regime, had a privileged role in these matters.

Moreover, in the wake of the Oslo Accord, there were increasing signals that Israel might reach an agreement with Arafat that would confer to the PLO the Hashemite monarchy's special responsibility for the Muslim holy sites in Jerusalem. According to Israeli intelligence director Efraim Halevy, it was this fear above all that that made King Hussein hasten to conclude a peace treaty with Israel.[96] Because losing his special role in Jerusalem would be damaging both for his domestic standing and his respect within the Arab world, it was imperative for him to reach an agreement with Israel that acknowledged his special rights and responsibilities.

There were, therefore, a number of distinct statist interests at stake for the king that could be safeguarded by making peace with Israel.

Assessment of Top-Down Explanations. Based on the foregoing, it can be seen that the Israeli-Jordanian peace settlement was undertaken due to statist motivations rather than societal pressures. Israel needed to concen-trate on greater threats. Jordan needed to do the same but also required US economic and military assistance and aimed to stabilize the regime eco-nomically and politically to secure the regime's hold on power. In contrast, societal attitudes, which in Jordan were hostile to peacemaking, did not motivate the treaty. In this regard, Asher Susser summed up the attitude of Jordanian society as follows: "Peace with Israel is the government's busi-ness, but the government can't force us to make peace with Israel. If the state wants to make peace with Israel as state business, it can, but we won't cooperate."[97] Former Mossad director Efraim Halevy similarly told me that "as with Egypt, this [the Israeli-Jordanian peace] is a treaty signed at the top, but from the middle-high echelon downward it was thought that it was bad."[98]

The Post-Transition Era

Having determined that the treaty was motivated by statist calculations, we will now turn our attention to the level of stability the treaty has enjoyed in the postagreement phase (i.e., whether it has been a stable peace, an enduring one, or simply a temporary respite from conflict) and whether statist and societal pressures explain that outcome.

In the two decades since the treaty, neither side has repudiated the treaty; the basic security and territorial components of the treaty have been respected; and Israel and Jordan have refrained from using force against each other. Yet we cannot consider this a stable peace because of mutual recriminations and political crises. Israel has been unhappy with Jordan's failure to take measures to normalize the peace through economic and cultural exchange, which I discuss below.[99] Jordanian dissatisfaction stems primarily from Israeli failure to consummate the Oslo Accord with a final status agreement with the Palestinian Authority and what Jordanians view as Israeli provocations against the Palestinians.[100] Moreover, the relationship has endured key crises, such as Prime Minister Benjamin Netanyahu's opening of a road near the Temple Mount in 1996 and his building of the Jerusalem settlement at Har Homa in 1997; the shooting and killing of seven Israeli schoolgirls by a Jordanian soldier at the border in 1997; Israel's 1997 attempted assassination of Hamas leader Khalid Mashal on Jordanian soil; and the collapse of the Israeli-PLO peace process with the outbreak of the al-Aqsa Intifada of September 2000.[101] Jordan even recalled its ambassador to Tel Aviv for an extended period from December 2008 until September 2012 to protest Israel's Operation Cast Lead in Gaza,[102] and it had delayed sending the new Jordanian ambassador to Tel Aviv for an extended period in October 2000 to protest the Israeli response to the 2000 Intifada.[103] In addition, in March 2013 and February 2014 nonbinding resolutions, the Jordanian parliament voted to expel the Israeli ambassador to Jerusalem to express disapproval of Israeli policy toward Jerusalem.[104] Clearly, while the peace settlement has endured, mutual recriminations and intense crises mean that it cannot be considered a stable settlement.

Does this enduring settlement correspond with continued statist pressures to maintain the peace treaty together with a failure to co-opt society with bottom-up measures, as I hypothesize in chapter 1? The evidence in this case is consistent with my hypothesis. As was the case with the Egyptian-Israeli treaty, many of the top-down pressures that motivated the Israeli-Jordanian settlement persisted after the treaty was signed and ensured that both parties continued to observe it. From the Israeli perspective, it still made good sense to maintain peaceful relations with Jordan, given that Jerusalem faced more threatening states in the region in Iraq, Syria, and Iran.[105] Jordan, too, as one of the weaker Arab states with potentially hostile states such as revolutionary Iran and Iraq in the neighborhood, had good reason to stick to the treaty, especially given the US commitment to it. Indeed, since the Jordanian monarchy's grand strategy in the era of American hegemony is to align itself with the United States, which is "too important of a player in the Middle East to be ignored," the importance that successive US presidents have placed on Arab-Israeli peacemaking made it essential for the kingdom to respect the treaty even in the face of events that strained bilateral relations.[106] In addition, the stability of the Jordanian regime has not improved. In fact, King Hussein's son and successor, King Abdullah II, does not enjoy the widespread legitimacy of his greatly loved father and has been fearful of being overtaken by the popular movements to overthrow autocratic Arab regimes, known as the Arab Spring, since December 2010.[107] Any move that would threaten the economic stability of Jordan, therefore, would be risky for him. The logic of greater threats, hegemonic incentives, and state survival still supports the Israeli-Jordanian peace treaty.

In contrast, although greater efforts were made to create some societal support for the treaty than we witnessed with the Egyptian-Israeli treaty—such as a bilateral trade and economic cooperation treaty signed in October 1995 and an upgraded bilateral trade agreement signed in December 2004—bottom-up mechanisms have continued to be noticeably absent in the over two decades since the Israeli-Jordanian treaty was concluded.[108] Thus, although the US-sponsored QIZ generated some economic cooperation between the two countries—particularly in the textile industry—for a few years until it was made largely redundant by a US-Jordanian free trade agreement signed in 2000, it never gained much societal traction. Only a small segment of Jordanian and Israeli business elites participated in the QIZ, with a high degree of participation by foreign companies, notably from China and India. Moreover, most small and medium-sized businesses in Jordan continued to oppose normalization with Israel in anticipation of a return to their traditional market in Iraq.[109] Consequently, by 2000, six years after the treaty, the most generous estimate of Jordanian exports to Israel is $78 million, or less than 0.4 percent of Jordanian GDP. The more conservative estimate is less than half that amount. Similarly, Israeli exports to Jordan that year amounted to no more than $70 million, or only 0.05 percent of Israeli GDP.[110] Rather than rising steadily, Jordanian exports (based on Jordanian figures) to Israel fluctuated thereafter, peaking at $159 million (0.8% of Jordanian GDP) in 2007, before dropping back to $75 million (0.25% of GDP) in 2011 and 2012.[111] It never reached 1 percent of either state's GDP, and therefore this cannot be judged an economically interdependent relationship. Israeli textile exports to Jordan and the number of Israeli firms doing business in Jordan also declined after 2002.[112] Overall, as Avraham Sela observes, "Jordanian hopes for the 'benefits of peace' in the form of foreign investments in tourism projects, trade exchange with and through Israel to the Mediterranean, and transit trade through Jordan to the Arab world, all of which were included in the political and military agreements signed between the two states, remained mostly on paper."[113]

Broader bilateral economic cooperation was prevented by the Jordanian professional bars, which, under pressure from an Islamist-led public anti-normalization campaign opposing the treaty, forbade their members to conduct business with Israel or face blacklisting and expulsion, which strips them of key social benefits such as their pension and health care.[114] As Russell Lucas observes, "Since membership in a professional association was mandatory for employment in certain professions, being expelled was tantamount to the loss of one's livelihood."[115] Consequently, these bans had a chilling effect on bilateral ties. Individuals and companies that do business with Israel also run the risk of being reported in their "list of shame," an online Internet list of normalizers who are viewed as traitors and become the targets of boycotts and protests.[116] In this context, few Jordanian businesses or individuals are willing to work with Israeli firms. Thus, for example, although a contract to install the air-conditioning system for the Ben Gurion Airport near Tel Aviv was initially awarded to a Jordanian company, that company concluded that Jordanian public and professional union attitudes toward Israel were too hostile, and, consequently, it backed out of the deal.[117]

The majority of the Jordanian business elite, moreover, continued to oppose normalization with Israel, especially after Netanyahu won the December 1996 Israeli election. In this climate, almost the entire Jordanian business sector boycotted the first Israeli trade fair in Amman, held in 1997.[118] Moreover, as the antinormalization movement in Jordan picked up steam, attacks on the Israeli embassy in Amman and the murder of an Israeli businessman in Jordan led the Israeli ambassador to warn Israelis not to visit Jordan.[119] Furthermore, the Israeli security climate, which requires careful monitoring of transborder movement and careful vetting of applicants for visas, has further discouraged Jordanians who might have been interested in economic, educational, or cultural exchanges.[120] These factors explain the low level of bilateral economic exchange between the two countries.

It is true that, in 1997, Israel agreed to reduce its allotment of US economic assistance in order to allow for additional US aid to Jordan. Nonetheless, this does not count as bilateral economic interaction, which could contribute to societal interaction, but rather, given that the aid comes from the US to the Jordanian government, it reinforces the top-down nature of the peace.[121]

Furthermore, as noted in the previous chapter, aside from the as yet politically insignificant Union for the Mediterranean, no regional institutions exist in the Middle East that include both Israel and the Arab states as members. There was an abortive attempt after the 1991 Madrid Conference to establish the Multilateral Working Group on Arms Control and

Regional Security, involving Israel, thirteen Arab states, a Palestinian delegation, and important extraregional actors (including the United States and Russia as co-gavel holders, the European Union, the Organization for Security and Co-operation in Europe, and the UN) in an effort to foster regional cooperation on security issues. This institution never gained any traction and has not met since 1995.[122] Consequently, there still has been no opportunity for international institutions to transform the nature of bilateral relations.

Finally, although the Jordanian regime is viewed as one of the most liberal in the Arab world, it still falls well short of the requirements for democracy. In this regard, the Polity IV data set gives the regime a −2 on its Polity scale for each of the years 1995 to 2006, after which it dropped to −3. This ranks Jordan as an anocracy, rather than a democracy.[123] Moreover, because of the widespread societal opposition to the treaty represented by the antinormalization campaign, the monarchy felt compelled to clamp down on freedom of expression in the country and to restrict opposition political parties. Significantly, the government revised the Press and Publications Law to prevent newspapers from printing anything disparaging about the monarchy, the security services, or "friendly states"— that is, Israel. The government also investigated and harassed political parties that criticized the treaty, forbade Islamic preachers who opposed peace with Israel from giving sermons in mosques, and clamped down on large protests and outspoken critics of the peace treaty.[124] Clearly, the Jordanian government fell short of the standards of modern democracy. No foundation, therefore, has been laid for a democratic peace to reinforce the peace treaty.

Consequently, the Israeli-Jordanian peace treaty has not become entrenched within Jordanian society nor even among the Israeli public. Certainly, the security components of the treaty have held, and war between the two states is quite unlikely. Furthermore, the two countries have established military-to-military contacts and cooperation over matters such as border surveillance, and they have also met regularly to manage water resources.[125] These contacts, however, remain at the state level, without engaging the two societies. Indeed, it is precisely because the security cooperation between the two countries is under the table that it can occur; in economic and cultural areas, where cooperation would be visible to the Jordanian public, little cooperation is occurring.[126] Perhaps as a result, while the Israeli public generally embraced the treaty—and on the whole viewed it far more favorably than the peace agreement with the PLO—they still did not rush to embrace the Jordanians.[127]

In Jordan, opposition to the treaty is widespread, particularly among Palestinians, those committed to political Islam, and those who view themselves as economically less secure; and it has united such disparate groups such as the Muslim Brotherhood and pan-Arabists, whose world views are ordinarily diametrically opposed.[128] Even students and professionals, who are cosmopolitan and should ordinarily be most supportive of peacemaking, are hostile to peace with Israel.[129] Moreover, Arab intellectuals and journalists in Jordan, as in the rest of the Arab world, strongly oppose normalization with Israel, which has never gained societal buy-in.[130] Jordanian societal hostility to peace with Israel is so deeply ingrained that it has generated public debate over and opposition to foreign policy and defense issues, such as Jordanian participation in joint maneuvers with Israeli and Turkish forces in the late 1990s, which had previously been considered outside the public purview.[131] Thus, although the monarchy desired a warmer peace with significant economic cooperation, the opposition of the Jordanian professional associations and widespread opposition within Jordanian society to normalization made a warm peace unlikely right from the beginning. Indeed, a 1997 public opinion poll, three years after the treaty, indicated that 81 percent of Jordanians continued to view Israelis as their enemies.[132] The Jordanian public, as a whole, continues to oppose normalization with Israel, especially since frustration over stalled progress in Israeli-Palestinian negotiations and renewed violence after the Camp David summit of 2000 further undercut popular support for the treaty in Jordan and strained relations between the two countries.[133] This is demonstrated by, among other indicators, the fact that in 2007, over a decade after the treaty, only 3,724 Jordanians visited Israel compared to 276,069 Israelis visiting Jordan.[134] It is clear that, as Ashton observes with considerable understatement, the king's "efforts to entrench the treaty at home met with only limited success."[135]

We can conclude, then, that Jordan-Israeli peace failed to stabilize in the post-treaty era, with continued crises and mutual recriminations, in the context of few efforts to socialize the settlement. Nonetheless, it has endured because both states continue to face top-down incentives to remain at peace with each other.

Overall, then, the Israeli-Jordanian peace settlement amounted to a top-down settlement driven by concerns over more dangerous threats the two rivals faced, common interests in securing American goodwill and economic incentives, and King Hussein's need to improve the desperate Jordanian economic situation, which could undermine his fragile hold on power. Bottom-up dynamics simply did not play a significant role. As the absence of check marks on the left side of table 4.1 indicates, there is no evidence that any of the bottom-up pressures specified in the theoretical overview existed at the time of the peace treaty. In contrast, all three top-down mechanisms were in play, most notably for Israel, the existence of more menacing threats, and for Jordan, the influence of the United States (the two shaded factors, in accordance with the convention I use throughout the book).

Table 4.1 Causes of the Israeli-Jordanian transition to peace

	Public opinion	Business pressures	Institutions	Improved state-to-nation balance	Greater threats	Great power pressures	Regime survival
Israel-Jordan	—	—	—	—	√	√	√

Table 4.2 Developments in the postagreement phase

	Democra-tization	Economic exchange	Regional institutions	Improved state-to-nation balance	Greater threats	Great power pressure	Regime survival
Israel-Jordan	—	—	—	—	√	√	√

As indicated by the partial shading in table 4.2, the Israeli-Jordanian peace treaty has endured but is not stable, indicating that although neither side repudiated the treaty and war has not recurred, crises and mutual re-criminations persist. Once again, the absence of check marks on the left side of the table highlights the lack of serious efforts to socialize the treaty through mechanisms derived by bottom-up approaches. Although the former rivals reached economic cooperation agreements, they failed to achieve significant levels of bilateral economic exchange. No liberal-democratic convergence occurred between the two regimes in the absence of meaningful democratization in Jordan. No significant regional institutions were developed to entrench a cooperative regional identity. The regional and bilateral state-to-nation imbalance remained as powerful as ever after the treaty. The treaty has remained in force, despite mutual recriminations and crises, because the top-down pressures that motivated it remain in force. Consequently, after two decades, peace is still only "skin deep," with cooperation at the governmental level but little societal participation or buy-in.

Having examined three case studies in great detail, in the next chapter I will round out my analysis of regional rivalries that ended with negotiated peace settlements in the twentieth century with a series of mini–case studies.

CHAPTER 5

Other Twentieth-Century Cases

The three detailed case studies presented in chapters 2–4 have uncovered a similar logic of peacemaking. The transition to peace in each case was a state-driven process for reasons of realpolitik and concerns over regime survival. The depth of peace and its prospects for endurance, however, depended on steps taken in the postagreement period to co-opt the rival societies and lead them to embrace the settlement. Where these steps were taken to convert the settlement to a bottom-up peace (Western Europe), the relationship between the regional rivals was transformed, stable peace developed, and the rivalry ended. Where peacemaking ended with the treaty (both Middle East settlements), the rivalry is merely suspended with the potential for it to be reignited when governments change or when popular pressures make it impossible for the leaders to maintain a top-down peace.

That all three settlements were subject to a similar logic is compelling evidence in support of a top-down model of peacemaking. Nonetheless, it is necessary to explore other instances of regional peacemaking to see if the model is generalizable beyond these three cases. To this end, this chapter provides a brief overview of the other key peace settlements between regional rivals in the twentieth century. Utilizing Paul Diehl and Gary Goertz's list of enduring rivalries, I round out the universe of twentieth-century cases in this chapter with examinations of the peace settlements between Ecuador and Peru (1998), Italy and Yugoslavia (1954), Bulgaria and Yugoslavia (1947), Russia and Turkey (1921), Ethiopia and Somalia (1988), and China and Japan (1978).[1]

Ecuador-Peru

Ecuador and Peru were rivals for a century and a half due to a territorial dispute over the territorial legacy of Spanish colonial lands in the Amazon basin. In principle, the two countries initially agreed to divide the border on the principle of *uti possidetis juris*, under which the newly independent countries would be entitled to all the lands under control of their preindependence colonial administration. The Spanish administrative records were unclear and often contradictory, however, and complicated by the fact that the border passed through sparsely populated regions with imprecise demarcations.[2] Consequently, Peru waged an inconclusive war with Gran Colombia (encompassing present-day Colombia, Ecuador, Panama, and Venezuela) in 1828–29 over the definition of its border. Following Ecuadorian independence from Gran Colombia in 1830, Ecuador and Peru concluded the July 1832 Treaty of Friendship, Alliance, and Commerce, which sought to stabilize the conflict by recognizing the "present limits" of the two countries as an interim border pending a final settlement. This agreement foundered, however, as the two sides disagreed on whether "present limits" referred to the boundaries at the time of signature (1832) or the territorial limits of the Spanish viceroyalties that preceded them.[3]

Over the next century, attempts to resolve the dispute through Spanish (1897–1910) and American (1936–38) arbitration and bilateral negotiations also failed to bear fruit, as Quito rejected arbitration decisions that denied Ecuador access to the Amazon River and both sides faced intense domestic opposition to negotiated concessions.[4] As a result, in July 1941 the dispute escalated to war. The better-prepared Peruvian army made significant gains in the war, capturing over four hundred square miles of territory in the first month. Under pressure from Argentina, Brazil, Chile, and the United States, however, the two combatants stopped fighting. Shortly thereafter, they concluded the 1942 Rio Protocol, guaranteed by Argentina, Brazil, Chile, and the United States, which set the parameters for a permanent settlement of the conflict based on a border line demarcated by technical experts.[5]

The Rio Protocol was short lived, however, as by 1946 more accurate mapping indicated that the demarcation line was based on flawed geographical assumptions.[6] Ecuador, therefore, claimed that the protocol needed to be renegotiated, especially since it had been compelled to sign the treaty under duress. The Peruvian government, though, insisted that the Rio Protocol had settled the border dispute and could not be altered.[7] To confirm this impasse, in 1960 Ecuadorian president José María Velasco Ibarra declared the Rio Protocol null and void.[8] Border clashes were frequent between the two states thereafter, most notably the 1981 Paquisha War—a clash over military outposts in the Cordillera del Condor—and the 1995 Cenepa War—another clash over military outposts in the disputed border region along the Cenepa River, which this time led to a general mobilization.[9]

On October 9, 1998, after a meeting with US president Bill Clinton, presidents Alberto Fujimori of Peru and Jamil Mahuad Witt of Ecuador announced that they had concluded an agreement to resolve the longstanding conflict. In essence, the Global and Definitive Peace Agreement, signed on

October 26 in Brasilia (the so-called Brasilia Accords), confirmed the Rio Protocol's border, as Peru wanted, while granting Ecuador navigation rights on the Amazon and one square kilometer of territory around Tiwinza.[10]

The case for a bottom-up settlement between Ecuador and Peru is weak. There is little evidence, for example, that public pressure motivated the settlement. In the years preceding the settlement, public sentiment in Ecuador, which made the most significant concessions as part of the 1998 agreement, continued to be hostile to Peru, which it viewed as an enemy country, and continued to demand an Ecuadorian sovereign outlet to the Amazon.[11] Indeed, President Abdala Bucaram's 1997 visit to Peru, which caused many Ecuadorians to label him a traitor, was one of the principal reasons for his impeachment.[12] Although Peru actually gave up very little as part of the final settlement, until January 1999 Peruvian public opinion polls showed that most Peruvians disapproved of the treaty, even if many who disliked it believed they had no choice but to accept it.[13] Furthermore, the agreement was met by protests in Peru, particularly in the Amazon jungle, where riots in the city of Iquitos killed or wounded scores of people and parts of the city were burned to protest the deal. Many Ecuadorians also protested the treaty.[14] Thus, although there is some indication that public attitudes were not as intractable as they had been in 1941, it appears that the leaders were more conciliatory than the public was.[15]

Pressure from domestic economic interests also cannot explain this settlement. The two countries had very little economic interaction prior to the treaty, which suggests that few vested interests in peace existed prior to the treaty.[16] Nonetheless, as I detail below, the peace agreement heralded a dramatic increase in their bilateral economic exchange, even if, in terms of percentage of GDP, it remains comparatively small. As Alan Henrikson observes, the prospects of decreasing military spending, integrating within the emerging Mercosur South American regional-trading institution, and increasing access to international loans and beneficial economic partnerships influenced the governments of Peru and Ecuador to sign the final agreement in 1998.[17] It appears, though, that these economic motivations were statist rather than societal. As David Mares and David Scott Palmer note, most in the business communities believed that, although peace would undoubtedly bring some economic gains to both countries, they "were unlikely to have a significant macroeconomic effect on either country," as even the most liberal estimate was that the conflict was responsible for a loss of only $35 million in bilateral trade annually.[18] Moreover, in her study of this case, Beth Simmons concluded that "no major social forces or partisan organizations in Ecuadorian society have advocated less than accepting sovereign access to the Amazon."[19] Consequently, Ronald Bruce St. John argues that the central role of Ecuadorian president Mahuad, whose preference for a peace agreement so that Ecuador "could get on with the real needs of the country, most especially economic reform and development" was the single most important factor that caused the agreement, suggests that Ecuadorian peacemaking originated with the government rather than societal elites.[20]

Finally, there is little evidence that regional institutions or a change in the state-to-nation balance brought about the treaty. Both Ecuador (2004) and Peru (2003) joined Mercosur after the peace treaty was signed. They were both members of the Organization of American States, which is a significant regional political organization. Nonetheless, despite a few notable exceptions, such as its role in the 2000 electoral crisis in Peru, it has typically been viewed as a weak institution that was, according to Clare Ribando, "mired in dissent and inaction."[21] Thus, it would be difficult to pin the treaty on the importance of OAS membership to the states' identities. The two countries were also members of the Andean Pact customs union, although that was not a very successful organization until it took steps, beginning in 1996, to transform itself into the Andean Community, with the eventual creation of an Andean common market in 2005, well after the peace treaty was signed.[22] Nor was the treaty preceded by any significant population or territorial exchange to repatriate a lost minority or states created to allow self-determination to a stateless population. Thus, of the bottom-up mechanisms, only economic pressures provide a plausible explanation of Ecuadorian-Peruvian peacemaking. Yet, the economic logic in this case would appear to have been of a top-down nature, driven by leaders rather than societal elites.

While the logic of greater threats was not a consideration in this episode, third-party involvement, particularly that of the United States and the other guarantors of the Brasilia Accords (Argentina, Brazil, and Chile), did play an important role in motivating and facilitating the settlement. Notably, they provided a military observer force—the Ecuador-Peru Military Observer Mission, which helped defuse the conflict from 1995 to 1998 when the risk of a Peruvian escalation was high. These countries also provided mediation, considerable procedural support, and arm-twisting to reach a settlement.[23] In this regard, it is no coincidence that the final settlement was announced following a meeting in Washington with President Clinton. The role of the guarantor representative from the United States, Luigi Einaudi, was of particular importance in suggesting formulations for overcoming disagreements and coaxing the two sides to find common ground.[24] Moreover, with US encouragement, the Inter-American Development Bank rewarded the agreement with a $500 million loan to the two countries, as part of a $3 billion commitment to develop the Ecuador-Peru borderlands.[25]

Governmental-survival motives also loomed large in both countries. In Ecuador, political and economic instability had prevailed since the early 1990s, and the country consequently went through five different presidents and seven finance ministers from 1995 to 1998 alone.[26] Bucaram was ousted in February 1997, not only because of his visit to Peru, but also because of public dissatisfaction with the economy. The subsequent Alarcón government lasted no more than a year, and under the new Mahuad government, the country was paralyzed by strikes and demonstrations against rising fuel prices. In this context, Mahuad viewed a peace treaty as a means of jump-starting the economic recovery, which would create political stability, as well.[27] As Simmons observes, Fujimori's impetus for peacemaking was motivated by domestic problems that made peacemaking rational, even if the public remained hostile to it. Even before the 1995 war, Fujimori wanted to resolve the conflict because he faced enormous challenges at home that made it risky to fight a border war with Ecuador. Notably, he had to deal with a disastrous economic situation—including his predecessor's legacy of a cumulative 2 million percent inflation from 1985 to 1990—widespread poverty, and internal unrest fanned by the Shining Path, a Marxist guerilla movement.[28] By 1998, he was faring quite poorly in public opinion polls and judged that the tangible payoffs of a peace treaty could propel him to another electoral victory.[29] Thus, top-down motivations appear to have brought about this settlement.

The peace settlement between Ecuador and Peru has been quite stable with no war or repudiation by either side and without large-scale crises or mutual recriminations. This stability occurred in the context of efforts by both governments to socialize the settlement, using bottom-up mechanisms to overcome residual societal hostility. Significantly, bilateral economic exchange has expanded exponentially, with Ecuadorian exports to Peru rising from $87 million in 1999 (amounting to a paltry 0.2% of Ecuadorian GDP) the year after the treaty to almost $1 billion in 2009 (an elevenfold increase, representing 1.6% of GDP) and Peruvian exports to Ecuador multiplying almost tenfold during the same period from under $60 million (or about 0.05% of Peruvian GDP) to about $570 million (or over 0.4% of GDP).[30] These percentages are nowhere near the 4 percent of GDP the Franco-German trade has achieved, but it does show a sharply increasing trend.[31] Moreover, the two countries joined Mercosur early in the new millennium, which helped both to cement growing bilateral trade ties and to institutionalize cooperation between regional states.[32] Even before joining Mercosur, the two countries agreed to cooperate together within the Andean Community (including Ecuador, Peru, Bolivia, and Colombia), which pledged to eliminate all duties of trade between member states.[33] Although Ecuador has not reliably entrenched a democratic regime, in light of these other positive developments, David Mares and David Palmer conclude that "the advances achieved in relations between Peru and Ecuador in the decade since the resolution of the border dispute offer clear signs that the problems that divided the two nations for so long have been overcome."[34] In this regard, although I have not been able to access indicators of Ecuadorian public opinion, there is evidence that

Peruvian attitudes toward Ecuador have improved in the postsettlement era.[35] Thus, although the two sides no longer face strong top-down imperatives to maintain the settlement, it appears to be stable for societal reasons.

Italy-Yugoslavia

The rivalry between Italy and Yugoslavia primarily concerned a territory known as the Julian region (Venezia Giulia in Italian and Julian March to Yugoslavians), upper Adriatic and Dalmatian territories that Italy claimed with the dissolution of the Austro-Hungarian Empire during World War I, which was home to both ethnic Italians and Slavic peoples. Under the Treaty of London, which Italy signed with the Triple Entente powers (Great Britain, France, and Russia) in 1915, Italy was supposed to receive Istria, northern Dalmatia, and a protectorate over Albania in return for its entry into the war against its former allies (Germany and Austria-Hungary).[36] US president Woodrow Wilson vetoed this agreement in negotiations over the Treaty of Versailles in 1919 because it would violate the principle of national self-determination by giving territories with a Serbo-Croatian majority to Italy.[37] Thereafter, Italy was eager to secure these territories. Although Italian-Serbian tensions appeared to abate after the Treaties of Rapallo (1920) and Rome (1924), in which Italy formally annexed much of the disputed territories, they flared anew once Fascist Italian leader Benito Mussolini entered into agreements with the Kingdom of Albania and Croatian separatists to limit the extent and influence of the Kingdom of Yugoslavia.[38]

During World War II, Italy participated in the Axis invasion of Yugoslavia, seizing control of parts of Slovenia and Croatia, and annexing the Dalmatian coast.[39] After Mussolini was deposed and Italy withdrew from the war, however, the Socialist Federal Republic of Yugoslavia reclaimed these territories as part of its Croatian and Slovenian Socialist Republics, and many ethnic Italians from Dalmatia, Istria, and Fiume fled to Italy. Most of the disputed territories, therefore, were in areas controlled by the Yugoslav army by the end of the war, although the Italians objected strongly.[40]

Most border questions were finally resolved after World War II in a series of agreements. To begin with, as part of the 1947 Treaty of Paris between the victorious Allied powers and Italy, Italy was forced to come to terms with its defeat in the war. Consequently, Italy accepted the war's territorial outcome, which placed most of Istria, the city of Zadar in Dalmatia, several Adriatic islands, and the Slovenian littoral under Yugoslavian control.[41]

The issue of Trieste was more complicated. Most of the Julian region—comprising the provinces of Trieste, Gorizia, Pola, and Carnero that were ceded to Italy after World War I—ended up under control of the Yugoslav army at the end of World War II. The British negotiated the so-called

Morgan Line to separate the Trieste territory into an Allied-occupied zone (Zone A) and a Yugoslav-occupied zone (Zone B). The Treaty of Paris formalized a UN-sponsored plan to create the Free Territory of Trieste out of these zones, with US and British forces administering the smaller Zone A, containing the city of Trieste, and the Yugoslav army administering the larger Zone B.[42] A failure to agree with the Soviet Union on a suitable candidate for governor as well as Yugoslav moves to establish a Communist administration in Zone B, however, led the tripartite powers (the United States, United Kingdom, and France) to issue a declaration calling for the return of Trieste to Italy. This declaration sparked widespread protests in Yugoslavia, which reinforced Tito's motivation to resist any such move. As a result of the split between Tito and Stalin, the tripartite powers suspended the declaration in an effort to gain Tito's favor, which led to domestic discontent in Italy. Moreover, in 1953, the Trieste crisis intensified, with rioting by pro-Italian forces in Trieste itself that made it difficult for the Americans and British to administer the territory. Yet the Anglo-American decision on October 8, 1953, to hand Zone A over to Italy was rebuffed by Tito, who warned that any entry of Italian troops into Zone A would be considered an invasion and met with force. Consequently, Washington and London, as the occupying powers of Zone A, initiated negotiations with Yugoslavia, the occupying power of Zone B, while negotiating privately with Italy to broker a compromise.[43]

In this context, on October 5, 1954, the United States, the United Kingdom, Italy, and Yugoslavia signed the London Memorandum, yielding Zone B and a few villages from Zone A to Yugoslavia and the bulk of Zone A, including the city of Trieste, to Italy. Italy forwent a share of Zone B in order to gain control of Punta Sottie, a small hill that overlooked the city of Trieste.[44]

It would be difficult to explain the settlement in terms of either joint democracy or public pressure for moderation. While Polity IV lists Italy as democratic in the early 1950s, Tito's Yugoslavia fell well short.[45] Regarding public attitudes, although it is difficult to find polling data on Yugoslav public opinion during this period, an Italian public opinion poll taken in October–November 1953 indicated that the majority of respondents wanted the return of all of the Trieste territory (including Zone B) to Italy in accordance with the tripartite declaration of 1948.[46] They clearly did not favor a compromise. Italian diplomats also indicated repeatedly to the Americans that the Italian leadership was more willing to consider a reasonable, workable compromise on the issue than the Italian public, which was unreasonable and emotional on the issue.[47] Furthermore, the widespread protests in 1952 in both Italy and Yugoslavia in response to Anglo-American efforts to broker a compromise indicate that the public was extremely nationalistic in both countries, pressuring Italian and Yugoslav leaders to be rigid rather than demanding compromise.[48] For this reason, all of the principal negotiators interviewed by John C. Campbell in the 1970s stressed that secrecy was an essential component of the negotiations, without which public hostility to compromise would have scuttled any prospect of a compromise.[49]

Nor did economic considerations play any significant role. Italy did not trade much with Yugoslavia before the agreement, so it had few vested interests in peacemaking. In 1954, for example, Italian exports to Yugoslavia totaled $27.8 million, or less than .06 percent of Italian GDP. At around $30 million, Yugoslav exports to Italy accounted for barely above 0.3 percent of Yugoslav GDP. Furthermore, the two states were not partners in any cooperative regional institutions at the time. Nor, for that matter, was there any restoration of the state-to-nation balance that made an agreement possible, as the Treaty of Paris and the Trieste agreement brought many Slavs under Italian rule and many Italians under Yugoslav sovereignty.[50] Thus, there was no bottom-up pressure to speak of for the treaty.

In contrast, in the context of the emerging Cold War, top-down pressures were quite significant. To begin with, the incentives for Western states, including Italy, to cooperate with Tito's Yugoslavia as a means of peeling it away from the Soviet Union, the far-greater threat, were considerable. Tito's split with Stalin similarly made it important for him to find a workable compromise with Italy to help establish good relations with the West.[51] Nor can the role of the United States and, to a lesser extent, Great Britain be underestimated. The Anglo-Americans managed the negotiations and acted as go-betweens with Italy and Yugoslavia. More significantly, Washington linked Yugoslavian concessions over Trieste to considerable economic incentives to Yugoslavia—including over $20 million in direct aid to pay for the construction of a port in Zone B and the promise of wheat aid in the amount of 500,000 tons—and to military assistance and support for a Balkan pact, thus, in Jean-Baptiste Duroselle's words, placing tremendous "economic pressure" on Tito to make concessions.[52] Indeed, the Eisenhower administration threatened both Tito and Italian prime minister Mario Scelba that if they failed to reach a fair compromise, their share of US aid could suffer.[53] There does not appear to be strong evidence that state-preservation motives played any role in this settlement.

After the London Memorandum, although Italian public opinion was dissatisfied with the extent of Rome's concessions, relations between the two countries improved. After a crisis in 1974, in which the Italian government made statements referring to Zone B as "Italian territory," the agreement, which remained in principle only a provisional settlement, was eventually formalized in the 1975 Treaty of Osimo, which also provided for protection for national minorities in the area and increased bilateral cooperation.[54] Although the treaty did include minor border changes in Italy's favor, these changes did not amount to a revision of the agreement, as the treaty "definitively sanctioned the territorial arrangement" of the London

Memorandum.[55] This treaty has held ever since and was confirmed in the early 1990s by the governments of both Italy and the relevant Yugoslav successor states (Croatia and Slovenia), despite the Italian extreme Right, and even many within the Italian mainstream, having called for its renegotiation with Zagreb and Ljubljana. To the extent that the Italian government wished to update the treaty to fit the new political reality after the dissolution of Yugoslavia, it was not to affect the territorial settlement but to secure compensation for refugee property, the protection of minorities, and greater economic cooperation.[56] This does not constitute a meaningful effort to revise the settlement. Therefore, since 1975, the treaty should be considered a stable one, even if there are still some bilateral irritations.

This stability coincided with efforts to engage Italian and Yugoslav society. Notably, within weeks of the agreement, businessmen from both sides began to explore trading opportunities and coordinate joint ventures.[57] Bilateral trade increased considerably and became of great importance to Yugoslavia, although it did not amount to much in terms of Italian GDP. Italian exports to Yugoslavia had jumped from under $28 million in 1954 (a paltry 0.06% of Italian GDP) to over $1.2 billion (0.25% of GDP). By 1992, the figure had doubled again to over $2.5 billion (still 0.25% of GDP) before dropping to near zero during the wars of Yugoslavian succession. More significantly in percentage terms, Yugoslavian exports to Italy grew from under $31 million in 1954 (0.3% of Yugoslavian GDP) to below $900 million in 1980 (0.9% of GDP) and to over $2.8 billion in 1992 (2.4% of GDP) before collapsing with the Yugoslav state.

Paradoxically, although the Italians in the affected area were quite unhappy with the treaty, the state-to-nation imbalance improved somewhat after the exodus of ethnic Italians from Yugoslav-controlled territory back to Italy, which had begun during the war, accelerated, totaling approximately 300,000.[58] Given that the final settlement left Italians under Yugoslav control and Slavs under Italian control, however, the state-to-nation imbalance was not eliminated. The two states did not join any significant regional institutions together, aside from the Conference on Security and Cooperation in Europe (later the Organization for Security and Cooperation in Europe), which was less of a coherent regional institution and more of a forum for dialogue.[59] Nor did the two states share democratic institutions, as according to Polity IV, Tito's Yugoslavia never ranked higher than −5 on the Polity scale, making it at best an anocracy.

Since Yugoslavia's dissolution, though, the two relevant successor states, Croatia and Slovenia, have both made the transition to democracy, making the three parties to the settlement democratic.[60] Moreover, since Slovenia's 2013 accession to the European Union, the three states are also all members of a highly salient cooperative regional institution. Consequently, there is support for the settlement from three of the four bottom-up mechanisms investigated.

Bulgaria-Yugoslavia

The rivalry between Bulgaria and Yugoslavia grew out of the 1877–78 Russo-Turkish War and, more specifically, the Treaty of Berlin that followed it.[61] A key provision of the treaty stripped Bulgaria of Macedonia, which had been awarded to Sofia as part of the Treaty of San Stefano only four months earlier.[62] Ever since, "the acquisition of the region has been the focal point of [Bulgaria]'s nationalist programmes and often a key factor in its domestic politics."[63] After the First Balkan War (1912–13), Serbia demanded all of Macedonia on the grounds that it needed access to the Adriatic Sea and that Bulgaria would be too powerful with Macedonia in its possession. During the resulting Second Balkan War of 1913, in which Bulgaria attacked Serbian and Greek armies in Macedonia, Bulgaria was defeated by a coalition of armies from Greece, Serbia, Turkey, Montenegro, and Romania. In the Treaty of Bucharest, which ended the war, the victors stripped Bulgaria of the lion's share of Macedonia.[64]

From then on, the rivalry simmered, with Sofia intent on regaining control of all of Macedonia. The Bulgarians entered World War I on the German side with the intent of defeating Serbia in order to recapture the province. After failing to regain its Macedonian territories, Bulgaria again aligned with Germany and the Axis powers in World War II, this time invading Yugoslavia and Greece (in concert with German, Italian, and Hungarian armies) and recapturing Macedonia. Nonetheless, its success was overturned by the 1945 Yalta conference, when Roosevelt, Churchill, and Stalin redrew the Balkan map to the benefit of those who fought on the side of the Allied powers.[65] As a consequence, the official postwar peace treaty signed with Bulgaria in 1947, the Bled agreement, restored the boundaries of that country to those of January 1, 1941—that is, without the bulk of Macedonia, which was integrated into Yugoslavia.[66]

Because the settlement amounted to a Bulgarian capitulation to Yugoslav demands, we must understand Bulgarian rather than Yugoslav motivations in this case. The Bulgarians signed the 1947 peace treaty for power-political reasons. Principally, before Tito's split from Stalin, Bulgarian Communist Party leader Georgi Dimitrov was pressed by Stalin and reluctantly agreed to transfer Macedonians in Bulgaria to the People's Republic of Macedonia as part of the Yugoslav federation. This would facilitate Stalin's goal of creating a united Balkan socialist republic. Given that the Soviet Union possessed and exercised overriding hegemonic authority within the Eastern bloc after World War II, Bulgaria had little choice but to obey Moscow, despite continued nationalist antipathies.[67] Consequently, under Soviet compulsion, Bulgaria subordinated its national interests in Macedonia to Soviet geostrategic interests and agreed to renounce its claims to Macedonia, thereby acceding to Yugoslavia's status quo.[68] Moreover, because the Bulgarian Communist Party was directed from Moscow, rather than locally, obeying Stalin's orders also served Dimitrov's personal interests of keeping power, since defying Stalin could have led to his removal from office.[69] In this regard, Bulgarian leaders faced both pressure from a key great power and threats to regime survival that compelled concessions to Yugoslavia, despite their being domestically unpopular and Dimitrov himself disliking them.

Because policymaking in the Stalinist Eastern bloc's authoritarian states was a top-down affair, with Moscow issuing orders to its hand-selected puppet governments, public opinion played no role in Bulgarian decision making. The Communist regime cracked down quite hard on the opposition and completely silenced the free press.[70] Indeed, as R. J. Crampton comments, public opinion had no role in policymaking, since, in Communist Bulgaria, "the chain of command was always vertical, from the center down; there were to be no horizontal links because the center could not tolerate the possibility of local conspiracies against it."[71] In Yugoslavia, where Tito's Communist regime became less authoritarian after 1953, at the time of the treaty it was still a system of one-party rule in which elections were uncontested and largely meaningless. The party approved a slate of candidates; opposition candidates were not allowed to run; and there was no secret ballot, as voters publicly dropped rubber pellets into "yes," "no," or "no candidate" boxes. In this context, the public had no meaningful say over policy, and public opinion was largely irrelevant.[72]

Nor did economic interests motivate the rapprochement. Bilateral trade mirrored diplomatic relations with Moscow, with Bulgarian-Yugoslavian trade being cut off after Tito's split with Stalin and being reinstated only after diplomatic relations improved. Indeed, IMF Direction of Trade Statistics record trade between Yugoslavia and Bulgaria as 0 for each of the years between 1950 and 1954. From Yugoslavia's perspective, moreover, there was no pressing need to renew economic relations with Bulgaria, since Tito had replaced the economic gains forgone as a result of his split with the Eastern bloc with lucrative trade with the West. As a result, even after Stalin's death, Yugoslavia still traded more with the West than it did the Comecon countries, and with Bulgaria far less than all other Eastern bloc states except for Albania and Romania.[73] Finally, at the time of the treaty, the two countries were part of one significant regional institution, the Cominform. This was a very weak institution established in 1947 that met once annually for four years, accomplishing little, before eventually being disbanded officially in 1956, after it was long forgotten.[74] Consequently, a strong sense of we-ness stemming from institutional membership cannot explain the rapprochement.

The only evidence consistent with a bottom-up approach is that, as part of the 1947 treaty, Bulgaria allowed the transfer of Macedonians from Bulgaria to the Republic of Macedonia, which mitigated the state-to-nation imbalance. This reluctant gesture, however, represented compliance with top-down pressure from Moscow. Moreover, it was a consequence of the treaty, rather than a precursor to it, so it would be difficult to see it as a cause of the treaty. Clearly, then, the peace treaty between the two countries grew out of top-down pressures, mainly emanating from Soviet pressure on Bulgaria to improve relations with Belgrade.

In this case, however, the 1947 treaty did not terminate the rivalry, as the soured relations between Yugoslavia and Moscow following the 1948 split between Tito and Stalin allowed Dimitrov to "rebaptise the 'Macedonians' as Bulgarians, while at the same time encouraging subversive elements inside the Socialist Republic of Macedonia itself in the hope of opening up a way for the region to be annexed" by Bulgaria.[75] Nonetheless, only a few years later, after Stalin's death, under Soviet pressure to improve relations with Yugoslavia in an effort to woo Tito back and heal the Soviet-Yugoslav split, Bulgaria was compelled to honor the treaty. As Dimitar Petkov observes, nothing before the death of Stalin in March 1953 suggested that an improvement of Bulgarian-Yugoslav relations was in the offing. Yet, shortly after his death, Moscow once again viewed the Macedonian issue as a means of healing the rift between Tito and the Soviet Union.[76]

After the mid-1950s, the two countries continued to adhere to the terms of the settlement, but although it endured, peace was not stabilized for decades. In fact, the Bulgarian state itself occasionally irritated bilateral relations by raising the issue of Macedonia in the postagreement era and expressing dissatisfaction with the treaty, which it wished to revise. In 1958, for example, after Soviet-Yugoslav relations soured following Tito's increased criticism of the Soviet system, the Bulgarian government challenged the legitimacy of the San Stefano borders and criticized the notion of a separate Macedonian nationality.[77] In the wake of the Warsaw Pact invasion of Czechoslovakia in 1968, Bulgarian leaders seized on the tensions between the conservative Soviet Union and moderate Yugoslavia to revive the issue of Greater Bulgaria.[78] Thus, whenever Belgrade and Moscow fought, the statist impetus for Bulgaria to accept the territorial status quo was undermined. These attempts to revise the treaty and occasional bilateral crises meant the settlement was far from stable. Overall, however, Bulgaria was compelled to adhere to the settlement throughout the Cold War owing to Soviet insistence and the Bulgarian leadership's utter dependence on Moscow.

While top-down pressures continued to support the settlement, the treaty was not socialized in any meaningful way during the Cold War. Neither of these Communist regimes counted as a democracy.[79] They did increase bilateral trade but not to any significant extent. In 1985—the high-water mark of bilateral trade during the Cold War—Yugoslavian exports to Bulgaria were worth $172 million (or only 0.15% of Yugoslavian GDP), while Bulgarian exports to Yugoslavia amounted to a paltry

$114 million (or only 0.26% of Bulgarian GDP). This hardly counts as a vibrant trading relationship. Nor were the two states members of the same powerful regional institution. Aside from the Conference on Security and Cooperation in Europe, hardly a well-institutionalized regime, the two states moved in very different circles. They also failed to resolve the state-to-nation imbalance, with thousands of Macedonians whom the Bulgarians refused to recognize as Macedonian remaining under Bulgarian control.[80]

With no efforts to socialize the treaty using bottom-up mechanisms, and with not even the Bulgarian state remaining committed to the terms of the settlement, it is not surprising that Bulgarian society never bought into the agreement and retained its hostility to independent Macedonia, the relevant successor state to Yugoslavia, in the early post–Cold War era. Indeed, as late as December 2012, only 8 percent of the Bulgarian public supported Macedonian candidacy for the European Union, with many opponents citing hostile attitudes toward Macedonia.[81] Moreover, although Bulgaria recognized the former Yugoslav Republic of Macedonia as an independent country, it refused to acknowledge the existence of a Macedonian nation.[82] For this reason, progress toward an agreement to improve bilateral relations between Bulgaria and Macedonia foundered for years during the 1990s on Bulgaria's refusal to publish the document in Macedonian, since it did not want to recognize the language officially.[83] Consequently, even after the dissolution of Yugoslavia, societal tensions continued to persist.

Nonetheless, the settlement between Bulgaria and Macedonia appears to have stabilized in the twenty-first century. Significantly, the governments of Bulgaria and Macedonia signed a joint declaration in 1999 stating that neither government had any territorial claims on the other.[84] In the ensuing fifteen-year period, neither government has attempted to revise the treaty, and their bilateral relationship has been free of crises and mutual recriminations. This newfound stability coincides with post–Cold War evidence of socialization. Since 2002, Bulgaria and Macedonia have both been classified as democratic states by Polity IV.[85] The economic relationship between these states has also improved. Macedonian exports to Bulgaria, for example, ballooned from about $20 million in 2001 (0.6% of Macedonia GDP) to almost $230 million in 2012 (2.4% of Macedonian GDP). Bulgarian exports to Macedonia similarly rose from about $108 million in 2001 (under 0.8% of Bulgarian GDP) to $520 million in 2012 (1% of Bulgarian GDP). Overall, while these numbers do not approach the degree of integration of the Franco-German economies, this is still a considerable increase in bilateral economic interaction. While there have not been any territorial or population changes that amount to a rectification of the state-to-nation balance, the Macedonian government implicitly recognized the small Macedonian minority in Bulgaria as Bulgarian in the 1999 declaration.[86] Thus, the state-to-nation imbalance has been papered over by the states, even if it has not been eliminated. Finally, Macedonia has applied for EU membership where it would join Bulgaria, which has been a member since 2007.[87] In this context, there is some evidence that societal attitudes are beginning to shift, as Bulgarian attitudes toward Macedonian membership in the EU have improved considerably since December 2012.[88]

Of course there is still an important statist reason to adhere to the peace agreement. After all, these small, economically weak post-Communist states depend on their ability to improve their economies and deliver the economic goods to their populations if they want to remain in power. To the extent that embedding themselves within the European Union is a necessary prerequisite for economic recovery, they must comply with European regulations requiring them to resolve their border disputes and treat minorities fairly.[89] Consequently, remaining at peace with Macedonia is consistent with state-survival imperatives, as well. Nonetheless, given the recent evidence of changing Bulgarian attitudes, there is reason to expect that the recent efforts to socialize the settlement will enable it to outlast this statist imperative.

Russia-Turkey

The longstanding rivalry between Russia and Turkey lasted for several centuries, recessing at times and re-emerging at others.[90] The essence of the rivalry, from the Russian perspective, was the Eastern Question, which related to the fate of the weakening and then collapsing Ottoman Empire, Russian access to the Bosphorus and the Dardanelles straits, and the fate of Slavs under Ottoman control in the Balkans, among other issues.[91] The last installment of the rivalry unfolded in the late nineteenth century as the demise of the Ottoman Empire accelerated. During this time period, Russia, which hoped to gain both influence in the Balkans at Turkey's expense and to secure access to the Mediterranean through the straits, fought the last of its thirteen wars with the Ottoman Empire.[92] Notably, Russia defeated the Ottomans decisively in the Russo-Turkish War of 1877–78 and imposed a large reparations indemnity on the Turks, which hampered the Ottoman economy and interfered with its development projects, especially construction of the Baghdad Railway.[93] When World War I broke out, Istanbul sided with the Central Powers, primarily because it feared Russia would use the war to grab Turkish territory in Anatolia and because Germany promised territorial gains at Russia's expense.[94] The war proved devastating for both regimes, as Russia collapsed into revolution and the Turkish defeat in war formally marked the transformation of the once great Ottoman Empire into modern-day Turkey.

Following World War I, the two belligerents took two major steps toward ending their rivalry. To begin with, the new Bolshevik regime in Russia exited the war by concluding the Treaty of Brest-Litovsk with the Central Powers on terms that were favorable to Turkey. In particular, Soviet Russia agreed to withdraw from Eastern Anatolia, which would be restored to Turkish control.[95] Three years later, the two countries signed the 1921 Treaty of Moscow, a peace treaty ending their state of war and committing the two new regimes to friendly relations.[96]

Although neither Russia nor Turkey could be classified as a democracy during this period, public opinion does appear to have played some role in the Russian decision to end the conflict in that the 1917 Revolution was sparked by war weariness and a public rejection of the sacrifices and privations of war.[97] Moreover, Turkish propaganda directed toward the Russian public and the new regime, labeling the war an imperialist endeavor, gained traction among Russian soldiers and the war-weary public at large.[98] The Turkish public, especially after the harsh treatment they received from the Allied victors of World War I, were more favorable toward the new Soviet regime than they had been toward czarist Russia.[99] In addition, an important factor that helped overcome Turkish hostility toward Russia was the 1918 return of Eastern Anatolia and its Turkish population, which alleviated the state-to-nation imbalance.[100] Economic considerations mattered, but these pertained more to the Turkish need for arms and money from Russia to help establish the new Turkish regime and the Bolshevik leadership's need to have commercial access to the straits, rather than any pressure from a business community. Allen Bodger describes Russian trade with Turkey—and, indeed, the entire Ottoman Empire—before World War I and the treaty as "miniscule," with Turkish exports to Russia at 6 percent of total Turkish exports (and therefore, a far smaller percentage of Turkish GDP, for which data is not available), well behind Turkish trade with geographically more removed Great Britain, Austria, France, Germany, and Italy. Russian exports to Turkey amounted to no more than 2.5 percent of all Russian exports (and therefore, a much smaller percentage of Russian GDP).[101] While Russian military officials in Turkey were eager to improve that situation, the Russian business community did not make it a high priority.[102] This suggests that there was little economic pressure for peacemaking, at least in Russia. Prior to the post–World War II world, there were no regional institutions to speak of; thus, institutional membership cannot have motivated peacemaking.

Bottom-up factors, particularly public attitudes and an improved state-to-nation balance, appear to have been relevant to peacemaking in this case. Nonetheless, a far more compelling strategic rationale drove Turkish and Bolshevik leaders. As a revolutionary regime that was recognized by very few states, Soviet Russia faced far too many enemies. Indeed, from 1919–1920, Moscow weathered an armed intervention on behalf of the counter-revolutionary White Russians by a multinational force led by Great Britain and France, leading the Bolsheviks to conclude that the whole world was against them.[103] Consequently, once it became clear that Lenin's preferred option—a Communist takeover of the unstable Turkish state—was foreclosed by the nationalist regime in Turkey, an agreement with Turkey to stabilize the southern border seemed to Russian leaders to be a wise course of action.[104]

The leadership of the new Turkish state, led by Mustafa Kemal Atatürk, also had strong statist motives for peacemaking. Turkey emerged from World War I "prostrate and exhausted, without an army and without any resources whatsoever; Istanbul and the government of the last Sultan were under the control of the Allied occupation force."[105] In these circumstances, the primary goal of the young Turks was to build an army and other national institutions, consolidate their power, and establish the new regime's independence. Peacemaking with Russia allowed them to focus on their inward-oriented mission without the distraction of a security threat from a great power to the north. In addition, the government in Ankara hoped to gain military and economic assistance from the Russians to help them build and maintain the Turkish armed forces. In particular, Atatürk asked Moscow for "five million pounds of gold, munitions, modern weapons, food, and sundries for the Eastern army."[106] Finally, since the Allied states actually represented a greater threat to the autonomy and independence of the new Turkish state than Bolshevik Russia, and since Mustafa Kemal judged that an alliance with Soviet Russia could help check Allied demands on Turkey, a logic of greater threats operated in the Turkish case, as well.[107]

Lenin and the Bolsheviks had similar state-building motives for making peace with Turkey, as they needed to focus their attention on consolidating their revolution and building the institutions of the Soviet state. State building and providing the Russian people with a regime that could govern effectively were of particular importance for regime survival in Soviet Russia. After all, Lenin was keenly aware that the czarist regime's failure to deliver effective government led to its overthrow and the murder of the czar and his family. Surely he could suffer a similar fate if he failed to consolidate his regime.[108] Thus, both regimes had reasons to make peace to consolidate their transitions and secure their power positions.

In the aftermath of the treaty, bilateral relations initially improved, with the two sides signing the Treaty of Friendship and Neutrality in December 1925.[109] By the late-1930s, however, Russo-Turkish relations began to sour because of the 1936 Montreux Convention on the Turkish Straits, which Moscow disliked because it gave Turkey control over whether and when Russian naval vessels could enter and transit the straits between the Black Sea and the Mediterranean.[110] Turkish neutrality during World War II, which the Soviets claimed favored Germany, further eroded bilateral relations. The relationship deteriorated so much that, in March 1945, Moscow renounced the 1925 treaty and told the Turks that friendly relations could be restored only if Turkey ceded territory in Eastern Anatolia to the (now)

Soviet Union and negotiated a new statute for the straits, which granted the USSR unrestricted access to them, a co-responsibility for administering them, and military bases in Turkish territory along the waterway.[111] These demands were at odds with the 1921 Treaty of Moscow. Turkish association with the West during the Cold War, epitomized by its entry into the North Atlantic Treaty Organization, institutionalized the rupture between Turkey and the Soviet Union.[112] As a result, although the two states did not resort to war with each other, the treaty was renounced and the peace settlement, therefore, was merely temporary.

Based on the information available in an era before public opinion polls were routinely conducted and trade statistics were regularly recorded., the treaty does not appear to have been socialized. According to Polity IV, neither regime even approached democracy during the period of the treaty, with neither country surpassing –6 on the Polity scale. Nor did the two countries belong to any cooperative regional institutions, which did not really come into existence until after World War II. It is difficult to get Russo-Turkish trade statistics for this period, but the available evidence suggests that, although the two sides did attempt to increase their bilateral trade, neither state was among the other's principal trading partners.[113] Finally, after the 1921 treaty, whose territorial components were confirmed by the 1921 Treaty of Kars, there were no significant territorial or population transfers affecting the Russo-Turkish state-to-nation balance until World War II.[114] As a result of this lack of socialization, the Turkish population was very critical of Russian behavior in World War II, particularly the Nazi-Soviet Pact of 1939, which it blamed for the outbreak of the war.[115]

Ethiopia-Somalia

The modern rivalry between Ethiopia and Somalia concerned the Ogaden territory, which Great Britain had ceded to Ethiopia together with the Haud grazing area when it administered British Somaliland after World War II.[116] Following the establishment of an independent Somalia (an amalgamation of British and Italian Somaliland) in 1960, the new Somali state made the restoration of the Ogaden, with its predominantly Somali population, and the disputed Haud area to Somalia a core component of Somali foreign policy, even enshrining it within article 4 of the new state's constitution.[117] Military clashes between Somalia and Ethiopia over these territories began within six months of Somali independence and escalated by 1963, with twelve thousand Somali insurgents in the Ethiopian-controlled Ogaden. By February 1964, these clashes had sparked a full-scale border war.[118]

Although the 1964 war ended quickly under pressure from the Organization for African Unity (OAU) for a negotiated settlement, negotiations went nowhere, and the conflict quickly got caught up within the superpowers'

Cold War competition over Africa. Initially, Somalia allied with the Soviet Union and Ethiopia with the United States. Especially after an October 1969 military coup put the socialist-leaning General Siad Barre in Mogadishu, Somalia reached out for and received Soviet arms and assistance. This patron-client relationship, culminating in the 1974 Treaty of Friendship and Cooperation, allowed Somalia to build up its military at Moscow's expense, in exchange for strategic concessions to the Soviets in Africa.[119] Ethiopia, meanwhile, lodged itself within the American camp, although it received considerably less weaponry and assistance from Washington.[120] During the mid to late 1970s, however, as Ethiopian human rights violations soured Washington's relations with Addis Ababa and a 1974 military coup overthrew Haile Selassie's US-aligned regime in Ethiopia, the new government of Mengistu Haile Mariam reached out to the Soviet Union and switched sides in the Cold War. The arms and assistance that the Ethiopians subsequently received from Moscow led Somali leaders to seek US assistance. During the mid to late 1970s, believing that Ethiopia was preoccupied with putting down domestic insurgencies, Somalia initiated another war over the Ogaden in July 1977. This war started well for Somalia, which quickly gained control over 90 percent of the Ogaden, but it then turned sour as a force led by Soviets and Cubans pushed the Somalis back out.[121]

After almost three decades of conflict, however, Ethiopia and Somalia signed a peace treaty on April 3, 1988, that provided for a mutual withdrawal of forces from the Ethiopian-Somali border, re-establishment of diplomatic relations, and an end to proxy warfare by both sides. Some also believe believed at the time that, in a secret clause, Barre renounced Somali claims to the Ogaden.[122]

The main reason the two sides agreed to terminate the rivalry in the mid-1980s was that both regimes faced intense domestic political crises that looked as if they could be resolved only if the protracted, costly conflict was ended. As Gebru Tareke observes, the Ogaden War "fatally wounded the regime in Mogadishu and may even have been the catalyst in the decomposition and demise of the Somali state."[123] The Somali defeat led to widespread public disillusionment and dissatisfaction with the government. A mere month after the end of the Ogaden War, Barre had to fend off an attempted coup. This was only the beginning of a much bigger opposition movement (the Somalia National Movement and the Somali Salvation Democratic Front), which the Ethiopian government provided support to, as a counterbalance to the Somalis' support for the Western Somali Liberation Front in eastern Ethiopia.[124] In the post-1980 period, especially after 1982, Barre's security agenda "had shifted from preserving Somalia's territorial integrity from Ethiopian encroachments and the liberation of the Ogaden to ensuring his own political survival."[125] For its part, the Ethiopian government was increasingly challenged by an insurgency by the Eritrean People's Liberation Front and the Tigrayan People's Liberation Front, which made significant gains on the battlefield against Ethiopian troops.[126] To some extent these internal challenges can be seen as more serious threats that the states had to respond to, which would be consistent with the greater-threat hypothesis. Because they were internal, however, they are less about international balancing and more about domestic challenges or omnibalancing.

As far as bottom-up mechanisms are concerned, there is little to suggest that society drove peacemaking in this case. To begin with, neither state could be classified as democratic in 1988 (Polity IV rated Ethiopia a –8 and Somalia a –7).[127] Although indicators of public opinion in both countries are not available, there is no indication of public pressures for peacemaking in existing studies of the conflict. Nor was there any significant economic exchange between these two persistently impoverished states. Indeed, according to the IMF Direction of Trade Statistics, as reported by Gleditsch, bilateral trade between Ethiopia and Somalia was close to zero for every year since 1982.[128] Nor was the state-to-nation imbalance, represented by the Somali population in the Ogaden, resolved prior to the treaty. Both states were members of the OAU, a relatively weak regional institution, and there is no evidence that this institution brought about a common identity between the two states that made the use of force anathema.[129] Instead, they resolved their conflict when the domestic political costs of continuing were too high and threatened the stability of both regimes.

In the absence of a coherent Somali state, however, the peace treaty never stabilized. Instead, widespread opposition to the treaty in the Ogaden led to the creation of an additional antigovernment opposition, the Somali Patriot Movement, which helped topple the Barre regime within the next few years, leaving Somalia in a collapsed state crisis.[130] The Mengistu regime in Ethiopia also fell, with Mengistu himself escaping into exile.[131] In this environment, with the Somali state fragmenting, Ethiopian troops entered Somalia in support of African Union efforts to fight Islamist insurgents in Somalia. This incursion, however, had less to do with the former rivalry and more to do with providing stability to an unstable neighbor and keeping the Islamists from power.[132] Nonetheless, there is no reason to believe that, if an effective Somali state were to re-emerge and institutionalize itself, Somali designs on the Ogaden would not resurface, as well. We must, therefore, judge the treaty to be at best a temporary expedient and at worst a failure.

In the absence of coherent states, no attempt was made to socialize the treaty, which may explain its fleeting nature. The peace treaty was never reinforced within Ethiopian or Somali public opinion, nor were business groups brought on board with meaningful bilateral economic exchange. Although Ethiopia and Somalia were members of the OAU and then the African Union, the fragmentary nature of these states prevented any kind of regional cooperative identity from taking hold in them. Moreover, the state-to-nation imbalance persists, given that a large community of ethnic Somalis in the Ogaden still reside under Ethiopian jurisdiction. In the absence of societal traction, the agreement could endure only as long as the states that concluded it.

China-Japan

The rivalry between China and Japan began in the nineteenth century after Japan modernized as part of the Meiji Restoration and pursued a course of militarism and imperialism in East Asia at Qing dynasty China's expense. The first significant clash occurred over Korea, which had been under Chinese suzerainty for centuries. In the First Sino-Japanese War (1894–95) Japan defeated China, securing the independence of Korea and acquiring Taiwan, the Liaodong Peninsula, the Penghu Islands, and a large indemnity from China.[133] Together with Japan's brutal treatment of Chinese civilians during this war, the notorious Port Arthur massacre (in which Japanese troops slaughtered the Chinese residents of Port Arthur after capturing the town), and the 1905 Russo-Japanese War, this territorial conquest sowed the seeds of Chinese hostility toward Japan.[134] The Chinese were forced to pay another large indemnity to Japan following the battles of the Boxer Rebellion of 1899–1901.[135] After World War I, the European victors compelled China to cede portions of Shandong Province to Japan and accept further Japanese inroads into Manchuria, despite China having joined the war on the Allied side.[136]

The already intense rivalry between China and Japan heated up again in the 1930s with the Japanese invasion of Manchuria and the declaration of a Japanese puppet state, Manchukuo, there. Then, in 1937, Japan seized on a pretext to invade the rest of China, commencing the Second Sino-Japanese War, which ended in 1945. During this protracted war, the Japanese initially conquered Shanghai, Nanjing, and other important Chinese cities. Their notoriously brutal occupation policies and war crimes, epitomized by their postvictory campaign of slaughter and torture in Nanjing (known as "the rape of Nanking" or "the Nanking massacre"), in which the Japanese military murdered as many as 300,000 civilians, raped tens of thousands of women, and looted and burned property on a massive scale, engendered bitter Chinese resentment that would last decades after the war ended with Japan's defeat after the United States entered World War II.[137] Indeed, this antipathy lasted through governmental changes in both countries, as Japan made the transition to liberal democracy and China underwent a Communist revolution.

The rivalry persisted as a cold one in the first two decades after World War II. In the 1970s, however, the two rivals made a concerted effort to improve bilateral relations. In 1972, Chinese premier Zhou Enlai and Japanese prime minister Kakuei Tanaka issued a joint communiqué announcing the normalization of relations between the two countries and committing both sides to establishing diplomatic relations and negotiating treaties on trade, navigation, aviation, and fishing rights.[138] Six years later, on August 12, 1978, they signed the Treaty of Peace and Friendship, committing the two countries to peaceful relations, respect for each other's sovereignty, peaceful resolution of disputes, further development of economic and cultural relations, and opposition to attempts by any country or group of countries to seek hegemony in Asia.[139]

From the point of view of the People's Republic of China, the principal motivation for resolving the conflict with Japan was to help balance against the Soviet Union, which its leaders viewed as its primary threat.[140] Although the Communist regime in China had a closer ideological affinity with the Soviet Union than with the United States, it officially viewed both superpowers as potential threats.[141] Moreover, after Stalin's death, de-Stalinization in the USSR led to tensions with the Chinese leadership under Mao Zedong, with Sino-Soviet competition in the third world and, in 1969, active skirmishes between the two countries on their borders, along which over a million soldiers were stationed.[142] By the late 1960s, as its relations with the Soviet Union continued to deteriorate, China began improving its relations with the United States.[143] In this context, it was essential for China to collaborate more closely with the West, including Japan, as a means of countering Soviet expansionism.[144] It is instructive in this regard that China insisted that the treaty would have to have an "anti-hegemonism" clause, implicitly directed against the Soviet Union and its expansionist policies in Asia.[145] Furthermore, China advanced the important objective of getting Japan to commit to the One China policy by granting recognition to the People's Republic of China and withdrawing it from Taiwan, which Beijing had made a prerequisite of normalization in 1972.[146] Since China was a revolutionary state with Taiwan as a competitor for diplomatic recognition, winning recognition from key states, such as Japan, was an important state-building motive for improving relations.

From the Japanese side, pressure on the governing Liberal Democratic Party from the business community, notably the Keidanren (Japanese federation of economic organizations), which expected that a peace treaty "would ease implementation of the long-term (1978–1985) bilateral trade agreement signed in February with Peking," was an important factor.[147] In addition, after President Nixon made his monumental 1971 opening to Communist China, the United States—Japan's primary ally—clearly favored a Sino-Japanese treaty, as it would demonstrate to China the advantage of alignment with the West.[148] The Chinese, too, were focused on Washington, and they believed that a treaty with Japan could help improve China's relationship with Japan's primary ally, the United States.[149]

This treaty cannot be explained in terms of joint democracy and democratic pressures. To begin with, while Japan had made the transition to democracy by 1978, China was not a democratic state, scoring a –7 (authoritarian) on the Polity IV rating scale.[150] Furthermore, the Chinese state was heavily centralized and autonomous; it simply did not consider public opinion or societal attitudes when making policy decisions, especially those regarding foreign affairs and national security.[151] Even in Japan, where the polity was democratic, the public was more attentive to quality-of-life issues such as the price of rice. Therefore, Yung H. Park concludes that for the Japanese government, even though the Japanese public was not unfavorable to China, "the China decision was made independently of the public mood."[152]

Assessing the commercial liberal argument is more complicated. There is evidence that the Chinese state may have been motivated by potential economic gains that could advance state interests. Significantly, bilateral economic relations flourished after the 1972 communiqué, with Chinese exports to Japan jumping at least fourfold from under $500 million in 1972 (0.2% of Chinese GDP) to at least $2 billion (0.4% of GDP).[153] Japanese exports to China, similarly, at least quintupled from $619 million (about 0.14% of Japanese GDP) in 1972 to at least $3 billion in 1978 (or less than 0.4% of GDP).[154] Although this was not huge in terms of GDP, it was clearly growing and creating vested interests in good bilateral relations. Furthermore, in February 1978, just six months before the signing of the peace treaty, the two countries signed a lucrative eight-year private trade agreement that envisioned $10 billion in trade each way over the next seven years.[155] Nonetheless, it would appear that these were state interests in economic gains for the purpose of advancing the Chinese economic development program—it needed Western loans and technology to modernize—rather than business interests motivating the state to make peace for their own parochial reasons.[156] In general, the Chinese state was not responsive to Chinese business interests. Indeed, given the structure of the Chinese economy in the 1970s, business interests in China were penetrated by the state in a clientalist system and had no ability to pressure the government.[157] From the Japanese perspective, however, as mentioned earlier, business interests did help drive Japanese progress toward the treaty, despite concerns that the antihegemony clause would imply that Japan sided with China against the Soviet Union.

At the time of the peace treaty, China and Japan did not belong to any of the same regional political, economic, or military organizations. Therefore, institutionalism played no role in motivating peacemaking. Since the treaty was not preceded by and did not involve territorial changes or population transfers, it cannot be explained by an improvement in state-to-nation balance.[158] In sum, therefore, top-down factors, in particular a greater Soviet threat and US encouragement, motivated Chinese leaders, while bottom-up motives, particularly business pressures, factored into Japanese decision making, together with top-down motives.

Since 1978, although the peace treaty has certainly held, the Sino-Japanese relationship has failed to develop into a stable peace. This occurred because the geostrategic imperatives for a close Sino-Japanese relationship have disappeared with the Soviet Union's collapse, only to be replaced by Japanese concerns about Chinese dominance of Asia and Chinese anxiety over Japanese intentions.[159] At the same time, the two sides have faced growing territorial antagonism over the sovereignty of the disputed Diaoyu/Senkaku Islands and their maritime boundary.[160] Increasing attempts by China since 2013 to assert and patrol a maritime boundary that conflicts with other states, including Japan, have threatened to inflame relations further, as has greater Chinese saber rattling over the disputed Diaoyu/Senkaku Islands.[161] Consequently, while a military conflict between the two remains unlikely for the foreseeable future—especially given that any conflict with Japan would inevitably involve China in a confrontation with the United States, a top-down motivation—the relationship cannot be termed stable, as it has been characterized by mutual recriminations and crises.

In this context, the states have not worked to socialize the peace agreement and have periodically stoked societal antagonism. Notably, the Japanese government has persistently inflamed Chinese sentiment by downplaying the atrocities that Japan committed in China. In this regard, reports in 1982 that the Japanese education ministry had published history textbooks that sanitized Japanese actions in Asia during World War II caused both public and official outrage in China.[162] Since then, Sino-Japanese political disputes over the memory of World War II have continued unabated, dominating bilateral relations and overshadowing the prospect of regional stability and prosperity in East Asia.[163] For example, although he made serious efforts to improve bilateral relations, Japanese prime minister Junichiro Koizumi, simultaneously inflamed Chinese opinion with his annual visits to the Yasukuni Shrine honoring the Japanese World War II war dead.[164] There is even reason to suspect that, rather than socializing the settlement, Chinese state elites actually cultivated anti-Japanese sentiment in order to redirect growing domestic anger against the Communist Party against an external target.[165] Consequently, public attitudes remain distrustful.[166]

Of the bottom-up mechanisms to engage society, therefore, only economic instruments have been utilized. Mutual democracy cannot bring about attitudinal change, since Communist China is not a democracy and is constantly assailed for human rights violations.[167] Although the two states have joined several regional international organizations—including Asia-Pacific Economic Cooperation, the East Asia Summit, the Asian Development Bank, and several ASEAN-associated groupings (the Regional Forum, ASEAN Plus Three, and the ASEAN Defense Ministers' Meeting-Plus)—these are not the same type of cohesive identity-and-cooperation inducing institutions as ASEAN itself or the European Union. Thus, while the economic relationship between China and Japan has grown by leaps and bounds, societal hostility still exists and the relationship is not warm.[168]

Overall, the cases of regional rivalry that resolved themselves with peace treaties examined in this chapter conform to the pattern identified in the previous chapters. In all of these episodes, the dynamics of the transition involved statist motivations, in which one or both rivals responded to greater threats, great power pressures, or the need to preserve their domestic power position through state building or alleviating economic crises. In most cases, societal pressures for peacemaking were completely absent; in others, the few societal pressures for peacemaking were merely elements that reinforced the far more politically significant statist pressures. Only in one case, which I will discuss shortly, did a bottom-up pressure—lobbying from the business community—play a meaningful, if not exclusive, role in motivating a peace treaty.

Table 5.1 presents these findings visually. For each case, the factors that were present at the time of the peace treaty are represented with a check mark. The most significant causal factors for each state in the dyad is shaded in gray. Because in the Ecuador-Peru and Ethiopia-Somalia cases the states were motivated by similar logics, only one factor is shaded. Similarly, because the Bulgaria-Yugoslavia case involved a unilateral compromise, only the Bulgarian motivation is shaded. As becomes readily apparent, all of the shading lies in the right three columns of the table, which represent statist top-down motivations. (The state-to-nation balance issue is listed as NA, or "not applicable" in the Sino-Japanese case, since the post–World War II rivalry developed in the absence of a state-to-nation imbalance.)

Only in the Sino-Japanese case did business pressures factor into the peacemaking process. Japanese business elites pressed the government for steps that would ease the implementation of bilateral economic arrangements

Table 5.1 Causes of the transitions to peace

	Public opinion	Business pressures	Strong regional institutions	Improved state-to-nation balance	Greater threats	Great Power pressures	Regime survival/ state building
Ecuador-Peru	—	—	—	—	—	√	√
Italy-Yugoslavia	—	—	—	—	√	√	—
Bulgaria-Yugoslavia	—	—	—	—	—	√	√
Russia-Turkey	√	—	—	√	√	—	√
Ethiopia-Somalia	—	—	—	—	—	—	√
China-Japan	—	√	—	NA	√	√	√

that promised to be very lucrative for Japan. Nonetheless, while this was not an unimportant influence, the business community's influence was insufficient to obtain a treaty. Without the Soviet threat and the US diplomatic opening to China, it is unlikely that China would have opted for a peace agreement with Japan. In the Russo-Turkish case, although favorable public attitudes preceded the settlement and an improvement in the state-to-nation balance accompanied it, neither of these factors played a decisive role in Russian or Turkish decision making. Consequently, these cases are largely consistent with the top-down pattern of peacemaking.

After these peace settlements were reached, they took divergent paths. Three became stable peace agreements. The Ecuador-Peru settlement and the Italo-Yugoslavian agreement remained largely stable with no wars between the signatories, no significant governmental attempts to revise the treaty by either party, and no significant mutual recriminations or high-level crises between the parties. It is true that in the early 1970s the Italian government sought to revise the Trieste settlement, but once it was confirmed by the Treaty of Osimo, the matter has remained closed for almost four decades, despite the opportunity for revision provided by the breakup of Yugoslavia. Consequently, I judge that to be a stable peace. In addition, since I divide the Bulgarian-Yugoslavian peace settlement into two periods—the Cold War period involving Bulgaria and Yugoslavia and the twenty-first century period involving Bulgaria and Macedonia—I judge the latter relationship to be stable, as the Bulgarian and Macedonian governments have renounced any territorial claims against each other and their relations have been free of crises and serious recriminations for an extended period.

In contrast, while China and Japan have not resorted to force and have respected the terms of the settlement, their relationship has been characterized by considerable mutual recriminations and crises over territorial issues, such as the Diaoyu/Senkaku Islands, and inflammatory actions. The Cold War peace between Bulgaria and Yugoslavia was enduring but unstable owing to Bulgarian attempts to revise the settlement in the decades following its signature, even though it did not result in renewed interstate violence. Consequently, while these treaties have endured, they cannot be termed stable. Finally, the Ethiopia-Somalia settlement, which has collapsed along with the Somali state and the presence of Ethiopian troops on Somali soil, and the Russo-Turkish treaty, which was terminated when Moscow renounced the 1925 Treaty of Friendship and made demands at odds with the 1921 Treaty of Moscow, have both relapsed into political conflict, if not war.

Table 5.2 distinguishes between the three postsettlement outcomes by shading the stable agreements dark gray, shading the enduring agreements light gray, and leaving the relapsed agreements unshaded. It then indicates the presence of both bottom-up mechanisms or strategies to entrench the

Table 5.2 Developments in the postagreement phase

	Democra-tization	Economic exchange	Regional institutions	Improved state-to-nation balance	Greater threats	Great Power pressure	Regime survival
Ecuador-Peru	—	√	√	—	—	—	—
Italy-Yugoslavia	√	√	—*	—	—	—	—
Bulgaria-Macedonia (21st century)	√	√	—*	—	—	—	√
China-Japan	—	√	—	—	√	—	—
Bulgaria-Yugoslavia (20th century)	—	—	—	—	—	√	√
Ethiopia-Somalia	—	—	√	—	—	—	√
Russia-Turkey	—	—	—	—	—	—	—

agreement and statist motives for adhering to the treaty with check marks. As is evident by the check marks on the left side of the chart but almost none on the right in the top three rows, the three stable agreements are those in which serious attempts to engage society took place, despite statist pressures to maintain the agreement having dissipated in two of the cases. The agreement between Ecuador and Peru was stabilized in the context of greatly increased bilateral economic exchange and emerging regional institutions, such as Mercosur. The Italo-Yugoslav settlement was followed up with increased economic interaction between the former rivals. After the collapse of Yugoslavia, the successor states to the peace settlement, Croatia and Slovenia, both made the transition to democracy, meaning that all parties to the agreement are now democratic, and very recently (hence the asterisk) they have all become members of the European Union. The relationship between Bulgaria and Macedonia has been consummated with democratization and economic exchange plus the prospects of Macedonia joining Bulgaria as an EU member (denoted with an asterisk, as it has not yet occurred).

The middle two agreements, which endured but did not stabilize, did not draw on a range of mechanisms derived by bottom-up approaches to bring society on board after the agreement. While the Sino-Japanese treaty was reinforced by reasonably large-scale economic exchange, the Chinese state has not democratized, and the institutions the two states are jointly members of are relatively weak consultative institutions rather than well-institutionalized regional frameworks. Consequently, Chinese and Japanese society are still hostile, and, if it were not for Japan's alliance with the United States and the expectation that a conflict with Japan would involve the United States, one could imagine China allowing the Diaoyu/Senkaku Islands dispute or the dispute over territorial waters and airspace to escalate. Until the twenty-first century, the settlement between Bulgaria and Yugoslavia had not been socialized with democratization, significant levels of bilateral trade, common regional institutions, or territorial or population transfers to improve the state-to-national balance. Instead, the treaty endured during the Cold War largely because of Soviet influence and the fear that challenging the Soviet Union would be a bad career move for Bulgarian leaders. Thus, all of these enduring but unstable agreements have been maintained largely due to the persistence of statist incentives to adhere to the treaties.

Finally, the Ethiopian-Somali and Russo-Turkish settlements also failed to socialize the agreements. Consequently, they fell apart when the statist interests that motivated them disappeared. In the Russo-Turkish case, neither state was democratic; they did not belong to cooperative regional institutions; they did not trade extensively; and they did not alter the state-to-nation balance significantly after the 1921 treaty. As a result, once the two nascent regimes stabilized and the Soviet Union no longer faced diplomatic isolation and the risk of imminent invasion, their competing interests trumped their reasons to cooperate with each other, although the Russo-Turkish relationship has improved somewhat, as Russia's adventure in Ukraine has strained Moscow's relationship with the West. In the case of Ethiopia and Somalia, aside from their membership in the African Union, the two weak/failing states were unable to socialize the treaty. Under these circumstances, when the Somali state collapsed, the new strategic imperative drove Ethiopia to act on its interests and forget the peace treaty.

Overall, these settlements are consistent with my staged theory of peacemaking between regional rivals. The peace agreements were achieved due to statist rationales, but those that became stable did so because of mechanisms to co-opt society in the postagreement era. In the concluding chapter, I will cumulate my case study findings and consider the implications for international relations theorists and for policymakers seeking to promote peace in troubled regions.

Peacemaking between Regional Rivals

Theoretical and Policy Implications

The three detailed case studies of Franco-German, Egyptian-Israeli, and Israeli-Jordanian peacemaking in this book reveal similar paths to a peace agreement despite their different regional contexts. Each of these three settlements was achieved owing to the efforts of the governments involved, state-survival goals, and international imperatives rather than pressures from peace-loving societies. They were top-down settlements rather than bottom-up ones. As these have been among the most successful and most dramatic cases of peacemaking between regional rivals (even if they vary in the depth of their peace agreements, or in Benjamin Miller's terms, the warmth of the peace), it leads us to believe that top-down approaches can be very successful.[1] In contrast, bottom-up dynamics did not bring about any of these settlements. Indeed, in none of these cases was there significant public support for peace in both states before the treaty, business interests that demanded peace to realize or protect economic gains, powerful regional institutions involving the rivals as members that created cooperative regional identities, or a congruent state-to-nation balance when the peace agreement was negotiated. Thus, these paths to peace suggested by the bottom-up literature clearly did not drive peacemaking.

The discussion of the six additional twentieth century cases in chapter 5 confirms this pattern. Indeed, in only one case (the Sino-Japanese treaty) did bottom-up pressures play a significant role. Even in that case, however, lobbying from Japanese business groups would have been insufficient to produce a peace treaty absent the powerful balance-of-power considerations that drove Chinese decision making. In all other cases, the dominant motives for peacemaking related to greater threats, great power pressures, and/or state survival. In fact, perhaps because security competition gets in the way of societal interaction, there is very little evidence of bottom-up pressures of any kind before the conclusion of these peace agreements. Table C.1 illustrates these findings strikingly, with the heavy balance of check marks (indicating the presence of a particular motivating factor at the time of the agreement) and shading (indicating the primary motives of each of the parties) on the statist side of the ledger.

It is interesting to note that even in the case of the Franco-German settlement, which was negotiated between two democratic states and is therefore the most favorable case for the bottom-up approach, top-down dynamics drove the peacemaking process. This is powerful evidence that peace between regional rivals is obtained through statist calculations. Nonetheless, to be fully confident in this generalization, we would need to examine more cases of peacemaking between democratic regional rivals. As it turns out, however, the empirical record simply does not provide us with many cases of peacemaking between democratic regional rivals. As I observe in the introductory chapter, there are only nine cases of peace treaties between regional rivals in the twentieth century that meet the theoretical criteria, only one of which was achieved between democracies (France and Germany), a case that clearly conforms to my expectations.[2] Because I did not select cases but am examining the entire universe of twentieth-century cases, this is not a deliberate selection bias but an artifact of the underlying set of cases. The paucity of peace treaties between democratic rivals may provide support for the hypothesis that democracies rarely become embroiled in rivalries with each other and, therefore, may provide some support for the democratic peace theory.[3] It also may simply reflect the fact that enduring rivalries are rare events; as with war, the odds of any two particular states becoming enduring rivals are very low. The odds of two democracies—until recently a relatively rare regime type— becoming embroiled in rivalries are far lower. So it should not surprise us that we have hardly any instances of intrademocratic regional rivalries. Regardless of the reason, the shortage of democratic regional rivalries terminating in peace treaties must be borne in mind when generalizing my findings. Nonetheless, the Franco-German case gives us some ground to conclude that even democratic states make peace in a statist manner in spite of societal opposition, a conclusion that is supported by the experience of peacemaking in other contexts that do not meet the selection criteria for this study.[4]

The similarity of peacemaking in these very disparate cases is all the more striking given the considerable variation in their regional circumstances. If peacemaking follows the same pattern in Europe as it does in the Middle East, where belligerents have far less in common culturally and religiously, and in sub-Saharan Africa, where states are weak and unstable, it suggests that this pattern is quite robust and generalizable.

Despite their similar paths to a settlement, these cases differ markedly in their postagreement experiences. After the Western European peace settlement was concluded, societal mechanisms helped socialize and stabilize

Table C.1 Causes of the transitions to peace

	Public opinion	Business pressures	Strong regional institutions	Improved state-to-nation balance	Greater threats	Great power pressures	Regime survival/ state building
France-Germany	—	—	—	Weak	√	√	√
Egypt-Israel	—	—	—	Weak	—	√	√
Israel-Jordan	—	—	—	—	√	√	√
Ecuador-Peru	—	—	—	—	—	√	√
Italy-Yugoslavia	—	—	—	—	√	√	—
Bulgaria-Yugoslavia	—	—	—	—	—	√	√
Russia-Turkey	√	—	—	√	√	—	√
Ethiopia-Somalia	—	—	—	—	—	—	√
China-Japan	—	√	—	NA	√	√	√

the settlement and ensure its survival beyond the founding realist and statist conditions.[5] Consequently, despite changes in government and governing parties within Western European states and despite changes in the statist founding conditions the settlement endures. The Italo-Yugoslavian and the twenty-first century Bulgarian-Macedonian relationship have also stabilized recently, as the states in question have democratized, increased bilateral trade, and sought a positive future within cooperative regional institutions.

In contrast, the Arab-Israeli settlements were not supported by strategies to engage society in their aftermath and, consequently, failed to achieve societal buy-in. These treaties, therefore, endure, despite frequent crises and mutual recriminations, only because the states continue to identify their own interests as tied up with the peace treaty, since they still face greater threats that they need to focus on and US pressure to remain at peace. Similarly, the Sino-Japanese treaty has endured, despite the absence of democratization and the failure of the two states to integrate in cohesive regional institutions. Thus, although the two states have increased their bilateral economic exchange considerably, the peace endures in the face of mutual recriminations and crises, primarily, it would seem, because of the presence of the United States as a greater potential threat for China that would no doubt become involved in any Chinese conflict with Japan. Before stabilizing after the disintegration of Yugoslavia, the Bulgarian-Yugoslavian settlement endured despite a lack of stability and Bulgarian attempts to revise the treaty, mainly because the Soviet Union—the undisputed Eastern bloc hegemon during the Cold War—insisted on it.

Finally, the Russo-Turkish and Ethiopian-Somali settlements were never societally entrenched and were maintained only by top-down motivations. Once these statist interests disappeared, the peace treaties were repudiated or ignored, making them only temporary expedients.

Table C.2 Developments in the postagreement phase

	Democra-tization	Economic exchange	Regional institutions	Improved state-to-nation balance	Greater threats	Great power pressure	Regime survival
France-Germany	√	√	√	Weak	—	—	—
Ecuador-Peru	—	√	√	—	—	—	—
Italy-Yugoslavia	√	√	—*	—	—	—	—
Bulgaria-Macedonia (21st century)	√	√	—*	—	—	—	√
Egypt-Israel	—	—	—	—	√	√	—
Israel-Jordan	—	—	—	—	√	√	√
China-Japan	—	√	—	—	√	—	—
Bulgaria-Yugoslavia (20th century)	—	—	—	—	—	√	√
Ethiopia-Somalia	—	—	√	—	—	—	√
Russia-Turkey	—	—	—	√	—	—	—

Table C.2 illustrates this dynamic visually. The stable settlements (darkly shaded) have their check marks concentrated on the left side, indicating that they endured in the presence of numerous societal strategies to entrench the treaties but largely in the absence of sustained statist pressures. The enduring treaties (lightly shaded) have their check marks concentrated on the right side, indicating that they were largely maintained by statist incentives in the absence of serious efforts to bring society on board. The temporary settlements (unshaded) have very few check marks, indicating the dearth of reasons to perpetuate the peace.

A few caveats are in order. First, while it would be convenient to identify a single top-down path to peace or prioritize the top-down pressures so that we could identify the specific conditions that bring about peace between regional rivals, the evidence in this book defies such a simplification. Although in almost all the cases I examined multiple top-down factors combined to inspire a peace treaty, the specific catalyst for peacemaking differed across the cases. In some cases, such as the settlements between Ethiopia and Somalia and between Ecuador and Peru, regime-survival motives played a dominant role in fostering peacemaking. In others, such as the Israeli-Jordanian and Bulgarian-Yugoslavian settlements, great power considerations—particularly a desire to satisfy the global hegemon or a great power with disproportionate influence in the region—acted as the catalyst. In still others, such as the Franco-German rapprochement and the Sino-Japanese treaty, the emergence of a greater threat to one or both parties was the principal motivation for peacemaking.

Moreover, none of the three top-down influences were significant in every case. Thus, for example, while a greater threat was significant in driving Franco-German rapprochement, it played no role in Egyptian-Israeli peacemaking. Even regime survival/statebuilding considerations, which factored into almost all of these cases, played a leading role in some cases, such as the treaty between Ecuador and Peru, a supporting role in others, such as the Israeli-Jordanian agreement, and no role in the Italo-Yugoslavian settlement. Consequently, while this research clearly supports the important generalization that peacemaking begins with states rather than societies, it does not allow further generalizations about the specific statist path to peace that must be followed. In other words, this research suggests that statist pressures are a necessary condition for peacemaking, but no specific kind of statist pressures are either individually necessary or sufficient conditions. This is both encouraging and discouraging. On the one hand, it is discouraging, since we cannot identify a single "silver bullet" strategy to achieve rivalry termination. On the other hand, it is encouraging that there are a variety of statist paths to peacemaking so that in the absence of a specific facilitating factor peace may still be built on other statist pressures.

The same cannot be said regarding the utility of particular postagreement strategies. In fact, several interesting conclusions are suggested by the cases of stable peace. First of all, contra Miller, none of the three stable agreements completely resolved their state-to-nation imbalances by the time the peace was stabilized. Consequently, we can rule out population or territorial transfers as a necessary condition of post-treaty stability. Furthermore, in each of these stable settlements, the former rivals engaged in significant postagreement economic exchange. This does not mean that generating economic interdependence is a prerequisite for stability, but it does appear to be a reasonable strategy to pursue after a peace treaty is signed, in concert with other bottom-up strategies to achieve a stable peace.[6] In addition, the experience of Ecuador and Peru provides additional support for Amitav Acharya's and Etel Solingen's claims that stable peace can occur even if one or more of the states involved is not democratic.[7]

Second, since this book has explored only cases of regional rivalries that terminated with peace treaties or their functional equivalent, we can reach conclusions about necessary conditions for transitions to peace, but we cannot engage in speculation about the sufficiency of particular paths to peace.[8] This would require an analysis of negative cases, especially "near misses" in which peace negotiations failed to yield an agreement. As indicated in the introduction, that will be the next phase of my research.

Finally, it must be remembered that societies can change their minds, too, so there is no guarantee that socialized agreements will last. International politics is dynamic, and there is no reason to expect that even the most stable of peace settlements, such as that between France and Germany, will last forever. These could conceivably be tested over the long term by dramatic changes in the international balance of power or perhaps extraordinary regional crises pertaining to shortages of critical resources or some other unforeseen event. Nonetheless, peacemaking that penetrates deeply into the societies of the former belligerents is more likely to endure crises, challenges, or governmental changes than treaties that remain unpopular long after their signature. This should especially be the case if the peace agreement is embedded within a network of regional or bilateral institutions and reinforced with lucrative bilateral economic exchange and measures to rectify ethnic grievances that fuel a state-to-nation imbalance. While we cannot talk about permanent peace, therefore, we can expect stable peace settlements that have been socialized to last for an extended period barring extraordinary changes in circumstance.

Theoretical Implications

My comprehensive study of successful agreements has implications not only for explaining the outbreak of peace but also for elucidating the causes of war. After all, theories of peace and theories of war are inextricably linked, as two sides of the same coin; a theory of peace necessarily subscribes to an underlying theory of war, and its policy prescriptions should be useful only if they negate a cause of war. In this regard, hegemonic stability theory, as advanced by Robert Gilpin and William Wohlforth, has an underlying theory of war that assumes that war is caused by anarchy in the international system and the constraints of the security dilemma.[9] To the extent that the hegemon can mitigate the condition of anarchy by altering the costs of defection and the benefits of cooperation, peace will be fostered, according to the theory.[10] In contrast, commercial liberals assume that war is the product of greed and opportunism, as rational actors calculate the likely costs and benefits of force and opt for war when they expect to gain wealth or territory. Consequently, the development of economic interdependence between states, which increases the opportunity costs of using force in terms of trade and investment forgone, can restrain states by making conquest less profitable.[11]

If peacemaking proceeds in stages, with a state-driven transition and, for stable peace settlements, a socialization process to change societal attitudes, what then does that say about the causes of war? It suggests that war initially has international structural causes but that it shapes the combatant states and societies in such as a manner as to perpetuate conflict long beyond the systemic conditions that inspired war. In other words, as Kenneth Waltz suggests, war begins with the permissive condition of international anarchy and the security dilemma it presents to states. Under these circumstances, as illustrated in figure C.1, states may be driven by scarcity—of territory, resources, and security—to wage war with each other. War, in and of itself, however, does not constitute a rivalry. Absent societal antipathy, when the international circumstances that compel war change—that is, when a greater threat to both states emerges or when stable borders are achieved—the warring states can lay down their arms and even cooperate

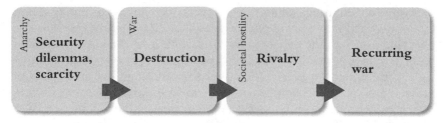

Figure C.1. The causes of war underlying my findings

to achieve common objectives, as occurred with regularity during the classical balance-of-power era in Europe.[12] Repeated war or particularly destructive war can create hostility in the combatant societies that outlasts changes in the international system. This hostility may derive from the intensity of conflict and the death toll it produces, the loss of culturally or historically important territory, or the creation of myths of national humiliation. Consequently, rivalries develop that take on dynamics of their own, especially in states that are at least partially beholden to their citizens in the making of security policy. When societal antipathies take hold, leaders may be unable to refrain from conflict, even if they judge war to be against the national interest, or they may refrain from making judicious compromises with the adversary for fear of being labeled traitorous and removed from power.[13] They therefore perpetuate the rivalry.

To break out of the vicious cycle of rivalry, two stages are thus necessary. First, the initial environmental conditions that originally pushed the states toward war need to be alleviated with the help of powerful third parties and the states themselves. They can do so by issuing security guarantees that alleviate the security dilemma or by providing economic and military incentives that offset the risks of cooperation. The bilateral push to war under anarchy may also be alleviated, at least in the short term, if other more pressing threats emerge, or if the states in question experience domestic political crises that present more immediate threats to state leaders than the traditional rival does. As indicated in this book, these developments may make it possible to de-escalate the rivalry and negotiate a peace settlement. Nonetheless, because the rival societies are likely to retain their hatred of the enemy, a peace treaty achieved in such a top-down manner will remain only skin deep, and the rivalry will endure unless the settlement is socialized and societal hostility is overcome. Consequently, utilizing postpeace strategies that target society, rather than the states involved, will be necessary to escape the inertia of rivalry and allow the states to put the conflict behind them when international circumstances allow. This is a more dynamic theory of both war and peace within international rivalries.

My empirical findings provide a further impetus for international relations scholars to move beyond the rigid theoretical paradigms that have dominated much of the debate in the field in the last century. In the three cases examined in detail in this book, peacemaking was not driven by a single paradigmatic logic. Instead, the different stages of peacemaking followed distinctly different logics. The transition phase, with its emphasis on common threats and hegemonic pressure, is largely consistent with the expectations of the realist paradigm, although the additional relevance of regime-survival motives reflects a domestic political dimension, as well. In the post-transition phase, however, the entrenchment of peace has little to do with realist mechanisms. Indeed, in the case of Western Europe, the realist dynamics that compelled peacemaking were distinctly weakened after the security settlement, yet the quality of peace improved over time. In the Middle Eastern cases, despite the persistence of realist incentives for cooperation between former enemies, the peace has remained rather tenuous. Realism, therefore, cannot explain the whole story of peacemaking. Instead, the socialization and incentive-changing mechanisms that entrench peace are more consistent with the constructivist and liberal paradigms.

These findings thus bolster calls to move beyond balkanized paradigms, or "isms," in the pursuit of greater nuance and explanatory power.[14] A more comprehensive and productive approach to understanding the politics of peacemaking between regional rivals would be to combine the insights of different theoretical approaches in a more synthetic theoretical framework. In this regard, my findings support scholars advocating eclectic theories of international politics.[15]

More specifically, my conclusions are consistent with one particular multiparadigmatic approach to foreign policy and international relations: the emerging approach of neoclassical realism. Neoclassical realists draw on the insights of liberal and constructivist theory, as well as *Innenpolitik* approaches that identify domestic political and institutional influences on foreign policy, but place these insights within a realist framework that acknowledges the primacy of international constraints and opportunities as determinants of state action. They posit that states construct foreign policy so as to respond appropriately to external challenges but must navigate their distinct domestic political environments to do so, which leads states to pursue unique national approaches to international challenges and occasionally causes surprising deviations from systemic imperatives.[16] Because my research concludes that peacemaking occurs, when it does, primarily because of reasons of state—largely geopolitical in nature—but that the nature of that settlement and the degree to which it is entrenched depends on the subsequent extent of societal engagement, it confirms that the external environment within which states interact has a dominant role in determining a state's security behavior, but that the nature of its policy responses to external pressures will be affected by state-society relations and the balance of societal attitudes.[17]

Policy Ramifications

In addition to its theoretical implications, this research also has important policy implications for third-party states and international institutions that seek to promote peacemaking between regional rivals. I will discuss several of these, including the need for secret negotiations; the importance of states; the need to match peace-promoting strategies to the specific stage of peacemaking; the utility of promoting peace with both incentives and disincentives; being attuned to opportune and inopportune moments for peacemaking; the fact that liberal states are unnecessary to achieve an agreement, although they are useful to cement agreements; and the need for regional frameworks.

KEEPING SOCIETIES OUT: THE NEED FOR SECRET NEGOTIATIONS

To begin with, peacemakers would do well to observe that peace settlements begin with states and not societies. The implication is that the key to stabilizing conflict-prone regions and dyads is to generate both incentives and pressure for hostile governments to cooperate and create conditions that encourage governments to negotiate and compromise with former enemies, even if such a course is domestically unpopular. To achieve this, third-party states and international institutions interested in promoting peacemaking need to pursue policies that might initially conflict with Western preferences and modi operandi. Despite the Western preference for open covenants openly arrived at, for example, the transition to peacemaking is actually facilitated by secrecy and, before an agreement is signed, threatened by domestic scrutiny. Secrecy allows the rival governments to fly under the radar of potential spoilers until after an agreement is reached and the leaders can present their societies with a complete agreement. Thus, when US secretary of state Dean Acheson refused to consider a French request for a secret agreement on German rearmament at the September 1950 NATO meetings, French foreign minister Robert Schuman and his government blocked progress on an open treaty—despite their conviction that German rearmament would serve French security interests—for fear that the government would fall.[18] In a similar vein, if Israeli prime minister Yitzhak Rabin had not repeatedly denied that his government was negotiating with the Palestinian Liberation Organization before the announcement of the 1993 Oslo Accord, domestic opponents would likely have scuttled the talks before an agreement was reached.[19] To create domestic political space for peacemaking, belligerent governments should be encouraged to negotiate secretly, outside the scrutiny of the public and the media, to prevent the content of agreements from becoming public and possibly tying leaders' hands.

This suggests that the project of regional peacemaking is likely to be complicated by technological innovations and practices that make it difficult for governments to keep secrets. In an era of Twitter and WikiLeaks, where private government policy papers and the content of secret negotiations can be published online without governmental consent, peace negotiators may be less willing to make domestically unpopular concessions for fear of being exposed. The example of Palestinian-Israeli negotiations, where Palestinian negotiator Saeb Erekat was publicly chastised after Al Jazeera released secret minutes indicating Erekat's willingness behind closed doors to consider a compromise on the Palestinian demand for a right of return, is instructive in this regard.[20] If negotiators and leaders cannot do their work outside the purview of the public, peace agreements, which of necessity require concessions, will be much harder to attain.

THE IMPORTANCE OF STATES

This book also highlights the importance of states in the peacemaking process. A key prerequisite for peacemaking is the existence of strong, well-institutionalized states on both sides of the conflict. States play central roles, both before an agreement is reached and afterward. Beforehand, states need to have the capacity to ignore or stifle domestic hostility toward the adversary and opt for unpopular compromises. This requires a high degree of stateness, principally the autonomy to enact policy when opposed or the capacity to buy off or silence opponents of peace.[21] Absent a sufficient degree of state insulation from societal forces, domestic spoilers and veto players are likely to interfere with peace negotiations and preclude compromises.[22] After a treaty is signed, the state must implement the agreement and ensure that spoilers are unable to scuttle it through violence or other means. Moreover, its role in socializing the treaty is of paramount importance. The state needs to play a leadership role in selling the treaty by providing economic payoffs to society, fostering constructive contacts between the two formerly rival societies, and working to defuse nationalist grievances.[23]

The discouraging implication is that peacemaking may be impossible in the absence of strong, coherent states. This may mean that in regions of failed states, failing states, and poorly institutionalized states, such as sub-Saharan Africa, it might be difficult to gain sufficient traction to overcome societal antipathy and reach peace treaties. Furthermore, it would be a challenge to entrench any agreements that are reached. Indeed, the treaty between Ethiopia and Somalia was not socialized, in large measure because of the fragmentary nature of the two regimes. As a corollary, if third parties wish to promote peace between rivals, one or more of which is not a state entity or does not have a well-institutionalized state apparatus, they would best serve the rivals by working on state building before initiating serious peace negotiations in order to increase the chances that their peacemaking efforts will gain sufficient traction. In this regard, peace between Israel and the Palestinian Authority should be quite difficult until the Palestinians develop adequate state capacity that could enable their leadership to reach unpopular compromises and bring a reluctant population on board.[24]

MATCHING STRATEGIES TO THE APPROPRIATE STAGE

Third parties must also distinguish between strategies that are appropriate for the transition stage and those that are appropriate for the postagreement stage. To promote a transition, it is necessary to tailor policies that influence state actors, particularly the leadership or the foreign policy executive, rather than the target state's society.[25] To this end, in the preagreement period economic incentives and economic assistance should be more attentive to the leadership's needs and objectives than to broader societal needs and development projects. This means that it is acceptable to extend foreign aid that will be devoted to regime survival, the security sector, or that will be used to buy the support of important sectors of the target polity rather than filtering down to benefit the people and the country as a whole. Although it might be unpalatable for Western governments to extend such aid—especially to regimes that are undemocratic and possess poor human rights records—it is precisely these grants that are most likely to gain policy traction with target regimes.

Furthermore, although bottom-up strategies designed to change societal attitudes, such as fostering cultural exchanges between the rival populations and encouraging joint ventures between them, pursuing democratization, and attempting to mitigate public hostility by enmeshing the states in regional institutions, are popular with Western governments and peoples, they are inappropriate at this stage. Attempting bottom-up peacemaking, particularly where nondemocracies are involved, can be both wasteful and even counterproductive, as it could interfere with the top-down efforts that are more likely to bring about successful agreements. To begin with, bottom-up measures push off the problem of peacemaking indefinitely. After all, societal change occurs in glacial time, over years, decades, and even generations; in contrast, statist agreements can proceed far more swiftly. In principle, if they are to succeed, bottom-up strategies require a considerable amount of time to change societal attitudes. Prejudices, hostility, and hatred do not abate overnight, especially within an entire population. It takes a considerable amount of time to change attitudes, as the Franco-German case demonstrates. Even under the most favorable of circumstances, it took about two decades to change French attitudes toward

West Germany from the early 1950s, when the majority of the French public eschewed even cordial diplomatic relations, to the 1970s, when a plurality of the French public viewed the FRG as France's best friend in Europe. This attitudinal change was facilitated by the peace settlement, which actually created better than cordial diplomatic relations between the two states. In the absence of such a settlement, if the two states remained in a state of war, that would only have reinforced societal hostility, making it incredibly unlikely that bottom-up strategies could have changed attitudes even as quickly as two decades. This means that in pinning our hopes on spreading peace through economic interdependence, democracy, or international institutions, we are abdicating any chance of success in the short run and condemning the rivals to conflict for years or decades.

In concept, bottom-up and top-down strategies can be pursued simultaneously, as they were in Western Europe after World War II, but that entails certain risks. First, if the third parties have limited resources to devote to peacemaking, diverting some to societal efforts from the more promising state-oriented trajectory could be unwise. Second, and more important, bottom-up strategies can undermine the governmental goodwill that is necessary by signaling a willingness to bypass the government and go directly to the people. After all, the leader of a nondemocratic state (such as a Sadat, a King Hussein, or a Tito) will view an attempt to democratize the rivals as an attempt to undermine his/her own hold on power. Such a leader may then identify cooperation with the outside power and the peacemaking process as counter to the leader's interests.

Third, if the leaders of the belligerent states are more willing to compromise than their societies, efforts to strengthen domestic actors either politically (through democratization) or economically (through the generation of economic interdependence) may undermine the leader's ability to commit to a peace of compromise. Promoting democratization to create opportunities for the public to press its leaders to make peace will also open up the same avenues of influence to opponents of the treaty, who may then serve as veto players, preventing a moderate leader (now or in the future) from making compromises for peace. Given the hostility of the Jordanian public to peace with Israel, for example, it would have been difficult for King Hussein to make peace with Israel if the Jordanian parliament were truly democratic and representative. Strategies that provide economic gains cannot restrict these gains to supporters of the treaty; therefore, they will also enrich opponents of the treaty, who may use their gains to act as spoilers. Moreover, as leaders are frequently motivated to engage in peacemaking by severe economic crises that threaten their hold on power, any attempt to provide broader economic benefits to the target society before an agreement might backfire by alleviating the economic crisis and rendering peacemaking unnecessary for the state. We can imagine, for example, that Sadat might have found it unnecessary to break with the rest of the Arab world by negotiating a peace treaty with Israel if Western aid had alleviated the Egyptian economic crisis in 1977.

For all these reasons, Western governments and international organizations need to overcome their unconditional love for people-to-people engagement and track-two diplomacy. These initiatives have their time and place, typically in building societal support after an unpopular agreement is reached. They are not high-probability strategies for securing a peace treaty and are, therefore, a waste of time and money in the preagreement stage. Similarly, integrating conflict-ridden states into international organizations without first securing a peace agreement is not an effective strategy for peacemaking. Including India and Pakistan in the ASEAN Regional Forum, for example, should not affect their willingness to make compromises for peace. While cohesive regional institutions can help stabilize peace agreements, it makes no sense to put the cart before the horse.

In the postagreement stage, the type of third-party support needed changes. At this point, the goal is to promote societal cooptation over time by providing a peace dividend; fostering bilateral contacts, joint ventures, and cultural exchanges between the former enemies; enmeshing the states in cooperative regional economic and political institutions; resolving ethnonationalist grievances between them; and, where lacking, promoting liberal democracy. Economic initiatives at this stage should be directed to the people, rather than the regime, to persuade them of the benefits of peace.

MIXING CARROTS AND STICKS

The case studies in this book indicate that states make the strategic decision to terminate rivalries primarily in response to threats, whether external—from other states or great powers—or internal—from domestic opponents, dissatisfied powerbrokers, or a disenchanted public. On the surface, that would suggest that the trick for outside actors to promote peace between a pair of rivals would be to accentuate the negative by issuing threats and imposing economic and other sanctions that could cause a deterioration in their domestic political environment. By keeping the heat on belligerent governments in that manner, they increase the likelihood that beleaguered leaders will choose peace to reduce their external vulnerability and domestic instability.

Yet these cases demonstrate that it makes sense to mix both carrots and sticks to coax leaders to peace.[26] After all, Sadat and King Hussein responded not only to US pressures but also to lucrative offers of economic and military aid that could alleviate their domestic economic woes. Similarly, the Marshall Plan was the decisive element that persuaded the French to permit the creation of the West German state and to rehabilitate that state economically, and the American security guarantee convinced them to proceed with German rearmament. The implication is that third parties, especially great powers that are likely to generate leverage over the rivals, can best promote peacemaking by employing sufficient coercion to maximize the potential security and regime survival costs of maintaining the feud, while at the same time offering the resources to help them overcome these threats if they make peace. Thus, the promise of economic and military incentives should go hand in hand with coercive instruments in the peacemaker's game plan.

CHOOSING THE RIGHT MOMENT

These peace settlements also suggest that third parties should distinguish between opportune and inopportune moments to press for top-down peace agreements. The conflict resolution literature addresses the issue of "ripeness," or the degree to which a conflict is ready for settlement.[27] In that literature, a conflict is ripe for resolution when a hurting stalemate has set in and both actors anticipate that they will suffer greater costs in the future if they do not resolve the conflict. The case studies presented in this book suggest several different hypotheses about the particular circumstances that facilitate peacemaking, or the nature of "ripeness," that have little directly to do with the costs of conflict itself.

1. When the adversaries face common threats that are more immediate and more threatening, they are more likely to bury the hatchet as a means of focusing on the greater threat. French and German leaders were inspired to cooperate with each other by the considerably greater threat posed to both countries by the Soviet Union. Jordanian and Israeli leaders recognized that other countries, such as Iraq, could potentially threaten their security to a greater extent. This suggests that the leaders of belligerent countries and interested third parties should pay attention to changes in the global and regional balance before investing significant political and economic capital on a peace initiative. The emergence of a rising threat to regional participants may bode well for peacemaking. In this regard, the rising power and regional activism of Iran in the new millennium, which threatens pragmatist Sunni regimes in the Middle East, may explain the genesis of the Saudi peace initiative toward Israel.[28] Moreover, it may present a galvanizing force for a United States or Middle East Quartet initiative in the region. Conversely, in the absence of a more compelling threat, peace negotiations are more likely to founder and may constitute a waste of resources. Under these circumstances, conflict management should take precedence over peacemaking until circumstances change.

2. International institutions and smaller states wishing to encourage peacemaking are likely to be more successful when the international system is unipolar, with an active and engaged hegemon that is willing to use its resources and reputation in support of peace.[29] Under these favorable circumstances, less powerful actors can provide some additional resources

and the unique advantages they have at their disposal—principally their legitimacy and any persuasive ability they derive from not being a great power and, consequently, being less threatening—to assist the hegemon in its efforts.[30] Conversely, in the absence of a hegemon, or if the world's leading power is uninterested in expending its resources to promote the regional peacemaking project, the prospects of a successful agreement are slimmer.

In this regard, the different attitudes of the United States toward Europe after the two world wars is instructive. The United States emerged from World War I as the leading power, in terms of aggregate economic resources, and it possessed the greatest military potential as a consequence. Yet the United States lapsed into isolationism after the war and did not endeavor, to any great extent, to keep Europe at peace during the 1920s and 1930s.[31] After World War II, however, the United Sates, as by far the dominant economic, political, and military power, engaged all its power resources to encourage a stable postwar order in Western Europe through tools such as Marshall Plan aid and an extended US military commitment to the Continent. It was no accident, therefore, that peacemaking was far more successful after World War II.

3. When belligerent states are led by moderate leaders, they are more likely to achieve peace agreements, as doves are more likely to contemplate peacemaking and their commitments are more credible to adversaries and third parties.[32] For example, Konrad Adenauer's well-known moderation made it possible for French, British, and American leaders to conclude security arrangements with Germany less than a decade after the German war crimes of World War II. Israel found it possible to make peace with Egypt under Sadat, who had early on in his tenure embraced UNSCR 242 encompassing the land-for-peace formula, and with King Hussein, who had long had clandestine ties with Israel. In contrast, Israeli negotiations with Syrian leader Hafez al-Assad, who had always pursued a hard line toward the Jewish state, failed to achieve results.[33] Although moderate leaders do not guarantee progress toward peace, when they are in power, peacemaking initiatives may succeed—if other conditions are favorable—and are worth pursuing. It may be folly, however, to push peace negotiations with leaders who are not apt to compromise. Indeed, that is precisely Dennis Ross's conclusion about the Camp David summit of 2000, whose failure he blames on the mistaken expectation that Palestinian leader Yasser Arafat was willing to make historic compromises for peace.[34] There have certainly been examples of more hawkish leaders making peace, including Israeli leader Menachem Begin in this book, but it is a lower probability strategy to invest scarce resources in promoting peace with hawks in power.

4. Highly autonomous states, whose domestic political institutions, decision-making procedures, and procedural norms limit the societal influence

over foreign policy, should be more likely to achieve successful peace agreements.[35] Since the three case studies of successful peace settlements in this book have confirmed classical realist expectations that the public is more bellicose than its leaders in postconflict situations, a key prerequisite for peacemaking is for the states involved to insulate moderate leaders (if there are any) from hostile domestic attitudes.[36] Autonomous leaders will be better able to escape domestic hostility toward the adversary if they believe a peace agreement is in the national interest (or in their own personal interest). It is precisely the autonomy of the Egyptian and Jordanian states that enabled Sadat and King Hussein to make peace with Israel when public attitudes in both countries were resolutely implacable. Both leaders shut out societal pressures when formulating their preferences and policies, and pursued their objectives despite objections from advisers and government ministers. They could only do so by virtue of their domination of the political processes in their states. In a similar vein, peacemaking works better with well-institutionalized states that possess the economic and coercive capacity to silence domestic opponents of compromise and/or have the legitimacy to pursue unpopular policies.[37]

In contrast, nonautonomous leaders who favor making concessions for peace are frequently stymied by domestic opposition. In this regard, the French experience after World War II is instructive. Three successive French leaders (Antoine Pinay, René Mayer, and Joseph Laniel) who supported the idea of a European Defense Community and believed that it was essential to rehabilitate Western Germany and integrate German forces in Western defense efforts nonetheless withheld the EDC treaty from the legislature for fear that it would be defeated by a National Assembly that was very anti-German.[38] It follows that efforts to promote peacemaking are more likely to bear fruit when the rival states are well institutionalized and able to act autonomously of society. Furthermore, to create the conditions for future peacemaking, even if the conditions are not currently conducive, outside actors should encourage rival states to insulate their executives. It is true that there are drawbacks of autonomy in terms of the corruption and trampling of accountability that can result, but if peacemaking is an important priority, it may be worth the risk.

5. When belligerent states face domestic political or economic crises because of the costs of conflict, they will be more receptive to peace overtures. As discussed in chapter 2, the French government's willingness to consider rehabilitating the West German economy and establishing a West German state was motivated by the devastating economic crisis France faced after World War II. Under these circumstances, the French government recognized that, if it wanted to receive critical American Marshall Plan aid, it had to accept German recovery and some degree of German partnership. Absent the economic dislocation caused by Sadat's *infitah* program and the bread riots it engendered, it is unlikely that Sadat would have embraced

the project of peacemaking with Israel. The damage inflicted on the Jordanian economy by the post–Gulf War sanctions on Iraq similarly reinforced pressure on King Hussein to make peace with Israel. Consequently, belligerents and interested third parties can capitalize on domestic economic and political difficulties in rival countries to jump-start peace negotiations with beleaguered leaders.

When circumstances are not conducive to peacemaking, any resources expended in an effort to promote an agreement will, at best, be wasted. It is possible, though, that the effort will be counterproductive, as granting economic or military incentives to a hard-line leader may strengthen his/her hold on power and prevent either moderate forces from achieving power or severe domestic economic crises that might compel peacemaking. Consequently, the best that third parties can do during inopportune moments, when the conflict is not ripe for resolution, is engage in conflict management.

Certainly, outside actors can endeavor to help create favorable domestic conditions for peacemaking in the rival states. Specifically, they can weaken a belligerent's economy by imposing economic sanctions on it, to be lifted only on the conclusion of a peace treaty, or they can help to engineer the success of moderate leaders by working behind the scenes to fund and promote moderate politicians. If they do so, they should simultaneously offer economic incentives, in terms of foreign aid, debt forgiveness, and/or trade and investment concessions as a reward for a peace agreement, amounting to a large peace dividend that would greatly ease the beleaguered government's difficulties. These strategies, however, entail important risks. Employing sanctions can engender resentment, which could discourage cooperation and may provide little benefit unless the sanctioners have sufficient economic leverage over the rivals to inflict significant harm on the target economy. Moreover, it might paradoxically generate greater governmental stability by spawning a rally around the flag against what may be seen as illegitimate foreign intervention.[39] Interfering in the selection of leaders, if discovered, is even more likely to generate resentment and the belief that cooperation with outside actors is antithetical to the regime's interests. Thus, outside actors should be cautious not to overplay their hands when using the policy tools available to them.

Liberal States Not Necessary but May Help in Post-Treaty Period

In this book I have shown that liberal states are not necessary for peacemaking. Having said that, since stabilizing peace requires the states involved to engage society with liberal mechanisms such as economic exchange and cooperative international institutions, democratic and/or liberal states may have a comparative advantage in promoting peace. After all, society is more likely to be receptive to state-led efforts to sell a peace agreement if it views that state as legitimate and if it perceives that it has a stake in the regime. At the same time, nondemocratic states may resist efforts to engage society in order to promote a peace treaty because of the considerable risks such a strategy could entail. Providing societal actors with the sense that they are politically consequential may lead to greater domestic demands on the regime and, in the worst case, may lead to calls to democratize and overthrow the state, which it may try to avoid at all costs. Finally, the prospects of achieving a "democratic peace" between former rivals is only possible if both states are democracies.

All things being equal, then, the presence of liberal states facilitates the entrenchment of top-down peace settlements. A top-down peace settlement involving at least one nondemocratic regime that is not followed up with processes of political liberalization and democratization might fail to gain societal traction, regardless of whether other economic and institutional strategies are pursued. As Galia Press-Barnathan argues, "without representative democracy, a peace forced from above cannot easily trickle down and win the hearts of the people."[40] This was the dynamic in the case of Jordan, where, despite efforts by the regime to pursue an economic relationship with Israel, the Jordanian public viewed the peace treaty as "the king's peace" and not representative of public opinion, which continued to resist normalization. Thus, while pressures for democratization may interfere with the first steps of peacemaking, it may be useful in the postagreement phase, in tandem with other treaty socialization strategies, to increase the likelihood that the settlement will endure.

It would be incorrect, however, to consider liberal states a prerequisite for a stable peace. Nondemocratic and illiberal states can also employ mechanisms derived from bottom-up approaches to help socialize peace settlements. Among the cases explored in this book, for example, Ecuador and Peru have been able to socialize the settlement despite Ecuador being neither fully liberal nor fully democratic. Italy and Yugoslavia were also able to stabilize their settlement starting in the mid-1970s, well before the relevant Yugoslav successor states democratized. Although they failed to achieve societal buy-in, perhaps because they employed only a few of the bottom-up strategies available to them, other illiberal states examined in this book also attempted to entrench peace by engaging society. For example, China extended bilateral trade ties with Japan after signing a peace treaty. Similarly, Ethiopia and Somalia entrenched themselves within the OAU, a cooperative regional organization, even if it was only a weak one. Thus, there is no reason to assume that illiberal states are incapable of socializing peace or that they will necessarily eschew societal engagement. Nor should the willingness of illiberal states to engage society surprise us. As neoclassical realist research indicates, just because a society is illiberal, it does not necessarily follow that societal attitudes are irrelevant, especially if the regime needs the support of key societal actors to maintain its hold on power.[41]

This raises an interesting question: Can authoritarian states engage society to sell a peace treaty and still remain authoritarian over time?[42] Although the possibility exists that societal engagement could eventually lead the state down the path of liberalization as society becomes empowered, in principle, authoritarian states should be able to create societal buy-in and still remain authoritarian. For example, Stalin rallied Russian society to support the "Great Patriotic War," yet he still kept an iron grip on the Soviet polity. By the same token, there is no reason why, for example, Sadat could not have fostered Egyptian societal support of peace with Israel without liberalizing political control in Egypt. How often societal engagement leads to liberalization and the conditions under which it will do so are interesting empirical questions that would be fruitful topics for future research.

The Need for Regional Frameworks

Finally, the empirical analysis in this book suggests that regional problems may require regional solutions in order to achieve more than a pragmatic realpolitik peace. The Franco-German conflict was effectively resolved with the consent and participation of all the Western European states and embedded within the context of broader Western European institutions. Consequently, there were no outstanding regional issues that prevented the peace settlement's entrenchment within the rival societies. The Ecuadorian-Peruvian settlement was embedded within Mercosur and other regional institutions to help make it a regional peace rather than simply a bilateral one. Conversely, the Egyptian-Israeli peace was simply bilateral, given that the other regional participants were unwilling to enter into serious negotiations. As a result, even though the two countries satisfactorily resolved the bilateral issues between them, the failure to resolve broader regional issues—including the Palestinian issue and the status of other Arab lands that Israel captured in 1967—prevented Egyptian society from embracing the treaty. A similar dynamic operated in the Israeli-Jordanian settlement, as enduring Israeli-Palestinian tensions undermined a broader societal reconciliation between the two countries. This does not mean that peacemaking between regional rivals should never be attempted on a bilateral basis. Even a cold peace that endures is better than continued hostilities. Nonetheless, we should not expect too much from a bilateral settlement that does not involve all the regional participants, especially if significant regional irritants remain.

Making peace is a difficult task, especially in the context of a bitter regional rivalry with intense mutual hatred. Many rivalries resist resolution for decades or longer, sometimes resulting in multiple wars. Nonetheless, rivalries do end, and when they do, as this book shows, they follow a similar path to peace by running through state interests. They follow different paths after making peace, depending on whether they socialize their top-down bargain within their societies. These are important insights that reveal much about the nature of interstate rivalries and their prospects for resolution.

Notes

Top-Down Peacemaking, Bottom-Up Peace

1. According to the program website, "this fund supports conflict mitigation and reconciliation programs and activities which bring together individuals of different ethnic, religious or political backgrounds from areas of civil conflict and war. These programs provide opportunities for adversaries to address issues, reconcile differences, promote greater understanding and mutual trust, and work on common goals with regard to potential, ongoing, or recent conflict." USAID Office of Conflict Management and Mitigation, December 11, 2012, http://www.usaid.gov/who-we-are/organization/bureaus/bureau-democracy-conflict-and-humanitarian-assistance/office (accessed May 15, 2014).

2. In 2010, the State Department gave the program a grant of at least $100,000. "Seeds for Peace 2010 Annual Report," http://www.seedsofpeace.org/annualreport.

3. Euro-Mediterranean Partnership, "Regional Co-operation: An Overview of Programmes and Projects," 18, https://ec.europa.eu/europeaid/sites/devco/files/publication-regional-cooperation-mediterranean-partnership-projects-2010_bn.pdf.

4. "Folding Together: 2004–5 Major Project," http://www.foldingtogether.org/major_project.htm.

5. "Cross Border Peace Dialogues Promote Peace among the East African Pastoral Communities," UN Development Programme in Uganda, September 19, 2013, http://www.ug.undp.org/content/uganda/en/home/presscenter/articles/2013/09/19/cross-border-peace-dialogues-promote-peace-among-the-east-african-pastoral-communities/.

6. In Obama's Nobel Prize speech, he stated, "I believe that peace is unstable where citizens are denied the right to speak freely or worship as they please, choose their own leaders or assemble without fear. Pent-up grievances fester, and the suppression of tribal and religious identity can lead to violence. We also know that the opposite is true. Only when Europe became free did it finally find peace." Nobel Lecture by Barack H. Obama, Oslo, December 10, 2009, http://www.nobelprize.org/nobel_prizes/peace/laureates/2009/obama-lecture_bn.html. Three years earlier, Bush asserted, "We have an opportunity to lay the foundation of peace for generations to come. Democracy can yield the peace we all want." Samantha L. Quigley, "Spread of Democracy Will Yield Peace, Bush Says," American Forces Press Service, February 17, 2006, http://www.defense.gov/news/newsarticle.aspx?id=14822.

7. "Remarks of Anthony Lake, Assistant to the President for National Security Affairs 'From Containment to Enlargement,'" Johns Hopkins University, School of Advanced International Studies, Washington, DC, September 21, 1993, https://www.mtholyoke.edu/acad/intrel/lakedoc.html.

8. Katrin Bennhold, "Sarkozy's Proposal for Mediterranean Bloc Makes Waves," *New York Times*, May 10, 2007, http://www.nytimes.com/2007/05/10/world/europe/10iht-france.4.5656114.html.

9. "Secretary of State Hillary Clinton's Remarks at African Union," Secretary Clinton blog, June 13, 2011, http://secretaryclinton.wordpress.com/2011/06/13/secretary-of-state-hillary-clintons-remarks-at-african-union/.

10. Paul Wehr, *Conflict Regulation* (Boulder, CO: Westview, 1979); and Richard L. Kuenne, "Conflict Management in a Mature Rivalry," *Journal of Conflict Resolution* 33, no. 3 (September 1989): 554–66.

11. For a discussion of the use of conflict management in the Arab-Israeli conflict, see Yaacov Bar Siman-Tov, "The Arab-Israeli Conflict: Learning Conflict Resolution," *Journal of Peace Research* 31, no. 1 (February 1994): 75–92.

12. Benjamin Miller, "Explaining Variations in Regional Peace: Three Strategies for Peacemaking," *Cooperation and Conflict* 35, no. 2 (June 2000): 155–91; and Alexander George, "From Conflict to Peace: Stages along the Road," *United States Institute of Peace Journal* 5, no. 6 (December 1992): 7–9.

13. This is the conceptualization of peace used by Charles Kupchan, *How Enemies Become Friends: The Sources of Stable Peace* (Princeton: Princeton University Press 2010).

14. For these reasons, I do not agree with those who criticize conflict management for merely perpetuating injustice and the underlying causes of war. See, e.g., Deiniol Lloyd Jones, "Mediation, Conflict Resolution and Critical Theory," *Review of International Studies* 26, no. 4 (October 2000): 647–62.

15. My focus on regional rivalries is consistent with a growing literature on regional rivalries and regional security complexes. See Barry Buzan and Ole Waever, *Regions and Powers: The Structure of International Security* (Cambridge: Cambridge University Press, 2003); Douglas Lemke, *Regions of War and Peace* (Cambridge: Cambridge University Press, 2002); Miller, "Regional Peace"; Arie M. Kacowicz, *Zones of Peace in the Third World: South American and West Africa in Comparative Perspective* (Albany: SUNY Press, 1998); David A. Lake and Patrick M. Morgan, "The New Regionalism in Security Affairs," in *Regional Orders: Building Security in a New World*, ed. David A. Lake and Patrick M. Morgan, 3–19 (University Park: Penn State University Press, 1997); and Norrin M. Ripsman and Steven E. Lobell, "Introduction: Conceptualizing the Political Economy of Regional Transitions," in *The Political Economy of Regional Peacemaking*, ed. Steven E. Lobell and Norrin M. Ripsman (Ann Arbor: University of Michigan Press, 2016).

16. Barbara Walter makes the claim that interstate war and civil war are two distinct phenomena, in part because of the difficulty of making credible commitments in the absence of states. Barbara Walter, "The Critical Barrier to Civil War Settlement," *International Organization* 51, no. 3 (June 1997): 335–64. For dissenting views, see R. Harrison Wagner, "The Causes of Peace," in *Stopping the Killing: How Civil Wars End*, ed. Roy Licklider, 235–68 (New York: New York University Press, 1993); and David A. Lake, "International Relations Theory and Internal Conflict: Insights from the Interstices," *International Studies Review* 5, no. 4 (December 2003): 81–89.

17. Buzan and Waever, *Regions and Powers*; Lake and Morgan, "New Regionalism," 11; Amitav Acharya, "The Emerging Regional Architecture of World Politics," *World Politics* 59, no. 4 (July 2007): 629–62; and T. V. Paul, "Regional Transformation in International Relations," in *International Relations Theory and Regional Transformation*, ed. T. V. Paul (Cambridge: Cambridge University Press, 2012), 4–6. On the distinctiveness of regional relations, see Raimo Väyrynen, "Regional Conflict Formations: An Intractable Problem of International Relations," *Journal of Peace Research* 21, no. 4 (November 1984): 340.

18. Jorge E. Dominguez, "Mice That Do Not Roar: Some Aspects of International Politics in the World's Peripheries," *International Organization* 25, no. 1 (Winter 1971): 1175–1208; and

William R. Thompson, "Regional Subsystem: A Conceptual Explication and a Propositional Inventory," *International Studies Quarterly* 17, no. 1 (March 1973): 89–117.

19. I thus depart from Etel Solingen's conception of a region as determined by the grand strategies of the governing coalitions of the states themselves. Etel Solingen, *Regional Orders at Century's Dawn: Global and Domestic Influences on Grand Strategy* (Princeton: Princeton University Press, 1998), 4.

20. This designation follows Leonard Binder's classic treatment of the Middle East, including Israel, as a region or "subordinate system." Leonard Binder, "The Middle East as a Subordinate International System," *World Politics* 10, no. 3 (April 1958): 408–29. For the argument that Israel cannot meaningfully be included in the Middle East region, see William R. Thompson, "The Arab Sub-System and the Feudal Pattern of Interaction: 1965," *Journal of Peace Research* 7, no. 2 (1970): 154.

21. Lake and Morgan, "New Regionalism," 12; and Patrick Morgan, "Regional Security Complexes and Regional Orders," in Lake and Morgan, *Regional Orders*, 28–29.

22. Johan Galtung, "Violence, Peace, and Peace Research," *Journal of Peace Research* 6, no. 3 (1969): 167–91.

23. Kupchan, *How Enemies Become Friends*; and Emanuel Adler and Michael Barnett, *Security Communities* (Cambridge: Cambridge University Press, 1998).

24. Kenneth Boulding, *Stable Peace* (Austin: University of Texas Press, 1978); Miller, "Regional Peace"; Benjamin Miller, *States, Nations, and the Great Powers* (Cambridge: Cambridge University Press, 2007); George, "From Conflict to Peace"; and Arie M. Kacowicz, introduction to *Stable Peace among Nations*, ed. A. Kacowicz, Y. Bar-Siman-Tov, O. Elgstrom, and M. Jerneck, 1–8 (Boulder, CO: Rowman & Littlefield, 2001). See also James P. Klein, Gary Goertz, and Paul F. Diehl, "The Peace Scale: Conceptualizing and Operationalizing Nonrivalry and Peace," *Conflict Management and Peace Science* 25, no. 1 (February 2008): 67–80; and Galia Press-Barnathan, *The Political Economy of Transitions to Peace: A Comparative Perspective* (Pittsburgh, PA: University of Pittsburgh Press, 2009), 9–13.

25. Barbara Geddes, "How the Cases You Choose Affect the Answers You Get: Selection Bias in Comparative Politics," *Political Analysis* 2, no. 1 (1990): 131–50; and Gary King, Robert O. Keohane, and Sidney Verba, *Designing Social Inquiry: Scientific Inference in Qualitative Research* (Princeton: Princeton University Press, 1994), 129–37.

26. See, e.g., Douglas Dion, "Evidence and Inference in the Comparative Case Study," in *Necessary Conditions: Theory, Methodology, and Applications*, ed. Gary Goertz and Harvey Starr, 95–112 (Lanham, MD: Rowman & Littlefield, 2003); Benjamin A. Most and Harvey Starr, "Case Selection, Conceptualizations, and Basic Logic in the Study of War," *American Journal of Political Science* 26, no. 4 (November 1982): 834–56; Jack S. Levy, "Case Studies: Types, Designs, and Logics of Inference," *Conflict Management and Peace Science* 25, no. 1 (February 2008): 8–9; and Alexander L. George and Andrew Bennett, *Case Studies and Theory Development in the Social Sciences* (Cambridge: MIT Press, 2005), 23–24.

27. Nathalie Japkowicz, "Supervised versus Unsupervised Binary-Learning by Feedforward Neural Networks," *Machine Learning* 42, nos. 1–2 (January 2001): 97–122; and Nathalie Japkowicz, Catherine Myers, and Mark Gluck, "A Novelty Detection Approach to Classification," in *Proceedings of the Fourteenth International Joint Conference on Artificial Intelligence*, ed. Chris S. Mellish (San Francisco, CA: Morgan Kaufmann 1995), 518. See also David Martinus Johannes Tax, "One-Class Classification: Concept-Learning in the Absence of Counter-Examples," (PhD diss., Delft University of Technology, 2001), homepage.tudelft.nl/n9d04/thesis.pdf.

28. Paul F. Diehl and Gary Goertz, *War and Peace in Enduring Rivalries* (Ann Arbor: University of Michigan Press, 2000), 145–46. Other lists of enduring rivalries exist. I chose Diehl and Goertz's over William Thompson's because Thompson defines rivalry more broadly in terms of strategic competition rather than the occurrence of war between the rivals. See William R. Thompson, "Identifying Rivals and Rivalries in World Politics," *International Studies Quarterly* 45, no. 4 (December 2001): 557–86. Since my focus is on peacemaking between regional rivals whose rivalries escalated to war, Goertz and Diehl's list was more appropriate for my purpose. D. Scott Bennett uses an approach similar to Diehl and Goertz's, focusing on conflict events

rather than strategic competition. See D. Scott Bennett, "Measuring Rivalry Termination," *Journal of Conflict Resolution* 41, no. 2 (April 1997): 227–54. They differ in their operationalizations of rivalry termination, which is not important for my case selection, since I study only those states that concluded a peace settlement. I chose Diehl and Goertz's list over Bennett's mainly because theirs was more recent.

29. This is one reason why I do not include the Treaty of Versailles, which functioned for a time as a peace treaty between France and Germany, because of France's use of force against Germany during the Ruhr occupation of 1923, only four years after the treaty's signature. As I indicate later, I also exclude this case, because the treaty was not freely negotiated by the two rivals.

30. Public opinion polls and reliable trade data are not available for some early twentieth-century rivalries, as well. Nonetheless, as I did not want to restrict my study merely to periods of bipolarity and unipolarity by focusing only on the post–World War II era, I concluded that it was useful to consider all rivalries within the twentieth century.

31. I am not referring merely to "power disparities," which are quite common and would include dyads such as France-Germany or China-Japan, but "considerable power disparities" or perhaps "step-level power disparities," in which one rival is an order of magnitude more powerful than the others, to make the two states clearly of unequal status. In other words, the difference between a great power and a second-ranking power, between a second-ranking power and a regional power, or between a regional power and a small state, or any other combination of this sort.

32. This follows Geoffrey Blainey's logic that war tends to erupt when both sides are confident that they can win—i.e., when there is a relative balance of power between the rivals. Geoffrey Blainey, *The Causes of War* (London: Free Press, 1973).

33. Excluding rivalries with considerable power disparities eliminates eight cases from consideration: USA-Cuba, USA-Ecuador, USA-Peru, Cyprus-Turkey, USSR-Norway, USSR-Iran, Iraq-Kuwait, and China-S. Korea. Given that none of these eight rivalries terminated in a peace treaty in the twentieth century, eliminating them does not actually affect the final (second) list of cases. That these asymmetric rivalries did not terminate in peace treaties, however, raises an important question. Why is it that none of these asymmetric rivalries terminated in a peace treaty or their functional equivalent? A possible answer is that asymmetric rivalries (such the USA-Cuba or Iraq-Kuwait) may persist for a while without war or peace because the greater power is not truly threatened by the weaker power and may thus largely ignore it until such time as it loses interest in the insignificant rivalry or has the opportunity to resolve the issue through force. For its part, the weaker rival does not have the power to compel the stronger rival to the bargaining table on acceptable terms. Consequently, the rivalry endures until external great powers intervene or until the greater power wins out by force or coercive bargaining. In contrast, symmetric rivalries represent high-level security threats for both parties, which makes both frequent warfare and peacemaking possible outcomes. I thank Bob Art for bringing this issue to my attention.

34. See, e.g., Barry Buzan, *People, States, and Fear: An Agenda for International Studies in the Post-Cold War Era*, 2nd ed. (Hertfordshire, UK: Harvester Wheatsheaf, 1991).

35. Inclusion of imposed treaties might bias my study in favor of top-down settlements.

36. George and Bennett, *Case Studies*, 205–32; and Steven Van Evera, *A Guide to Methodology for Students of Political Science* (Ithaca: Cornell University Press, 1997), 64–67.

37. Marc Trachtenberg, *The Craft of International History: A Guide to Method* (Princeton: Princeton University Press, 2006); and Norrin M. Ripsman and Jean-Marc F. Blanchard, "Contextual Information and the Study of Trade and Conflict: The Utility of an Interdisciplinary Approach," in *Beyond Boundaries? Disciplines, Paradigms, and Theoretical Integration in International Studies*, ed. Rudra Sil and Eileen M. Doherty, 61–62 (Albany: SUNY Press, 2000).

38. Miller, *States, Nations, Great Powers*.

39. It would be incorrect to say that stability is a bottom-up process. As we shall see, the role of states in promoting and socializing peace is critical. States must use methods generated from bottom-up theories to help achieve societal buy-in. I thank Charles Pentland for helping me flesh out this aspect of the argument.

1. Regional Stabilization in International Relations Theory

1. On enduring rivalries, see Paul F. Diehl, "Introduction: An Overview and Some Theoretical Guidelines," in *The Dynamics of Enduring Rivalries*, ed. Paul F. Diehl, 1–25 (Urbana: University of Illinois Press, 1998); Charles S. Gochman and Zeev Maoz, "Militarized Interstate Disputes, 1916–1976," *Journal of Conflict Resolution*, 28, no. 4 (December 1984): 585–616; Paul Diehl and Gary Goertz, *War and Peace in International Rivalry* (Ann Arbor: University of Michigan Press, 2001); John A. Vasquez, "Distinguishing Rivals That Go to War from Those That Do Not," *International Studies Quarterly* 40, no. 4 (December 1996): 531–58; and William R. Thompson, "Identifying Rivals and Rivalries in World Politics," *International Studies Quarterly* 45, no. 4 (December 2001): 557–86.

2. Stephen M. Walt, *Revolution and War* (Ithaca: Cornell University Press, 1996).

3. See, e.g., Dilip Hiro, *The Longest War: The Iran-Iraq Military Conflict* (New York: Routledge, 1991), 27–39.

4. On the importance of regional hegemony or "subparamountcy" in the Argentine-Brazilian rivalry, see Norman A. Bailey, *Latin America in World Politics* (New York: Walker, 1967), 55–60; and Wayne A. Selcher, "Brazilian-Argentine Relations in the 1980s: From Wary Rivalry to Friendly Competition," *Journal of Interamerican Studies and World Affairs* 27, no. 2 (Summer 1985): 26–28. This rivalry was also complicated by cultural and linguistic divisions between the Spanish-speaking world and the Portuguese-speaking world. Jack Child, *Geopolitics and Conflict in South America: Quarrels among Neighbors* (New York: Praeger, 1985), 98–99.

5. Ron Hassner, for example, notes that conflicts over territory that blend national and religious claims are more difficult to resolve. *War on Sacred Grounds* (Ithaca: Cornell University Press, 2009). Cf. Louis Kriesberg, "Intractable Conflicts," *Peace Review* 5, no. 4 (December 1993): 417–21.

6. George H. Gallup, *The Gallup International Public Opinion Polls: France, 1939, 1944–1975*, vol. 1 (New York: Random House, 1976), 141.

7. Mia M. Bloom, "Palestinian Suicide Bombing: Public Support, Market Share, and Outbidding," *Political Science Quarterly* 119, no. 1 (Spring 2004): 61–88.

8. See, e.g., Randall L. Schweller, "Neoclassical Realism and State Mobilization: Expansionist Ideology in the Age of Mass Politics," in *Neoclassical Realism, the State, and Foreign Policy*, ed. Steven E. Lobell, Norrin M. Ripsman, and Jeffrey W. Taliaferro (Cambridge: Cambridge University Press, 2009), 234, 247.

9. I. William Zartman, "Conflict Management: The Long and the Short of It," *SAIS Review* 20, no. 1 (Winter–Spring 2000): 227–35.

10. J. David Singer, "The Level-of-Analysis Problem in International Relations," *World Politics* 14, no. 1 (October 1961): 77–92; David Dessler, "What's at Stake in the Agent-Structure Debate," *International Organization* 43, no. 3 (Summer 1989): 441–73; and Jennifer Sterling Folker, "Realist Environment, Liberal Process, and Domestic-Level Variables," *International Organization* 41, no. 1 (March 1997): 1–26.

11. Michael W. Doyle, "Kant, Liberal Legacies, and Foreign Affairs: Part 1," *Philosophy and Public Affairs* 12, no. 3 (1983): 205–35; Michael W. Doyle, "Kant, Liberal Legacies, and Foreign Affairs: Part 2," *Philosophy and Public Affairs* 12, no. 4 (1983): 323–53; Michael W. Doyle, "Liberalism and World Politics," *American Political Science Review* 80, no. 4 (1986): 1151–61; Bruce M. Russett, *Grasping the Democratic Peace* (Princeton: Princeton University Press, 1993); and John M. Owen, "How Liberalism Produces Democratic Peace," *International Security* 19, no. 2 (Fall 1994): 87–125. Critics of democratic peace theory include Christopher Layne, "Kant or Cant: The Myth of the Democratic Peace," *International Security* 19, no. 2 (Fall 1994): 5–49; Raymond Cohen, "Pacific Unions: A Reappraisal of the Theory That 'Democracies Do Not Go to War with Each Other,'" *Review of International Studies* 20, no. 3 (July 1994): 207–23; Joanne Gowa, "Democratic States and International Disputes," *International Organization* 49, no. 3 (Summer 1995): 511–22; and Errol Henderson, *Democracy and War: The End of an Illusion?* (Boulder, CO: Lynne Reinner, 2002).

12. See, e.g., Russett, *Grasping the Democratic Peace*, 38–40.

13. Zeev Maoz and Bruce Russett, "Normative and Structural Causes of Democratic Peace, 1946–1986," *American Political Science Review* 87, no. 3 (September 1993): 624–38; William J.

Dixon, "Democracy and the Peaceful Settlement of International Conflict," *American Political Science Review* 88, no. 1 (March 1994): 14–32; and Owen, "Liberalism Produces Democratic Peace," 93–104.

14. D. Scott Bennett, "Democracy, Regime Change, and Rivalry Termination," *International Interactions* 22, no. 4 (December 1997): 369–97. This is consistent with Gary Goertz and Paul Diehl's observation that civil wars that lead to regime change in one or more states embroiled in an enduring rivalry can lead to rivalry termination by replacing the old regime with one more compatible with the rival state. Gary Goertz and Paul F. Diehl, "The Initiation and Termination of Enduring Rivalries: The Impact of Political Shocks," *American Journal of Political Science* 39, no. 1 (February 1995): 30–52, esp. 38.

15. Anthony Lake, Assistant to the President for National Security Affairs, "From Containment to Enlargement," Johns Hopkins University, School of Advanced International Studies, Washington, DC., September 21, 1993, http://www.mtholyoke.edu/acad/intrel/lakedoc.html (accessed August 28, 2011), now available at http://fas.org/news/usa/1993/usa-930921.htm.

16. "Polity IV Project: Political Regime Characteristics and Transitions, 1800–2012," http://www.systemicpeace.org/inscr/inscr.htm (accessed December 8, 2013).

17. See Michael W. Doyle, *Ways of War and Peace: Realism, Liberalism, and Socialism.* (New York: Norton, 1997), 230–50; Robert O. Keohane, "International Liberalism Revisited," in *The Economic Limits to Modern Politics*, ed. John Dunn (Cambridge: Cambridge University Press, 1990), 186–87; Erik Gartzke, "The Capitalist Peace," *American Journal of Political Science* 51, no. 1 (January 2007): 166–91; and John Mueller, "Capitalism, Peace, and the Historical Movement of Ideas," *International Interactions* 36, no. 2 (June 2010): 169–84. Critics of commercial liberalism include Kenneth N. Waltz, *Theory of International Politics* (Reading, MA: Addison-Wesley, 1979), 138; Barry Buzan, "Economic Structure and International Security: The Limits of the Liberal Case," *International Organization* 38, no. 4 (Autumn 1984): 597–624; and Norrin M. Ripsman and Jean-Marc F. Blanchard, "Commercial Liberalism under Fire: Evidence from 1914 and 1936," *Security Studies* 6, no. 2 (Winter 1996–97): 4–50.

18. See Brian M. Pollins, "Conflict, Cooperation, and Commerce: The Effect of International Political Interactions on Bilateral Trade Flows." *American Journal of Political Science.* 33, no. 3 (August 1989): 737–61. In actuality, the relationship between conflict and economic exchange is somewhat more complex. As Katherine Barbieri and Jack S. Levy indicate, trade frequently continues, albeit at a much restricted rate, between belligerents in wartime. Katherine Barbieri and Jack S. Levy, "Sleeping with the Enemy: The Impact of War on Trade," *Journal of Peace Research* 36, no. 4 (July 1999): 1–17. Moreover, third parties may have reasons to increase their economic relationships with one or both of the belligerents, while corporate investors may have already priced in the costs of conflict and, therefore, are not chased away by it. Norrin M. Ripsman and Christopher Way, "International Political Tensions and Foreign Investment" (paper presented at the annual meeting of the International Studies Association, Montreal, Canada, March 16–19, 2011). Nonetheless, it is reasonable to expect that, on average, the use of force should have a dampening effect on bilateral and probably also international economic exchange.

19. This logic underlies those who argued that the City of London sought to restrain the British government from war with Germany because of the financial losses they expected as a result of war. See, e.g., Paul A. Papayoanou, "Interdependence, Institutions, and the Balance of Power: Britain, Germany, and World War I," *International Security* 20, no. 4 (Spring 1996): 42–76.

20. David H. Bearce, "Grasping the Commercial Institutional Peace," *International Studies Quarterly* 47, no. 3 (September 2003): 347–70; Luigi Manzetti, "The Political Economy of Mercosur," *Journal of Inter-American Studies and World Affairs* 35, no. 4 (Winter 1993–94): 109; and Kusuma Snitwongse, "Thirty Years of ASEAN: Achievements through Political Cooperation," *Pacific Review* 11, no. 2 (1998): 183–94.

21. Dale Copeland, for example, argues that rather than interdependence itself causing peace, it is the expectations of economic gains that leads to peaceful relations between states. Dale C. Copeland, *Economic Interdependence and War* (Princeton: Princeton University Press, 2014).

22. See, e.g., Galia Press-Barnathan, "The Neglected Dimension of Commercial Liberalism: Economic Cooperation and Transition to Peace," *Journal of Peace Research* 43, no. 3

(May 2006): 261–78; and Galia Press-Barnathan, *The Political Economy of Transitions to Peace: A Comparative Perspective* (Pittsburgh, PA: University of Pittsburgh Press, 2009). Etel Solingen makes a related argument that links peaceful regional orders to the dominance of an internationalist coalition that expects to gain through cooperation. Etel Solingen, *Regional Orders at Century's Dawn: Global and Domestic Influences on Grand Strategy* (Princeton: Princeton University Press, 1998).

23. These thresholds are practical starting points for assessing the bilateral economic relationship, but they are, of course, not definitive. As Jean-Marc F. Blanchard and I have argued elsewhere, to gauge a bilateral economic relationship effectively, one would need to assess the nature of goods being traded, whether they are strategic goods or not, and whether substitutes and alternative suppliers are available, among other issues. "Measuring Economic Interdependence: A Geopolitical Approach," *Geopolitics and International Boundaries* 1, no. 3 (Winter 1996): 225–46; and Jean-Marc F. Blanchard and Norrin M. Ripsman, "Rethinking Sensitivity Interdependence: Assessing Trade, Financial, and Monetary Linkages between States," *International Interactions* 27, no. 2 (June 2001): 95–127. Nonetheless, as my purpose here is not to engage in a systematic test of the commercial liberal argument but to compare various top-down and bottom-up approaches, reliance on the more conventional "trade as a percentage of GDP" measure is more practical and warranted.

24. See Alexander Wendt, *Social Theory of International Politics* (Cambridge: Cambridge University Press, 1999), esp., 297–308; and Audie Klotz, *Norms in International Relations: The Struggle against Apartheid* (Ithaca: Cornell University Press, 1995), 25–27. For a critical take on institutionalism as a path to peace, see John J. Mearsheimer, "The False Promise of International Institutions," *International Security* 19, no. 3 (Winter 1994–95): 5–49.

25. Wendt, *Social Theory of International Politics*, chap. 7.

26. Technically, this is might be considered a top-down mechanism rather than a bottom-up one, as institutions and elites act on societal interests from without the state. See, e.g., Vincent Pouliot, *International Security in Practice: The Politics of NATO-Russia Diplomacy* (New York: Cambridge University Press, 2010). I thank Michael Lipson and Vincent Pouliot for bringing this to my attention. Nonetheless, as the dominant source of political pressure for policy change in this causal path is societal attitudes, which then compel state restraint, rather than state-level decisions despite societal attitudes, it too is truly a bottom-up mechanism.

27. Cameron G. Thies, "Explaining Zones of Negative Peace in Interstate Relations: The Construction of a West African Lockean Culture of Anarchy," *European Journal of International Relations* 16, no. 3 (September 2010): 391–415.

28. Emanuel Adler and Michael Barnett, "Security Communities in Theoretical Perspective," in *Security Communities*, ed. Emanuel Adler and Michael Barnett, 3–28 (Cambridge: Cambridge University Press, 1998).

29. Bruce Russett and John R. Oneal, *Triangulating Peace: Democracy, Interdependence, and International Organizations* (New York: Norton, 2001).

30. Amitav Acharaya, *Constructing a Security Community in Southeast Asia: ASEAN and the Problem of Regional Order* (London: Routledge, 2001). See also Solingen, *Regional Orders*, 3.

31. Edward D. Mansfield and Jon C. Pevehouse, "Trade Blocs, Trade Flows, and International Conflict, *International Organization* 54, no. 4 (Autumn 2000): 775–808; and Edward D. Mansfield, Jon C. Pevehouse, and David H. Bearce, "Preferential Trading Arrangements and Military Disputes," in *Power and the Purse: Economic Statecraft, Interdependence, and International Conflict*, ed. Jean-Marc F. Blanchard, Edward D. Mansfield, and Norrin M. Ripsman, 93–118 (London: Frank Cass, 2000).

32. Benjamin Miller, *States, Nations, and the Great Powers* (Cambridge: Cambridge University Press, 2007).

33. In this regard, Miller's argument is consistent with Chaim Kaufmann's claim that the only viable solution to ethnic conflicts is to separate the warring groups geographically. Chaim Kaufmann, "Possible and Impossible Solutions to Ethnic Civil Wars," *International Security* 20, no. 4 (Spring 1996): 136–75.

34. See, e.g., Lloyd E. Ambrosius, *Woodrow Wilson and His Legacy in American Foreign Relations* (New York: Palgrave MacMillan, 2002), chap. 9.

35. For discussions of state autonomy, see Eric A. Nordlinger, *On the Autonomy of the Democratic State* (Cambridge: Harvard University Press, 1981); and Atul Kohli, "Democracy and Development," in *Development Strategies Reconsidered*, ed. John P. Lewis and Valeriana Kallab, 153–82 (New Brunswick, NJ: Transaction Books, 1986). On the impact of state autonomy on foreign security policy, see Norrin M. Ripsman, *Peacemaking by Democracies: The Effect of State Autonomy on the Post-World-War Settlements* (University Park: Penn State University Press, 2002).

36. Jean-Marc F. Blanchard and Norrin M. Ripsman, "A Political Theory of Economic Statecraft," *Foreign Policy Analysis* 4, no. 4 (October 2008): 371–98.

37. The Almond-Lippmann consensus, for example, is that American public opinion is rather ignorant on matters of foreign policy and has no influence on US foreign policy choices. Ole R. Holsti, "Public Opinion and Foreign Policy: Challenges to the Almond-Lippmann Consensus," *International Studies Quarterly* 36, no. 4 (1992): 439–66; Ole R. Holsti, *Public Opinion and American Foreign Policy* (Ann Arbor: University of Michigan Press, 1996).

38. Walter Lippmann, *Essays in the Public Philosophy* (Boston: Little, Brown and Co., 1955), 18–21; and Reinhold Niebuhr, *The Structure of Nations and Empires* (New York: Scribner, 1959), 197.

39. On balance-of-power theory, see Hans J. Morgenthau, *Politics among Nations*, 6th ed. (New York: McGraw-Hill, 1985); Waltz, *Theory of International Politics*; Edward Vose Gulick, *Europe's Classical Balance of Power* (New York: Norton, 1967); and T. V. Paul, James Wirtz, and Michel Fortmann, eds., *The Balance of Power: Theory and Practice in the Twenty-first Century* (Stanford: Stanford University Press, 2004). For the logic of balance-of-threat theory, see Stephen M. Walt, *The Origins of Alliances* (Ithaca: Cornell University Press, 1987), 21–28.

40. D. Scott Bennett, "Security, Bargaining, and the End of Interstate Rivalry," *International Organization* 40, no. 2 (June 1996): 157–83, esp. 163–64, 178.

41. See Goertz and Diehl, "Initiation and Termination," 35–37; and Diehl and Goertz, *War and Peace*, 221–39.

42. Paul Kennedy, *Strategy and Diplomacy, 1870–1945* (London: George Allen and Unwin, 1983), 18; and Paul W. Schroeder, "Munich and the British Tradition," *Historical Journal* 19, no. 1 (March 1976): 224.

43. Joseph Kostiner and Chelsi Mueller, "Egyptian and Saudi Intervention in the Israeli-Palestinian Conflict (2006–09): Local Powers' Mediation Compared," in *International Intervention in Local Conflicts: Crisis Management and Conflict Resolution since the Cold War*, ed. Uzi Rabi (London: I. B. Tauris, 2010), 202, 210; and Frederic Wehrey, Theodore W. Karasik, Alireza Nader, Jeremy Ghez, Lydia Hansell, and Robert A. Guffey, *Saudi-Iranian Relations since the Fall of Saddam: Rivalry, Cooperation, and Implications for US Policy* (Santa Monica, CA: RAND Corporation, 2009), 86.

44. The best statement of this argument is Robert Gilpin, *War and Change in World Politics* (Cambridge: Cambridge University, 1981). See also Stephen D. Krasner, "State Power and the Structure of International Trade," *World Politics* 28 (April 1976): 317–47; A. F. K. Organski and Jacek Kugler, *The War Ledger* (Chicago: University of Chicago Press, 1980); William C. Wohlforth, "The Stability of a Unipolar World," *International Security* 24, no. 1 (Summer 1999): 5–41; and Stephen G. Brooks and William C. Wohlforth, *World Out of Balance: International Relations and the Challenge of American Primacy* (Princeton: Princeton University Press, 2008). Critics of the logic of hegemonic stability theory include Duncan Snidal, "The Limits of Hegemonic Stability Theory," *International Organization* 39, no. 4 (Autumn 1985): 579–614; and Kenneth N. Waltz, "Structural Realism after the Cold War," *International Security* 25, no. 1 (Summer 2000): 5–41.

45. For the comparison of international cooperation to the prisoner's dilemma game, in which each side fears that their cooperation will be reciprocated with defection (the "sucker's payoff" or most disastrous outcome), see Kenneth A. Oye, "Explaining Co-operation under Anarchy," in *Cooperation under Anarchy*, ed. Kenneth A. Oye, 1–24 (Princeton: Princeton University Press, 1986).

46. Glen D. Camp, "Greek-Turkish Conflict over Cyprus," *Political Science Quarterly* 95, no. 1 (Spring 1980): 50; and T. W. Adams, "The American Concern in Cyprus," *Annals of the American Academy of Political and Social Science* 401, no. 1 (May 1972): 101.

47. See, e.g., Robert O. Keohane, *After Hegemony* (Princeton: Princeton University Press, 1984); and Benjamin Miller, *When Opponents Cooperate: Great Power Conflict and Collaboration in World Politics* (Ann Arbor: University of Michigan Press, 1995), 89–124.

48. Nathalie Tocci, "The EU and the Middle East Quartet: A Case of (In)effective Multilateralism," in *Multilateralism in the Twenty-first Century: Europe's Quest for Effectiveness*, ed. Caroline Bouchard, John Peterson, and Nathalie Tocci (New York: Routledge, 2014), 278.

49. Stefan Brem, "Conclusion: Is There a Future for Non-Hegemonic Cooperation? Explaining Success and Failure of Alternative Regime Creation," in *Cooperating without America: Theories and Case Studies of Non-Hegemonic Cooperation*, ed. Stefan Brem and Kendall Stiles (London: Routledge, 2009), 175.

50. Charles Kupchan, *How Enemies Become Friends: The Sources of Stable Peace* (Princeton: Princeton University Press 2010).

51. See, e.g., Andrew Kydd, "Sheep in Sheep's Clothing: Why Security Seekers Do Not Fight Each Other," *Security Studies* 7, no. 1 (Autumn 1997): 114–55; Evan Montgomery, "Breaking Out of the Security Dilemma: Realism, Reassurance, and the Problem of Uncertainty," *International Security* 31, no. 2 (Fall 2006): 151–85; and Shiping Tang, *A Theory of Security Strategy for Our Time: Defensive Realism* (London: Palgrave Macmillan, 2010). Theories of reassurance signaling are realist in that they are consistent with defensive structural realism. Defensive realists assume that the international system provides few incentives for expansionism; therefore, states would be better served by eschewing conquest in favor of moderate grand strategies. See Jeffrey W. Taliaferro, "Security-Seeking under Anarchy: Defensive Realism Reconsidered," *International Security* 25, no. 3, (Winter 2000–2001): 152–86. Under these conditions, the key to mitigating the security dilemma that states face is to signal one's benign intentions to other states in order to alleviate their insecurity about the signaler's motives. Given that Kupchan, Kydd, Tang, Montgomery, and others expect that long-term trust, cooperation, and even a degree of harmony of interests can occur between states as a result of effective signaling, these theories end up leaving the realm of realism, since realists do not believe that states are capable of trust in an anarchic international environment. See Norrin M. Ripsman, "Two Stages of Transition from a Region of War to a Region of Peace: Realist Transition and Liberal Endurance," *International Studies Quarterly* 49, no. 4 (December 2005): 671–74.

52. Kupchan, *How Enemies Become Friends*, 39.

53. Montgomery, "Security Dilemma," 178–83.

54. Kupchan, *How Enemies Become Friends*, 41–54.

55. Kupchan, *How Enemies Become Friends*, 37. This reasoning is consistent with the "reduce enemies" logic of appeasement. Norrin M. Ripsman and Jack S. Levy, "Wishful Thinking or Buying Time? The Logic of British Appeasement in the 1930s," *International Security* 33, no. 2 (Fall 2008): 155–56.

56. See Gideon Rose, "Neoclassical Realism and Theories of Foreign Policy," *World Politics*. 51, no. 1 (October 1998): 144–72; and Norrin M. Ripsman, Jeffrey W. Taliaferro, and Steven E. Lobell, *Neoclassical Realist Theory of International Politics* (Oxford, UK: Oxford University Press, 2016).

57. Norrin M. Ripsman, "Neoclassical Realism and Domestic Interest Groups," in Lobell, Ripsman, and Taliaferro, *Neoclassical Realism*, 170–93.

58. Bruce Bueno de Mesquita and Randolph M. Siverson, "War and the Survival of Political Leaders: A Comparative Study of Regime Types and Political Accountability," *American Political Science Review* 89, no. 4 (December 1995): 841–55; Bruce Bueno de Mesquita, Alastair Smith, Randolph M. Siverson, and James D. Morrow, *The Logic of Political Survival* (Cambridge: MIT Press, 2003); and Giacomo Chiozza and H. E. Goemans, "Peace through Insecurity: Tenure and International Conflict," *Journal of Conflict Resolution* 47, no. 4 (August 2003): 443–67.

59. See Jack S. Levy, "The Diversionary Theory of War," in *The Handbook of War Studies*, ed. Manus I. Midlarsky, 259–88 (Boston: Unwin Hyman, 1989); Alastair Smith, "Diversionary Foreign Policy in Democratic Systems," *International Studies Quarterly* 40, no. 1 (1996): 133–53; and Sara McLaughlin Mitchell and Brandon C. Prins, "Rivalry and Diversionary Uses of Force," *Journal of Conflict Resolution* 48, no. 6 (December 2004): 937–61.

60. Richard Ned Lebow, "The Search for Accommodation: Gorbachev in Comparative Perspective," in *Understanding the End of the Cold War*, ed. Richard Ned Lebow and Thomas Risse, 167–86 (Baltimore: Johns Hopkins University Press, 1995).

61. Steven R. David, "Explaining Third World Alignment," *World Politics* 43, no. 2 (January 1991): 233–56. Of course, if the rival is not similarly willing to cooperate, or if the bargain is too lopsided in favor of the traditional rival, the leader may suffer removal from office anyway. See Michael Colaresi, "When Doves Cry: International Rivalry, Unreciprocated Cooperation, and Leadership Turnover," *American Journal of Political Science* 48, no. 3 (July 2004): 555–70.

62. On peace dividends, see Alex Mintz and Chi Huang, "Defense Expenditures, Economic Growth, and the 'Peace Dividend,'" *American Political Science Review* 84, no. 4 (December 1990): 1283–93.

63. This logic is explored in Steven E. Lobell and Norrin M. Ripsman, eds., *The Political Economy of Regional Peacemaking* (Ann Arbor: University of Michigan Press, 2016).

64. In this regard, Stephen Walt notes: "But a state that has just undergone a revolution is rarely ready for war, and it would be foolhardy indeed for a victorious revolutionary movement to risk its newly won position in a test of strength with a powerful neighbor. Revolutionary leaders may use tensions with other states to cement their hold on power, but we would expect them to focus primarily on internal problems and to avoid a direct clash of arms." Walt, *Revolution and War*, 10. Although she does not discuss the implications for rivalry termination, Theda Skocpol also notes that institutionalizing the new regime is by far the highest priority for a new revolutionary regime. Theda Skocpol, *States and Social Revolutions: A Comparative Analysis of France, Russia, and China* (Cambridge: Cambridge University Press, 1979), 286.

65. Ripsman, *Peacemaking by Democracies*. Since I conceptualize and operationalize autonomy structurally and a priori, rather than based on outcomes, an autonomous leader, with the structural power to act independently, could still bow to domestic pressures if he/she judged that the costs of using his/her autonomy (in terms of electoral reprisal, for example) in this issue area would be too high. Thus, autonomy can facilitate top-down peacemaking but does not preclude bottom-up peacemaking.

66. For this reason, as I elaborate elsewhere, liberal and constructivist theorists (although they differ) have deeper conceptions of trust in international relations than do realist theorists, who believe that trust is, at best, fleeting, given that the anarchic nature of the international system does not allow much room for states to trust one another. Ripsman, "Two Stages of Transition," 672–74. See also Aaron Hoffman, *Building Trust: Overcoming Suspicion in International Conflict* (Albany: SUNY Press, 2005), 1–6.

67. Andrew Hurrell, "Explaining the Resurgence of Regionalism in World Politics," *Review of International Studies* 21, no. 4 (October 1995): 358. See also Ole Waever, "Insecurity, Security, and Asecurity in the West European Non-War Community," in Adler and Barnett, *Security Communities*, 74–75.

68. Kupchan, *How Enemies Become Friends*. A third possibility exists that societal mechanisms precede statist mechanisms. That path, however, would make little sense, as it would be unnecessary for great power pressures or threat calculations to reinforce the peace settlement if underlying societal attitudes and identities have embraced it. Moreover, since statist calculations are of shorter term in duration than attitudinal changes, they are ill equipped to institutionalize agreements.

69. Keohane, *After Hegemony*.

2. Franco-German Peacemaking after World War II

1. For an overview, see Kalevi J. Holsti, *Peace and War: Armed Conflicts and International Order, 1648–1989* (Cambridge: Cambridge University Press, 1991).

2. On the Franco-German rivalry, see Paul R. Hensel, "The Evolution of the Franco-German Rivalry," in *Great Power Rivalries*, ed. William R. Thompson, 98–104 (Columbia: University of South Carolina Press, 1999).

3. See, e.g., René Albrecht-Carrié, *A Diplomatic History of Europe since the Congress of Vienna* (New York: Harper, 1973), 164–67; Allan Mitchell, *Bismarck and the French Nation, 1848–1890* (New York: Pegasus, 1971), 107–13; and Raymond Poidevin and Jacques Bariéty, *Les relations franco-allemandes, 1815–1975* (Paris: Armand Colin, 1977), 91–141.

4. Paul W. Schroeder, "The Lost Intermediaries: The Impact of 1870 on the European System," *International History Review* 6, no. 1 (February 1984): 1–27, esp. 14–15.

5. On German strategic calculations prior to World War I, see Terence Zuber, *Inventing the Schlieffen Plan: German War Planning, 1871–1914* (Oxford: Oxford University Press, 2001); Stephen Van Evera, "The Cult of the Offensive and the Origins of the First World War," *International Security* 9, no. 1 (Summer 1984): 58–107; and Jack Snyder, *The Ideology of the Offensive: Military Decision Making and the Disasters of 1914* (Ithaca: Cornell University Press, 1984), 107–56.

6. The label "hereditary enemies" is drawn from Julius W. Friend, *The Linchpin: French-German Relations, 1950–1990* (New York: Praeger, 1991), 1.

7. For the texts of these agreements, see multiple entries, United States Department of State, *Foreign Relations of the United States* (*FRUS*), 1952–1954, vol. 5 (Washington, DC: US Government Printing Office, 1983), 1338–66.

8. G. John Ikenberry, *After Victory: Institutions, Strategic Restraint, and the Rebuilding of Order after Major Wars* (Princeton: Princeton, 2001), 164–65, 213; Bruce Russett and John R. Oneal, *Triangulating Peace: Democracy, Interdependence, and International Organizations* (New York: Norton, 2001), 158; and John MacMillan, *On Liberal Peace: Democracy, War and International Order* (New York: Tauris, 1998), esp. 168–71.

9. In July 1947, for example, foreign minister Georges Bidault told the US ambassador to Paris that his government agreed that "the reconstruction of Germany is an element of European reconstruction" provided it did not take precedence over French recovery. Caffery to Marshall, July 11, 1947, *FRUS*, 1947, vol. 2, 983–86. His successor in 1948, Robert Schuman, was even more heavily committed to German recovery as a means of avoiding a resurgence of German nationalism. Raymond Poidevin, *Robert Schuman* (Paris: Imprimerie nationale, 1986), 212.

10. John H. Backer, *Winds of History: The German Years of Lucius DuBignon Clay* (New York: Van Nostrand Reinhold, 1983), 14; and Thomas Alan Schwartz, *America's Germany: John J. McCloy and the Federal Republic of Germany* (Cambridge: Harvard University Press, 1991), 30.

11. Cabinet Minutes (CM) (48) 2, January 8, 1948, Great Britain, Public Records Office.

12. McCloy to Truman, Sept. 10, 1950, Harry S Truman Presidential Library (HSTL), President's Secretary's Files (PSF), subject file: Foreign Affairs, Germany.

13. Acheson to Truman, June 16, 1950, HSTL, PSF, subject file: NSC meetings, meeting 60, July 6, 1950.

14. See, e.g., Note from the Commander-in-Chief of French Forces in Germany to the Ministère des Affaires Etrangères (MAE), May 22, 1952, France, MAE, Europe 1944–1960, Allemagne, dossier 1068, 59.

15. In February 1952, when the National Assembly authorized the government to negotiate the European Defense Community treaty, it attached fourteen preconditions for German rearmament. These included an Anglo-American guarantee in case Germany violated the treaty; active British participation in the EDC; a requirement that German forces must never outnumber the French army in Europe; and an agreement that Germany must never be allowed a national army or general staff and could not join NATO. See French Representative Hervé Alphand's Report to the Government, May 10, 1952, MAE, Europe 1944–1960, Allemagne, 1067.

16. Vincent Auriol, *Journal du septennat, 1947–1954*, vol. 7, *1953–1954* (Paris: Librarie Armand Colin, 1971), 126. See also, 46–48, 423.

17. George H. Gallup, *The Gallup International Public Opinion Polls: France, 1939, 1944–1975*, vol. 1 (New York: Random House, 1976), 141.

18. A public opinion poll indicated that 63% of decided French respondents opposed German participation compared to 37% who favored it. Herbert Tint, *French Foreign Policy since the Second World War* (London: Weidenfeld and Nicolson, 1972), 53. See also Marc Trachtenberg, *A Constructed Peace: The Making of the European Settlement, 1945–1963* (Princeton: Princeton University Press, 1999), 109.

19. Jean Stoetzel, "The Evolution of French Opinion," in *France Defeats EDC*, ed. Daniel Lerner and Raymond Aron (New York: Praeger, 1957), 84.

20. See, e.g., Norrin M. Ripsman, "Peacemaking and Democratic Peace Theory: Public Opinion as an Obstacle to Peace in Post-Conflict Situations," *Democracy and Security* 3, no. 1 (January 2007): 98–99.

21. That many French people made the parallel between the Weimar regime and the Adenauer regime is emphasized by Jean-Baptiste Duroselle, "German-Franco Relations since 1945," *Review of Politics* 14, no. 4 (October 1952): 509.

22. Norrin M. Ripsman, *Peacemaking by Democracies: The Effect of State Autonomy on the Post-World-War Settlements* (University Park: Penn State University Press, 2002), 208–12; and David Clay Large, *Germans to the Front: West German Rearmament in the Adenauer Era* (Chapel Hill: University of North Carolina Press, 1996), 200–23.

23. This is not intended as evidence against the claims of democratic peace theory. After all, its proponents maintain that only long-established stable democracies are subject to its logic. Therefore, they would not necessarily expect the recent German transition to democracy to cause an immediate pacification of the region. Bruce M. Russett, *Grasping the Democratic Peace* (Princeton: Princeton University Press, 1993), 16; and Michael Doyle, "Kant, Liberal Legacies, and Foreign Affairs: Part 1," in *Philosophy and Public Affairs* 12, no. 3 (1983): 205–35. This is only a further reason, however, to reject the hypothesis that common democratic regimes caused Franco-German peace.

24. See Ikenberry, *After Victory*, 185–86.

25. Karl Deutsch and Alexander Eckstein, "National Industrialization and the Declining Share of the International Economic Sector, 1890–1959," *World Politics* 13, no. 3 (January 1961): 267–99; and Richard N. Rosecrance, Alan Alexandroff, Wallace Koehler, John Kroll, Shlomit Laqueur, and John Stocker, "Whither Interdependence?" *International Organization* 31, no. 3 (Summer 1977): 425–71.

26. William Diebold, Jr., *The Schuman Plan: A Study in Economic Cooperation, 1950–1959* (New York: Praeger, 1959), 78–112.

27. Frank Roy Willis, *France, Germany, and the New Europe, 1945–1967* (Oxford: Oxford University Press, 1968), 236.

28. French exports to the FRG in 1954 totaled over $350 million, making up only 0.6% of French GDP. Within ten years, in 1964, that figure nearly quintupled to almost $1.6 billion, or a more significant 1.4% of GDP. Similarly, German exports to France in 1954 were worth $345 million, or just under 0.6% of German GDP. Within ten years of the peace settlement that quintupled to almost $1.9 billion, or 1.4% of GDP. Trade and trade as a percentage of GDP figures are calculated with figures from Kristian S. Gleditsch, "Expanded Trade and GDP Data," *Journal of Conflict Resolution* 46, no. 5 (October 2002), 712–24; and the associated data set at http://privatewww.essex.ac.uk/~ksg/exptradegdp.html (accessed May 22, 2014). Trade and GDP figures are in current US dollars. Where there is a discrepancy between the trade figures reported by the two partners, I have selected figures only for years in which the disagreement does not exceed 10% of the reported total and have then averaged the figures reported for each country. To determine exports as a percentage of GDP, current GDP is calculated by multiplying current GDP per capita by the country's population. This method and this data set are used throughout this chapter and this book, except for figures later than 2000 not covered by the Gleditsch data, for which IMF figures are used.

29. Galia Press-Barnathan, *The Political Economy of Transitions to Peace: A Comparative Perspective* (Pittsburgh: University of Pittsburgh Press, 2009), 140–42; and Alistair Cole, *Franco-German Relations* (Harlow, UK: Pearson Education, 2001), 22–24.

30. John Gillingham, *Coal, Steel, and the Rebirth of Europe, 1945–1955: The Germans and the French from Ruhr Conflict to Economic Community* (New York: Cambridge University Press, 1991), 217–27.

31. Poidevin, *Robert Schuman*, 247–48.

32. Backer, *Winds of History*, 12–14, 52–58; Schwartz, *America's Germany*, 30–31; and Jean Edward Smith, *The Papers of General Lucius D. Clay: Germany 1945–1949*, vol. 1, (Bloomington: Indiana University, 1974), 43–49.

33. Marc Hillel, *L'Occupation française en Allemagne* (Paris: Balland, 1983); and Frank Roy Willis, *The French in Germany* (Stanford: Stanford University Press, 1962). The French also refrained from joining the bizone because they did not wish to preclude a Four Power agreement including the Soviet Union.

34. John Gimbel, *The Origins of the Marshall Plan* (Stanford: Stanford University, 1976).

35. For details on the French reticence to rehabilitate Germany after the war and its accession to the London Accords of June 1948, see Ripsman, *Peacemaking by Democracies*, 136–50.

36. Ripsman, *Peacemaking by Democracies*, 176–87.

37. Jean Monnet, *Memoirs*, trans. Richard Mayne (London: Collins, 1978), 284–94; Rene Lucien Daniel Massigli, *Une comédie des erreurs, 1943–1956: souvenirs et reflexions sur une étape de la construction européenne* (Paris: Plon, 1978), 185–202; Irwin M. Wall, *The United States and the Making of Post-War France, 1945–54* (Cambridge: Cambridge University, 1991), 189–94; Schwartz, *America's Germany*, 101–5; Friend, *Linchpin*, 17–20; and Roger Bullen and M. E. Pelly, eds., *Documents on British Policy Overseas* [DBPO], ser. 2, vol. 1 (London: Her Majesty's Stationery Office), xiii.

38. As Schuman's Mouvement républicain populaire (MRP) colleague warned, "Britain . . . is separated from Europe, and the Americans are pressing us to take command of it. If we refuse, the United States will bestow this leadership role on Germany within six months." Quoted in William I. Hitchcock, *France Restored: Cold War Diplomacy and the Quest for Leadership in Europe, 1944–1954* (Chapel Hill: University of North Carolina Press, 1998), 114.

39. Monnet, *Memoirs*, 289–93; and Gillingham, *Coal, Steel*, 229–30.

40. Diebold, *Schuman Plan*, 28–42.

41. Gillingham, *Coal, Steel*, 235–37.

42. Ibid., 232–34.

43. Andrew Moravcsik, *The Choice for Europe: Social Purpose ad State Power from Messina to Maastricht* (Ithaca: Cornell University Press, 1998), 86–158.

44. Cf. Gillingham, *Coal, Steel*, 152–54; Poidevin, *Robert Schuman*, 244–45; and Sebastian Rosato, *Europe United: Power Politics and the Making of the European Community* (Ithaca: Cornell University Press, 2011).

45. See, e.g., Ole Waever, "Insecurity, Security, and Asecurity in the West European Non-War Community," in *Security Communities*, ed. Emanuel Adler and Michael Barnett, 3–28 (Cambridge: Cambridge University Press, 1998).

46. Alexander Wendt, *Social Theory of International Politics* (Cambridge: Cambridge University Press, 1999), chap. 6.

47. McCloy to Truman, Sept. 10, 1950, HSTL, PSF, subject file: Foreign Affairs, Germany, 6–7.

48. Public Records Office, Kew Gardens, England, CAB 129, Cabinet Papers, CP (50) 80, April 26, 1950.

49. See discussion later in this chapter and Ripsman, *Peacemaking by Democracies*, 205–12. The National Assembly defeated the treaty in large measure because they continued to distrust the nation that had "invaded us in 1792, in 1814, in 1815, in 1870, in 1914, and in 1940." Alexander Werth, *Lost Statesman: The Strange Story of Pierre Mendès-France* (Ann Arbor: University Microfilms, 1980), 183.

50. Miller, *States, Nations, and the Great Powers* (Cambridge: Cambridge University Press, 2011), 358–59.

51. Ibid., 358.

52. Jacques Freymond, *The Saar Conflict 1945–1955* (London: Stevens & Sons, 1960), xi. For similar assessments, see Hans-Peter Schwarz, *Konrad Adenauer: A German Politician and Statesman in a Period of War, Revolution and Reconstruction*, vol. 1 (Oxford: Berghahn, 1995), 488; and Richard L. Merritt, "Political Perspectives in Germany: The Years of Semisovereignty, 1949–1955," *Historical Social Research*, no. 13 (January 1980): 22.

53. Jonathan Rynhold, "The German Question in Central and Eastern Europe and the Long Peace in Europe after 1945: An Integrated Theoretical Explanation," *Review of International Studies* 37, no. 1 (January 2011): 258–59; and Freiherr von Braun, "Germany's Eastern Border and Mass Expulsions," *American Journal of International Law* 58, no. 3 (July 1964): 747–50.

54. See the discussion later in this chapter.

55. Tom Buchanan, *Europe's Troubled Peace: 1945 to the Present*, 2nd ed. (Chichester, UK: Wiley-Blackwell, 2012), 34; and Simon Duke, *United States Military Forces and Installations in Europe* (New York: Oxford University Press, 1989), xii.

56. Trachtenberg, *Constructed Peace*, 66–78, 95–103.

57. Charles de Gaulle, *War Memoirs*, vol. 3 (New York: Simon and Schuster, 1960), 239–40; Meeting between de Gaulle and Truman, Aug. 22, 1945, de Gaulle, *War Memoirs*, vol. 5 (New York: Simon and Schuster, 1960), 283–87; and Memorandum by the French delegation to the CFM, Sept. 13, 1945, *FRUS*, 1945, vol. 3, 869–71.

58. Trachtenberg, *Constructed Peace*, 70. See also Georges-Henri Soutou, "Le Général de Gaulle et l'URSS, 1943–1945: Idéologie ou équilibre européen?" *Revue d'histoire diplomatique* 108, no. 4 (1994): 347–53.

59. See, e.g., "France's German Policy," ORE 39–48, December 29, 1948—Papers of Harry S Truman, HSTL, PSF, subject file: Intelligence, box 255.

60. Wall, *United States and Post-War France*, 133. See also Tint, *French Foreign Policy*, 124.

61. Wall, *United States and Post-War France*, 133; and Georges Bidault to Secretary of State George Marshall, March 4, 1948, Archives nationales, Papiers Georges Bidault, 457 AP 25.

62. "The Ambassador in France (Caffery) to the Secretary of State, June 2, 1948, *FRUS*, 1948, vol. 2, 317. Bidault and Defense Minister Pierre-Henri Teitgen had previously expressed a similar view, calling for US military support to help overcome a "fear psychosis" in France stemming from a widespread concern that the United States would abandon France and Western Europe to a Soviet onslaught. "The Ambassador in France (Caffery) to the Under Secretary of State (Lovett), January 29, 1948, *FRUS*, 1948, vol. 3, Western Europe, 616–22, quote at 620. See also Georges Bidault, *Resistance: The Political Autobiography of Georges Bidault* (New York: Praeger, 1967), 155–56.

63. James McAllister, *No Exit: America and the German Problem* (Ithaca: Cornell University Press, 2002), 147–48.

64. John W. Young, *France, the Cold War, and the Western Alliance, 1944–49: French Foreign Policy and Post-War Europe* (New York: St. Martin's, 1990), 202; and Wall, *United States and Post-War France*, 93, 167.

65. Young, *France, Cold War, Western Alliance*, 203.

66. Wall, *United States and Post-War France*, 133.

67. Monnet, *Memoirs*, 290–91.

68. General de Gaulle initially declared that "to make France's recovery possible, the German collectivity must lose its capacity for aggression." De Gaulle, *War Memoirs*, vol. 3, 51. To this end, postwar French policy on Germany, which did not alter until 1950, was that Germany should remain demilitarized, occupied, and divided (239–40); and "Mémorandum de la délégation française au sujet de l'Allemagne," April 1946, British Public Records Office, FO371/ 55842—C4621/2860/18.

69. Notably, Generals Stehlin, Ely, de Lattre de Tassigny, and eventually even de Gaulle himself concluded early on that some form of controlled German military participation was essential for Western defense. See Pierre Guillen, "Les chefs militaires français, le réarmement de l'Allemagne et la CED, 1950–1954," *Revue d'histoire de la deuxième guerre mondiale et des conflits contemporains* 33 (January 1983): 3–33; Large, *Germans to the Front*, 37; Scott Erb, *German Foreign Policy: Navigating a New Era* (Boulder, CO: Lynne Rienner, 2003), 28; Michael Creswell and Marc Trachtenberg, "France and the German Question, 1945–1955," *Journal of Cold War Studies* 5, no. 3 (Summer 2003): 19; and Robert McGeehan, *The German Rearmament Question* (Urbana: University of Illinois Press, 1971), 16–17.

70. Reiner Pommerin, "The United States and the Armament of the Federal Republic of Germany," in *The American Impact on Postwar Germany*, ed. Reiner Pommerin (Providence: Berghahn Books, 1995), 24; and Creswell and Trachtenberg, "German Question," 19.

71. Large, *Germans to the Front*, 32–38; Georges-Henri Soutou, "France and the German Rearmament Problem," in *The Quest for Stability: Problems of West European Security, 1918–1957*, ed. R. Ahmann, A. M. Birke, and M. Howard (London: Oxford, 1993), 497; Georgette Elgey, *La république des contradictions, 1951–1954* (Paris: Fayard, 1968), 215; and

James S. Corum, "Adenauer, Amt Blank, and the Founding of the Bundeswehr, 1950–1956," in *Rearming Germany*, ed. James S. Corum (Leiden, Netherlands: Koninklijke Brill, 2011), 33.

72. Thomas A. Schwartz, "The 'Skeleton Key': American Foreign Policy, European Unity, and German Rearmament, 1949–54," *Central European History* 19, no. 4 (December 1986): 373–74.

73. "United States Minutes of the Second Meeting between President Truman and Prime Minister Pleven, Cabinet Room of the White House, January 30, 1951, 11 a.m.–12:30 p.m.," *FRUS*, 1951, vol. 4, 315–28.

74. Norrin M. Ripsman, "The Curious Case of German Rearmament: Democracy and Foreign Security Policy," *Security Studies* 10, no. 2 (Winter 2001): 1–47; Ripsman, *Peacemaking by Democracies*, 190–216; and Hitchcock, *France Restored*, 133–202.

75. Alfred Grosser, "France and Germany: Divergent Outlooks," *Foreign Affairs* 44, no. 1 (October 1965): 29; and Manfred Wilke, *The Path to the Berlin Wall: Critical Stages in the History of Divided Germany* (New York: Berghahn Books, 2014),131–32.

76. Large, *Germans to the Front*, 65.

77. Eric D. Weitz, "The Ever-Present Other: Communism in the Making of West Germany," in *The Miracle Years: A Cultural History of West Germany, 1949–1968*, ed. Hanna Schissler (Princeton: Princeton University Press, 2001), 220–21.

78. Konrad Adenauer, *Memoirs, 1945–53*, trans. Beate Rum von Oppen (Chicago: Henry Regnery, 1965), 78.

79. Ibid., 166.

80. Ernest R. May, "The American Commitment to Germany, 1949–1955," in *American Historians and the Atlantic Alliance*, ed. Lawrence S. Kaplan (Kent, OH: Kent State University Press, 1991), 63.

81. Adenauer, *Memoirs*, 273.

82. Jeffrey Herf, *Divided Memory: The Nazi Past in the Two Germanys* (Cambridge: Harvard University Press, 1997), 269.

83. Miller, *States, Nations, Great Powers*, 356–57; and John J. Mearsheimer, *The Tragedy of Great Power Politics* (New York: Norton, 2001), 256–57.

84. Gimbel, *Origins of the Marshall Plan*.

85. See, e.g., Bidault to the American, British, and Soviet Ambassadors, August 7, 1945, *Documents français relatifs à l'Allemagne* (Paris: Imprimerie Nationale, 1947), 7–10.

86. US Ambassador in Paris Bruce Caffery to Secretary of State George Marshall, July 11, 1947, *FRUS*, 1947, vol. 2, 983–86.

87. See Secretary of State George Marshall to Acting Secretary of State Robert A. Lovett, December 8, 1947, *FRUS*, 1947, vol. 2, 754; Marshall to Lovett, December 13, 1947, *FRUS*, 1947, vol. 2, 769; Vincent Auriol, *Journal du septennat, 1947–1954* (Paris: Librarie Armand Colin, 1970), 138–39, 184–86; and Note MAE, May 4, 1948, MAE, Secrétariat Générale 1945–1966, dossier Allemagne 6, 349–57.

88. See Memorandum of a Conversation between Byrnes and Bidault, September 24, 1946, *FRUS*, 1946, vol. 5, 607–10; and Acheson to US Ambassador to Great Britain, Lew Douglas, October 31, 1949, *FRUS*, 1949, vol. 3, 492–94.

89. Ripsman, *Peacemaking by Democracies*, 148. That the Americans offered these concessions to overcome French resistance to the broader German project is explicitly indicated in HSTL, "France's German Policy."

90. Jacques Dalloz, *Georges Bidault: Biographie politique* (Paris: L'Harmattan, 1992), 192. See also MAE Note, June 5, 1948, MAE, Secrétariat Générale 1945–1966, dossier Allemagne 6, 435; and Auriol, *Journal du septennat*, vol. 1948, 265–66.

91. Georges-Henri Soutou, "La sécurité de la France dans l'après-guerre," in *La France et l'OTAN 1949–1996*, ed. Maurice Vaïsse, Pierre Mélandri, and Frédéric Bozo (Brussels: Complexe, 1996), 26–32.

92. On the French government's conclusion as early as September 1950 that German rearmament was necessary, see Sir Gladwyne Jebb to Minister of State Kenneth Younger, September 16, 1950, *DBPO*, series 2 (1950–1955), vol. 3, 63; and "Rearmament Allemand," MAE Note, September 10, 1950, MAE, Europe 1944–1960, Allemagne, 185, 284–85. On French military opinion, see the sources in note 69 of this chapter.

93. Ripsman, *Peacemaking by Democracies*, 190–212.

94. In this regard, a large segment of the National Assembly believed it was essential to secure an Anglo-American guarantee against future German militarism before signing the EDC treaty. Alphand's Report to the Government, May 10, 1952, MAE, Europe 1944–1960, Allemagne, 1067. See President Vincent Auriol's summary of the May 23, 1952, cabinet meeting, in which Auriol, Air Minister Pierre Montel, and others expressed fears that the guarantees in the treaty did not sufficiently protect France from either renewed German militarism or German attempts to draw the alliance into a war to regain German territory in the east. Auriol, *Journal du septennat*, vol. 6, *1952* (Paris: Armand Colin, 1970), 346–51. On Auriol's reservations, see also Papers of Dean Acheson, Princeton Seminars, July 8–9, 1953, HSTL, wire 5, 15–17.

95. See, e.g., Trachtenberg, *Constructed Peace*, 117–18.

96. On the agreement on Western defense arrangements reached at the London Conference of September 1954, see *FRUS*, 1952–1954, vol. 5, 1338–66.

97. Minutes of the 216th Meeting of the NSC, October 6, 1954, *FRUS*, 1952–1954, vol. 5, 1378–84; and Memorandum of Conversation between Dulles and SACEUR Greunther, September 27, 1954, *FRUS*, 1952–1954, vol. 5, 1281–83.

98. Dulles to Bruce, July 13, 1953, *FRUS*, 1952–1954, vol. 5, 796; and Tint, *French Foreign Policy*, 51.

99. On the threat of unilateral action, see Dulles to US Emb. in Paris, May 18, 1954, *FRUS*, 1952–1954, vol. 5, 956–57; Meeting between MacArthur and Laniel, April 14, 1954, Dulles Papers, Eisenhower Library Collection, White House Memoranda, Princeton; and Meeting between Dulles, Hagerty and the President, April 19, 1954, Dulles Papers, Eisenhower Library Collection, White House Memoranda, Princeton. On the "agonizing reappraisal" threat, see Bonnet to the MAE, March 29, 1954, MAE, Europe 1944–1960, Généralités, CED, 27; John Foster Dulles Oral History Collection, Princeton University, Réné Mayer, 6; John Foster Dulles Oral History Collection, Princeton University, Ogden Reid, 3–4; and *FRUS*, 1952–1954, vol. 5, 868.

100. Ripsman, *Peacemaking by Democracies*, 207–12. On the impact of American pressure in general, see Pierre Guillen, "La France et l'intégration de la FRA dans L'OTAN," *Guerres mondiales et conflits contemporains*, no. 159 (July 1990): 77.

101. The divisions in the French cabinets, many of which split apart, are documented in the cabinet meetings summarized in Auriol, *Journal du septennat*.

102. On the remarkable continuity between Bidault and Schuman and their independence from French societal attitudes, see Gillingham, *Coal, Steel*, 150.

103. On the dynamic between French leaders who tried to negotiate independently and the French legislature, see Ripsman, *Peacemaking by Democracies*, chap. 4.

104. Warren F. Kimball, *Swords or Ploughshares? The Morgenthau Plan for Defeated Nazi Germany, 1943–1946* (Philadelphia: Lippincott, 1976); and Morgenthau to Roosevelt, September 5, 1944, *FRUS*, Conference at Quebec, 1944, 101–6.

105. Ripsman, *Peacemaking by Democracies*, 190.

106. Willis, *New Europe*, 62; and Adenauer, *Memoirs*, 79, 193–94.

107. Willis, *New Europe*, 63; Haig Simonian, *The Privileged Partnership: Franco-German Relations in the European Community, 1969–1984* (Oxford: Clarendon Press, 1985), 32–33; and Adenauer, *Memoirs*, 193–205.

108. See, e.g., Catherine Kelleher, *Germany and the Politics of Nuclear Weapons* (New York: Columbia University Press, 1975), 19–20.

109. Young, *France, Cold War, Western Alliance*, 127–28.

110. Marie-Renée Valentin, "Les grèves des cheminots français au cours de l'année 1947," *Le mouvement social*, no. 130 (January–March 1985): 55–80; and Young, *France, Cold War, Western Alliance*, 165–68.

111. Hitchcock, *France Restored*, 64–67; Alan S. Milward, *The Reconstruction of Western Europe, 1945–51* (Berkeley: University of California Press, 1984), 1–55; George Ross, *Workers and Communists in France: From Popular Front to Eurocommunism* (Berkeley: University of California Press, 1982), 51; and Harold Callender, "France Seeking Solvency amid a Welter of Strikes: Battle to Safeguard Economy by Drastic Financial Reforms Is Not Yet Won," *New York Times*, June 22, 1947, from ProQuest Historical Newspapers, *New York Times (1851–2010)*, 101.

112. On the French postwar labor shortage, see James R. McDonald, "Labor Immigration in France, 1946–1965," *Annals of the Association of American Geographers* 59, no. 1 (March 1969): 116–17; and Frances Lynch, "France," in *Government and Economies in the Postwar World: Economic Policies and Comparative Performance, 1945–85,* ed. Andrew Graham with Anthony Seldon (London: Routledge, 1990), 60.

113. "Weekly Summary Excerpt, December 2, 1947, Results of the Communist Strikes in France," in *Assessing the Soviet Threat: The Early Cold War Years,* ed. Woodrow J. Kuhns (Washington, DC: Center for the Study of Intelligence, Central Intelligence Agency, 1997), 156.

114. John W. Young, *Britain, France and the Unity of Europe* (Leicester: Leicester University, 1984), 57–58; and Wall, *United States and Post-War France,* 67.

115. Young, *France, Cold War, Western Alliance,* 231.

116. Friend, *Linchpin,* 38.

117. Philip H. Gordon, *France, Germany, and the Western Alliance* (Boulder, CO: Westview, 1995), 9–13; Patrick McCarthy, "Condemned to Partnership: The Franco-German Relationship, 1944–1983," in *France-Germany, 1983–1993: The Struggle to Cooperate,* ed. Patrick McCarthy (New York: St. Martin's, 1993), 10–12; and Hans-Peter Schwarz, *Konrad Adenauer: From the German Empire to the Federal Republic, 1876-1952,* vol. 2 (Providence: Berghahn, 1997), 364–67. On de Gaulle's dismissal of the smaller European states as insufficient for furthering French interests, see Erik Jones, "Small Countries and the Franco-German Relationship," in McCarthy, *France-Germany, 1983–1993,* 114–16.

118. As Adenauer informed the Americans, "there was no question of Germany being subordinate to France. Nevertheless, because of the recent past, it was impossible for Germany to take over the leadership of Europe. Consequently the only possibility remaining was 'for France to take on this leadership in a very moderate form.'" Schwarz, *Konrad Adenauer,* vol. 1, 612, 614–15.

119. Noted commentator on French foreign policy Alfred Grosser describes "a sort of gentleman's agreement" made between de Gaulle and Adenauer. "The Federal Republic would aid France in her Atlantic and European ambitions, and France would give firm support to the Eastern policies of the Federal Republic." *French Foreign Policy under de Gaulle* (Boston: Little, Brown, 1965), 66–67.

120. De Gaulle antagonized Great Britain by opposing British entry into the EEC and the United States by withdrawing from NATO and pursuing an independent nuclear policy. In addition, the "empty chair crisis" badly strained French relations with Italy and the Netherlands. Bonn, thus, remained France's closest ally.

121. David Lawday, "The Odd Couple," *Economist,* May 26, 1979, 27–36. See also David P. Calleo and Eric R. Stahl, eds., *Europe's Franco-German Engine* (Washington, DC: Brookings Institution Press, 1998).

122. See Friend, *Linchpin,* 26–77; and Gordon, *Western Alliance,* 17–24.

123. Commenting on French relations with Germany in his blueprint for French foreign policy at the dawn of the Gorbachev revolution, Mitterrand wrote, "France does not have a better, more reliable friend in Europe, where it has many excellent ones." François Mitterrand, *Réflexions sur la politique extérieure de la France* (Paris: Fayard, 1986), 95.

124. Simonian, *Privileged Partnership,* 117–20. Michel Jobert—a close adviser to Pompidou and his future foreign minister—concluded of Brandt's move, "Germany was already dreaming of the future; of a neutrality which would free it from Europe and lend it weight vis à vis Moscow" (153). Pompidou signaled his displeasure with a veiled threat to recognize the government of East Germany. See "M. Brandt remercie M. Pompidou," *Le Monde,* September 25, 1971, 1.

125. See, e.g., André Fontaine, "L'Allemagne à la dérive?" *Le Monde,* January 15, 1983, 1–2.

126. See, e.g., André Fontaine, "La Politique étrangère de M. Pompidou," *Le Monde,* February 3, 1970, 1–2; André Fontaine, "Les relations franco-allemandes: Entre la 'suite' et le 'requiem,'" *Le Monde,* January 26, 1983, 1–2; Edouard Balladur, "L'Europe sous la pression allemande," *Le Monde,* December 1, 1989, 1, 5; and Alfred Grosser, "Allemagne: Peur, déssaroi et raison," *Le Monde,* December 20, 1989, 2.

127. See, e.g., Willis, *New Europe,* 312–65; and Poidevin and Bariéty, *Relations franco-allemandes,* 335–36.

128. John Newhouse, *Collision in Brussels: The Common Market Crisis of June 30, 1965* (New York: Norton, 1967).

129. Andreas Wenger, "Crisis and Opportunity: NATO's Transformation and the Multilateralization of Détente, 1966–1968," *Journal of Cold War Studies* 6, no. 1 (2004): 22–74, esp. 33–34.

130. Simonian, *Privileged Partnership*, 26; and Gisela Hendriks and Annette Morgan, *The Franco-German Axis in European Integration* (Cheltenham, UK: Edward Elgar, 2001), 80–82.

131. Gordon, *Western Alliance*, 9–11.

132. On the sources of political conflict between France and Germany during the Cold War, see Stephen A. Kocs, *Autonomy or Power? The Franco-German Relationship and Europe's Strategic Choices, 1955–1995* (Westport, CT: Praeger, 1995); and McCarthy, "Condemned to Partnership."

133. On the trials and tribulations in US-Japanese relations, see Michael J. Green and Patrick M. Cronin, eds., *The US-Japan Alliance: Past, Present, and Future* (New York: Council on Foreign Relations, 1999); Michael Schaller, ed., *Altered States: The United States and Japan since the Occupation* (New York: Oxford University Press, 1997); and Roger Buckley, *US-Japan Alliance Diplomacy, 1945–1990* (Cambridge: Cambridge University Press, 1992).

134. See Norman Hillmer, *Partners Nevertheless: Canadian-American Relations in the Twentieth Century* (Toronto: Copp Clark Pitman, 1989).

135. The ups and downs of the Anglo-American special relationship are detailed in C. J. Bartlett, *The Special Relationship: A Political History of Anglo-American Relations since 1945* (Essex, UK: Longman, 1992); and John Dumbrell, *A Special Relationship: Anglo-American Relations in the Cold War and After* (New York: St. Martin's, 2001).

136. Sebastian Rosato, "Europe's Troubles: Power Politics and the State of the European Project," *International Security* 35, no. 4 (Spring 2011): 45–86.

137. Pierre Hassner, "Perceptions of the Soviet Threat in the 1950s and the 1980s: The Case of France," in *The Changing Western Analysis of the Soviet Threat*, ed. Carl Cristoph Schweitzer (London: Pinter, 1990), 171–74.

138. Mearsheimer, *Tragedy of Great Power Politics*, 256–57, 386–92.

139. William P. Mako, *US Ground Forces and the Defense of Central Europe* (Washington, DC: Brookings Institution Press, 1983), 4, 8.

140. Total European defense spending in 1952 was $10.2 billion in current dollars compared to $47.9 billion spent by the United States. *NATO Letter*, January 1963 (Paris: NATO Information Service, 1963), 26. By 1979, European spending jumped to $91.8 billion in current dollars, whereas the United States increased spending at a slower rate to $122.3 billion. *NATO Review*, February 1981 (Brussels: NATO Information Service, 1981), 32.

141. See, e.g., Stanley R. Sloan, "The Political Dynamics of Defense Burden Sharing in NATO," in *Evolving European Defense Policies*, ed. Catherine M. Kelleher and Gale A. Mattox, 79–98 (Lexington, MA: Lexington Books, 1987).

142. Paul Kennedy, *The Rise and Fall of the Great Powers: Economic Change and Military Conflict from 1500 to 2000* (New York, Vintage Books, 1989), 413–37.

143. William James Adams, *Reconstructing the French Economy: Government and the Rise of Market Competition since World War II* (Washington, DC: Brookings Institution Press, 1989), 4–5.

144. Jean-Pierre Dormois, *The French Economy in the Twentieth Century* (Cambridge: Cambridge University Press, 2004), 116.

145. Robert Gildea, *France since 1945* (New York: Oxford University Press, 2002), 93.

146. On the Fifth Republic, see Dorothy Maud Pickles, *The Fifth French Republic: Institutions and Politics* (London: Taylor & Francis, 1962). Of course, as the widespread political protests of 1968 indicate, the Fifth Republic did not banish instability completely from the French political scene. It did, however, provide a greater measure of stability than the fragile Fourth Republic.

147. For comparable Franco-German figures, see John E, Farquharson and Stephen C. Holt, *Europe from Below: An Assessment of Franco-German Popular Contacts* (London: Allen & Unwin, 1975), 89; and Willis, *New Europe*, 227–35.

148. Farquharson and Holt, *Europe from Below*, 90–91; and Simonian, *Privileged Partnership*, 25.

149. On bilateral tensions over economic issues, especially the French fear of being dominated by Germany, see Farquharson and Holt, *Europe from Below*, 90–92; Julius Weis Friend,

Unequal Partners: French-German Relations, 1989–2000 (Washington, DC: Center for Strategic and International Studies, 2001), 10; and Tint, *French Foreign Policy*, 100. On joint ventures, see German Federal Foreign Office, "France, Political Relations," November 2013, http://www.auswaertiges-amt.de/EN/Aussenpolitik/Laender/Laenderinfos/01-Nodes/Frankreich_node.html (accessed May 6, 2014).

150. Derek H. Urwin, "From a Europe of States to a State of Europe? An Historical Overview of the Uniting of Western Europe," in *The European Union Handbook*, ed. Jackie Gower, 3–15 (Chicago: Fitzroy Dearborn, 2002); and Clive Archer, *The European Union* (New York: Routledge, 2008), 19–58.

151. Simonian, *Privileged Partnership*, 6.

152. Of those polled with opinions, 16% reported that they had a "good opinion" of West Germany, while 42% reported that they had a "bad opinion." See the poll reported in *Sondages*, 1964, no. 3 (1964): 55, which presents data from multiple years.

153. An April 1956 public opinion poll, for example, reported that 39% of decided French respondents had "not much confidence" in West Germany, while a further 41% had "no confidence at all." *Sondages*, 1955, no. 4, 35.

154. A "good opinion" was reported by 58%, compared to only 11% who reported a "bad opinion." *Sondages*, 1964, no. 3, 55. This positive figure dropped off somewhat after the "empty chair crisis" in the EEC in 1965, but positive responses continued to overwhelm negative ones by at least 2 to 1. See *Sondages*, 1969, no. 1, 45.

155. *Sondages*, 1967, no. 4, 83.

156. In the January 1971 survey, 25% of decided respondents named Germany as France's best friend in Europe, compared to the 29% who selected Belgium. In comparison, only 17% named third-place Great Britain, only 8% chose fourth-place Switzerland, and only 6% selected fifth-place Italy. *Sondages*, 1971, no. 2, 157.

157. *Sondages*, 1972, no. 4, 31.

158. "Les français voient l'est en rose," *Libération*, October 4, 1989, 7.

159. "Les déclarations de M. Mitterrand," *Le Monde*, December 12, 1989, 1–2; "L'Allemagne ne peut pas détenir l'arme nucléaire," *Le Monde*, December 12, 1989, 2; and Claire Trean, "Paris veut associer Varsovie aux discussions sur l'Allemagne," *Le Monde*, March 11–12, 1990, 1–2.

160. Alan Riding, "Clamor in the East, Fear in Paris," *New York Times*, November 9, 1989, A13, from LexisNexis.

161. Gorbachev told German foreign minister Hans-Dietrich Genscher that Mitterrand had asked him to prevent German reunification. Friend, *Linchpin*, 82. For these reasons, both Mitterrand and French foreign minister Roland Dumas kept insisting during the weeks following the Berlin Wall's collapse that "German rearmament was not an immediate concern." See "La réunification de l'Allemagne ne peut être un problème d'actualité déclare M. Dumas," *Le Monde*, November 17, 1989, 3; and "M. Roland Dumas juge que les conditions ne sont pas réunies pour mettre fin à la division de l'Allemagne," *Le Monde*, December 10, 1989, 6.

162. "Ce qui compte, c'est la détermination du peuple allemand," *Le Monde*, November 5–6, 1989, 5.

163. See, e.g., "MM. Kohl et Mitterrand sont d'accord sur l'idée de confédération européenne," *Le Monde*, January 6, 1990; and "L'appartenance à l'OTAN est 'la destination naturelle' de l'Allemagne unie, estime M. Mitterrand," *Le Monde*, May 14, 1990, 4.

164. "M. Mitterrand: la nécessité d'une défense commune de l'Europe s'impose 'avec plus de force,'" *Le Monde*, February 15, 1990, 2; and Serge Schmemann, "Billions in Help for East Germany Approved by Bonn," *New York Times*, February 15. 1990, A1, from LexisNexis.

165. "Le chef de l'état apelle les français à avoir 'confiance en eux-mêmes,'" *Le Monde*, March 27, 1990, 2–4.

166. It is true that the German and French leaders, Kohl and Mitterrand, helped steer the process of German reunification to a stable conclusion. Kohl helped by signaling that Germany would renounce its claims to territory in neighboring states and would play by Western rules of international relations, privileging European integration over an exclusive concentration on German traditional interests. Alistair Cole, *Franco-German Relations: Political Dynamics of the European Union* (New York: Routledge, 2014), 19–20; and William E. Paterson and Gordon

Smith, "German Unity," in *Developments in German Politics*, ed. Gordon Smith, William E. Paterson, Peter H. Merkl, and Stephen Padgett (London: Macmillan, 1992), 15. Mitterrand, after initially vacillating, pursued a conciliatory policy, not opposing German reunification provided that it "must also serve the purpose of European integration." In this manner, he assured the French public that German reunification would be controlled by European institutions. Richard F. Kuisel, *The French Way: How France Embraced and Rejected American Values and Power* (Princeton: Princeton University Press, 2012), 137–38. There is no question, however, that societal attitudes had changed, as well.

3. The Egyptian-Israeli Peace Treaty

1. The roots of the Arab-Israeli conflict are discussed in Ian J. Bickerton and Carla Klausner, *A Concise History of the Arab-Israeli Conflict*, 4h ed. (New York: Prentice Hall, 2002); and Walter Laqueur and Barry Rubin, eds., *The Israeli-Arab Reader: A Documentary History of the Middle East Conflict* (New York: Penguin Books, 1995).

2. On the Sinai War, see Benny Morris, *Israel's Border Wars, 1949–1956: Arab Infiltration, Israeli Retaliation, and the Countdown to the Suez War* (Oxford: Oxford University Press, 1967); and Jack S. Levy and Joseph R. Gochal, "Democracy and Preventive War: Israel and the 1956 Sinai Campaign," *Security Studies* 11, no. 2 (Winter 2001–2): 1–49.

3. See Michael B. Oren, *Six Days of War: June 1967 and the Making of the Modern Middle East* (Oxford: Oxford University Press, 2002); William B. Quandt, *Peace Process: American Diplomacy and the Arab-Israeli Conflict since 1967* (Washington, DC: Brookings/University of California, 2001); and Avraham Sela, "Politics, Identity and Peacemaking: The Arab Discourse on Peace with Israel in the 1990s," *Israel Studies* 10, no. 2 (Summer 2005): 23.

4. Kirk J. Beattie, *Egypt during the Sadat Years* (New York: Palgrave, 2000), 137–217; Raymond Hinnebusch, Jr., *Egyptian Politics under Sadat: The Post-Populist Development of an Authoritarian-Modernizing State* (Boulder, CO: Lynne Rienner, 1988), 57–63; Michael N. Barnett and Jack S. Levy, "Domestic Sources of Alliances and Alignments: The Case of Egypt, 1962–73," *International Organization* 45, no. 3 (June 1991): 386–93; and Thomas Lippman, *Egypt after Nasser: Sadat, Peace, and the Mirage of Prosperity* (New York: Paragon House, 1989), 83–116.

5. Mohamed Heikal, *The Road to Ramadan* (New York: Quadrangle, 1975), 20; Hani Shukrallah, "Political Crisis/Conflict in Post-1967 Egypt," in *Egypt under Mubarak*, ed. Charles Tripp and Roger Owen (New York: Routledge, 1989), 70; and Barnett and Levy, "Domestic Sources of Alliances and Alignments," 387–89.

6. See Alvin Z. Rubinstein, *Red Star on the Nile: The Soviet-Egyptian Influence Relationship since the June War* (Princeton: Princeton University Press, 1977), chaps. 5–6; Heikal, *Road to Ramadan*, 171–77; Ismail Fahmy, *Negotiating for Peace in the Middle East* (Beckenham, UK: Croom Helm, 1983), 103; Anwar el-Sadat, *In Search of Identity* (New York: Harper & Row, 1978), 225–26; and Hamied Ansari, *Egypt: The Stalled Society* (Albany: SUNY Press, 1986), 176–77.

7. Naphtali Lau-Lavie, *Balaam's Prophecy: Eyewitness to History, 1939–1989* (New York: Cornwall Books, 1998), 370.

8. Shibley Telhami, *Power and Leadership in International Bargaining: The Path to the Camp David Accords* (New York: Columbia University Press, 1990), 67–71.

9. Raphael Israeli, *Man of Defiance: A Political Biography of Anwar Sadat* (Totowa, NJ: Barnes & Noble Books, 1985), 216–20; and "Official Working Visit by Egyptian President Anwar Sadat [in April 1977]," Memorandum from Secretary of State Cyrus Vance to President Jimmy Carter, n.d., Jimmy Carter Presidential Library [hereafter, JCPL], RAC Collection, ESDN NLC-133-157-3-3-4, 27.

10. Interview with William Quandt, former National Security Council office director for Middle Eastern Affairs (1977–79), February 19, 2008.

11. See, e.g., Anwar el-Sadat, "Where Egypt Stands," *Foreign Affairs* 51, no. 1 (October 1972): 120.

12. See Rubinstein, *Red Star on the Nile*, chaps. 5–6; Kenneth W. Stein, *Heroic Diplomacy: Sadat, Kissinger, Carter, Begin, and the Quest for Arab-Israeli Peace* (London: Routledge, 1999), x; and Quandt, *Peace Process*.

13. See, e.g., Fahmy, *Negotiating for Peace*, 33–34; and Quandt, *Peace Process*, 190.

14. World Bank, "World Development Indicators (WDI) and Global Development Finance (GDF) Databases," http://databank.worldbank.org.

15. See, e.g., Ansari, *Egypt*, 185–93.

16. David Hirst and Irene Beeson, *Sadat* (London: Faber and Faber, 1980), 244.

17. Israeli, *Man of Defiance*, 216–19.

18. Mohamed Heikal, *Secret Channels: The Inside Story of Arab-Israeli Peace Negotiations* (London: Harper Collins, 1996), 248; Mark N. Cooper, *The Transformation of Egypt* (Baltimore: Johns Hopkins University Press, 1982), 247–54; and Ansari, *Egypt*, 187.

19. On the proposed conference, see Moshe Dayan, *Breakthrough: A Personal Account of the Egypt-Israel Peace Negotiations* (New York: Knopf, 1981), 10; and Quandt, *Peace Process*, 180–87.

20. Fahmy, *Negotiating for Peace*, 257–58; and Boutros Boutros-Ghali, *Egypt's Road to Jerusalem: A Diplomat's Story of the Struggle for Peace in the Middle East* (New York: Random House, 1997), 44.

21. Ibrahim A. Karawan, "Sadat and the Egyptian-Israeli Peace Revisited," *International Journal of Middle East Studies* 26, no. 2 (May 1994): 253. Sadat repeatedly emphasized to American diplomats that he "could not accept Arab dictation of what [Egypt] can and cannot accept." William Quandt, *Camp David: Peacemaking and Politics* (Washington, DC: Brookings Institution, 1986), 135.

22. Interview with Avraham Sela, officer in the Research Division of the Israeli Defense Force Intelligence Branch, 1970–1986, June 23, 2008.

23. For the text of the treaty, see "Peace Treaty between Israel and Egypt," March 26, 1979, http://www.mfa.gov.il/mfa/foreignpolicy/peace/guide/pages/israel-egypt%20pea ce%20treaty.aspx. On the normalization agreements and economic/cultural agreements, see "Progress in Egyptian-Israeli Normalization Arrangements," attachment to Sol M. Linowitz (Personal Representative of the President for the Middle East Peace Negotiations) to Carter, January 12, 1981, JCPL, Plains file, subject file: Mid East, 10-77-1/82, 2–3.

24. It is significant, in this regard, that Muslim Brotherhood Egyptian president Muhammed Morsi assured the United Nations in 2012 that his government, too, would not seek to alter the Egyptian-Israeli peace treaty. Geoff Dyer, "Morsi Uses UN Speech to Attack Israel," *Financial Times*, September 26, 2012, http://www.ft.com/intl/cms/s/0/0fd26a2e-0803-11e2-a2d8-00144feabdc0.html#axzz29OF9z4ph (accessed October 14, 2012).

25. The Polity scale, which I use throughout this book, ranges from –10 (full autocracy) to +10 (full democracy). Regimes scoring between –10 and –6 are classed as autocracies. Those scoring between –5 and +5 are classed as anocracies. Finally, those scoring between +6 and +10 are judged to be democracies. Polity IV data are from http://www.systemicpeace.org/inscr/inscr.htm (accessed May 2, 2011).

26. Raymond H. Anderson, "Egyptians Voting Today in Presidential Plebiscite on Successor to Nasser," *New York Times*, October 15, 1970, 4; "Egypt Renominates Sadat for 6 Years in Presidency," *New York Times*, September 18, 1976, p. 4; and Alvaro Marques and Thomas B. Smith, "Referendums in the Third World," *Electoral Studies* 3, no. 1 (April 1984): 95.

27. Maye Kassem, *Egyptian Politics: The Dynamics of Authoritarian Rule* (Boulder, CO: Lynne Reinner, 2004), 55–56.

28. See John Waterbury, *The Egypt of Nasser and Sadat: The Political Economy of Two Regimes* (Princeton: Princeton University Press, 1983), 350–51; and Raymond William Baker, *Egypt's Uncertain Revolution under Nasser and Sadat* (Cambridge: Harvard University Press, 1978), 125–26.

29. Hinnebusch, *Egyptian Politics under Sadat*, 72.

30. Ibid., 44.

31. See, e.g., Adeed I. Dawisha, *Egypt in the Arab World: The Elements of Foreign Policy* (London: Macmillan, 1976), 107; Salwa Sharawi Gomaa, *Egyptian Diplomacy in the Seventies: A Case Study in Leadership* (PhD diss., University of Pittsburgh, 1986); and Baker, *Egypt's Uncertain Revolution*, 158. For a somewhat critical perspective, see Karawan, "Sadat and the Egyptian-Israeli Peace Revisited."

32. "An In-depth Study of the Voting Public in Israel, July 1977," attachment to Jim Fallows to Zbigniew Brzezinski and Carter, July 18, 1977, JCPL, National Security Affairs [hereafter, NSA] file, Brzezinski Material, country file: Israel, box 35, Israel, 7/77.

33. "Information Items," Zbigniew Brzezinksi to Carter, December 5, 1977, JCPL, RAC Collection, ESDN NLC-1-4-6-16-3, 1; and "Evening Report," Memo from the Middle East Desk to Brzezinski, May 31, 1978, JCPL, RAC Collection, ESDN NLC-10-12-1-22-2, 2.

34. Polls showed that 59.8% believed that "setting up new settlements during the negotiations with Egypt is not justified (21.6% believe it is justified; 18.6 undecided)." Gary Sick to Zbigniew Brzezinski, March 27, 1977, JCPL, RAC Collection, ESDN NLC-10-10-2-13-3, 2.

35. Dayan, *Breakthrough*, 194. Opponents of the treaty—particularly of the evacuation of Israeli settlements in the Sinai—existed among the public, the Knesset, and even the government itself. (Likud/Herut coalition members of the Knesset, Geula Cohen and Moshe Shamir, resigned from the Likud Party because of the peace treaty.) Overall, however, the treaty was received as legitimate by the Israeli public. See Yaacov Bar Siman-Tov, *Israel and the Peace Process, 1977–1982: In Search of Legitimacy for Peace* (Albany: SUNY Press, 1994), 138–242.

36. Vance to Carter, November 9, 1978, JCPL, RAC Collection, ESDN NLC-15-123-4-8-7, 2.

37. Dayan, *Breakthrough*, 193–94.

38. According to an Israeli public opinion poll taken in March 1980, 68% of respondents reported that they were happy with the treaty, whereas only 17.6% said that they were dissatisfied. The popularity of the key Israeli government ministers who negotiated the treaty spiked, as well. Vance to US Embassy Rome, March 12, 1980, JCPL, RAC Collection, ESDN NLC-16-127-3-27-2.

39. Morris B. Abram to Carter, July 5, 1977, JCPL, NSA file, Brzezinski Material, country file: Israel, box 35, Israel, 7/77.

40. While reliable public opinion polls for Egypt at the time do not exist, Raymond Hinnebusch discusses surveys of Egyptian students, who would have been the most Westernized and supportive of Sadat, which indicate that less than one-third of this group favored moving out of step with the Arab states and signing a separate peace. Hinnebusch, *Egyptian Politics under Sadat*, 235.

41. White House Memorandum, November 17, 1977, JCPL, RAC Collection, ESDN NLC-1-4-4-50-7, 1. Egyptians thronged the streets to greet Sadat as a hero on his return from Jerusalem. In reality, however, this result was manufactured by a mixture of repression (preventing protests) and incentives (providing a paid day off from work, food, and transportation to those who attended the welcome gathering). Judith Tucker, "While Sadat Shuffles: Economic Decay, Political Ferment in Egypt," *MERIP Reports*, no. 65 (March 1978), 3–9. Moreover, there was significant opposition among the political elite, particularly the National Progressive Unionist Party—many of whose members were arrested due to their anticipated opposition—and even within Sadat's inner circle itself. Notably, Foreign Minister Ismail Fahmi resigned over the trip, as he believed it played into Israeli hands and demonstrated naïve over-reliance on the United States. Kirk J. Beattie, *Egypt during the Sadat Years* (New York: Palgrave, 2000), 231–32; and Hinnebusch, *Egyptian Politics under Sadat*, 72–73. Thus, while Hinnebusch and others take the government-inspired public expression of support as genuine, there is reason to believe that public and elite attitudes were in reality much more critical.

42. Draft of cable from Weizman to Gamasy, sent to Foreign Ministry, April 24, 1978, Israel State Archives, Foreign Ministry files, Cairo file, het tsadi-6864/4.

43. Ezer Weizman, *The Battle for Peace* (New York: Bantam Books, 1981), 293.

44. "Top Secret Daily Paper," May 9, 1978, Israel State Archives, Foreign Ministry files, Cairo file, het tsadi-6864/4. See also General Gamasy's letters to Defense Minister Ezer Weizman of May 18 and May 25, 1978 in Israel State Archives, Foreign Ministry files, Cairo file, het tsadi-6864/4.

45. Interview with William Quandt, February 19, 2008.

46. In selling the treaty, they also emphasized that the treaty would not prevent Egypt from going to war with Israel if Israel were to attack Syria. Assistant Secretary of State for Near East Affairs Hal Saunders and Economics Officer Thomas R. Reynders to Secretary of State Cyrus

Vance and the White House, March 20, 1979, JCPL, RAC Collection, ESDN NLC-SAFE-17C-18-23-2-7, 1–3 (quotes at 1).

47. Although Vance reported "initial elation over acceptance of the treaty" in Egypt, he observed that support had faded as the nature of the autonomy agreement became clear. Vance to US Embassy Rome, March 12, 1980, 5. In a March 1980 NSC meeting, Carter noted "that Sadat was getting into trouble at home; with the military, with the university students, and among government bureaucrats, because he is embarrassed almost daily by the peace process." "National Security Council Meeting," March 18, 1980, JCPL, RAC Collection, ESDN NLC-17-2-19-4-7, 3.

48. On the Arab boycott, see Gil Feiler, *From Boycott to Economic Cooperation: The Arab Boycott of Israel* (London: Taylor & Francis, 1998).

49. See Kristian S. Gleditsch, "Expanded Trade and GDP Data," *Journal of Conflict Resolution* 46, no. 5 (October 2002): 712–24; and the associated data set at http://privatewww.essex.ac.uk/~ksg/exptradegdp.html (accessed May 22, 2014), which utilizes IMF data. Zero trade might be a slight underestimate, but it clearly implies that the two states did not trade significantly before the treaty.

50. Interview with Alan Baker, legal adviser to the Israeli foreign ministry (former member of the Legal Advisor's staff, Israeli foreign ministry during the late 1970s), June 21, 2004.

51. Galia Press-Barnathan, *The Political Economy of Transitions to Peace: A Comparative Perspective* (Pittsburgh: University of Pittsburgh Press, 2009), 39.

52. Ibid., 40.

53. Ruth Arad, Seev Hirsch, and Alfred Tovias, *The Economics of Peacemaking: Focus on the Egyptian-Israeli Situation* (New York: St. Martin's Press, 1983), 87.

54. Ibid., 136–37.

55. Sadat and his foreign ministers consistently pressed for the return of the Sinai in return for security arrangements but without normalization or even the exchange of ambassadors. They argued that normalization could be discussed at some future time, perhaps five years after the implementation of the security treaty. See "Memorandum of Conversation," April 4, 1977, *Foreign Relations of the United States, 1977–1980*, vol. 8, *Arab-Israeli Dispute, January 1977–August 1978* [hereafter, *FRUS*, vol. 8] (Washington, DC: US Government Printing Office, 2013), 173, 175; "Memorandum of Conversation," August 1, 1977, *FRUS*, vol. 8, 379–80; "Memorandum of Conversation," September 24, 1977, *FRUS*, vol. 8, 574; and Dayan, *Breakthrough*, 81.

56. Interview with former ambassador Robbie Sabel, member of Israeli delegation for negotiating the peace treaties with Egypt and Jordan, June 23, 2008.

57. Press-Barnathan, *Transitions to Peace*, 37.

58. Interview with Alan Baker, June 21, 2004.

59. Arad, Hirsch, and Tovias, *Economics of Peacemaking*, 136.

60. Interview with Dan Patir, former press secretary for Prime Minister Menachem Begin, June 20, 2004.

61. Telephone interview with Ezer Weizman, former Israeli defense minister, June 22, 2004.

62. On the weakness of the Arab League and institutions of Arab unity in the face of competing national and sectarian aspirations, see Avraham Sela, *The Decline of the Arab-Israeli Conflict: Middle East Politics and the Quest for Regional Order* (Albany: SUNY Press, 1998).

63. At the first secret meeting in Morocco between Israeli foreign minister Moshe Dayan and Egyptian deputy premier Hassan Tuhami in September 1977, for example, Tuhami emphasized that full Israeli withdrawal was Sadat's sine qua non for peace. He told Dayan that Sadat was eager to start a dialogue with Israel, "but only after Begin agreed to the principle of total withdrawal from the administered territories would Sadat meet with Begin and shake his hand. Israel's withdrawal was the basic problem. Its solution was the key to peace . . ." Dayan, *Breakthrough*, 47.

64. See, e.g., Kenneth W. Stein, "Continuity and Change in Egyptian-Israeli Relations, 1973–97," *Israel Affairs* 3, nos. 3–4 (1997): 298–99, 303; and Stein, *Heroic Diplomacy*, 22.

65. Interview with William Quandt, February 19, 2008. Former Israeli deputy defense minister Mordechai Zippori similarly told me that the Israeli government calculated that "without

Egypt, it would be almost impossible [for there] to be a war." Interview with Mordechai Zippori, former Israeli deputy defense minister, June 17, 2004. See also Quandt, *Peace Process*, 190.

66. Bar Siman-Tov, *Peace Process*, 20–21.

67. On Egypt's other national security threats, see Quandt to Deputy National Security Advisor David Aaron, August 16, 1977, JCPL, NSA file, Brzezinski Material, country file: Egypt, box 18; Embassy in Washington to Foreign Ministry, "The Topics of the Agreements to be Publicized at 12:00 Our Time," September 18, 1978, Israel State Archives, Foreign Ministry files, United States file, het tsadi-6867/1; and Jimmy Carter, *Keeping Faith: Memoirs of a President* (Toronto: Bantam Books, 1982), 283–84.

68. Joseph Finklestone comments: "For Sadat it was obvious that '90 per cent of the cards are in American hands' and the Arabs would achieve precisely nothing without American aid. He never stopped hammering home this point. His later achievement of signing a treaty with Israel and regaining all Egyptian land, he attributed almost entirely to holding fast to this truth." *Anwar Sadat: Visionary Who Dared* (London: Frank Cass, 1996), 159. See also William J. Burns, *Economic Aid and American Foreign Policy toward Egypt, 1955–1981* (Albany: SUNY Press, 1985), 177.

69. Stein, *Heroic Diplomacy*, 9 (italics in original).

70. Cited in Stein, "Continuity and Change," 300.

71. Heikal, *Secret Channels*, 248. Quandt believed that Sadat wanted to emulate the US relationship with Israel, especially because US economic aid would solve Egypt's underdevelopment problem. Interview with William Quandt, February 19, 2008.

72. Janice Gross Stein, "The Political Economy of Security Agreements: The Linked Costs of Failure at Camp David," in *Double-Edged Diplomacy: International Bargaining and Domestic Politics*, ed. Peter B. Evans, Harold K. Jacobson, and Robert D. Putnam (Berkeley: University of California Press, 1993), 89.

73. William Quandt made the link between US aid and Egyptian moderation explicit in a background paper for Carter's meeting with Congressman William Lehman regarding Egypt. He stated: "Sadat has been willing to take the lead in the Arab world in talking peace with Israel, and we intend to encourage him in that direction. . . . Our aid to Egypt is meant to help support moderate forces in the Arab world and help President Sadat deal with his urgent domestic problems." Quandt to NSC staff member Michael Hornblow, February 14, 1977, JCPL, White House Central file [hereafter, WHCF], subject file: Countries, box CO-23, CO 45 1/20/77-3/3, 1/77. See also Brzezinski to Carter, November 7, 1979, JCPL, NSA file, Brzezinski Material, country file: Egypt, box 19.

74. Chief presidential speechwriter James Fallows to Carter, March 31, 1977, JCPL, WHCF, subject file: Countries, box CO-23, CO 45 1/20/77–3/31/77; and Patrick Clawson and Zoe Danon Gedal, *Dollars and Diplomacy: The Impact of US Economic Initiatives on Arab-Israeli Negotiations* (Washington, DC: Washington Institute for Near East Policy, 1999), 63–65.

75. Carter to Church, April 2, 1979, JCPL, WHCF, subject file: Countries, box CO-24, CO 45 1/1/79–6/30/79.

76. "Foreign Assistance and Related Programs Appropriation Bill, 1980," June 11, 1979, JCPL, NSA file, Brzezinski Material, country file: Egypt, box 18, 45.

77. Clawson and Gedal, *Dollars and Diplomacy*, 64.

78. "President's Journal, Middle East Trip," March 8, 1979, JCPL, RAC Collection, ESDN NLC-128-9-9-1-0, 8–9.

79. "Meeting of the Departmental Leadership," August 31, 1978, Israel State Archives, Foreign Ministry files, Office of the Minister Moshe Dayan, het tsadi-6913/1.

80. Interview with William Quandt, February 19, 2008.

81. Lau-Lavie, *Balaam's Prophecy*, 400.

82. On Carter's pledge to the American Jewish community, see "Integrated Analysis of Israeli Security Assistance Programs for FY 1980," Morris Draper (NEA) to Mr. Ericson (PM), October 13, 1979, JCPL, RAC Collection, ESDN NLC-25-53-7-14-4, 6. On Carter's desire to play a "positive and active role" and the US strategy of "developing and exploiting the pressure that Sadat has put on Begin," see Secretary of State Cyrus Vance to Ambassador, December 13, 1977, JCPL, NSA file, Brzezinski Material, country file: Israel, box 35, Israel, 11–12/77.

83. Jimmy Carter, *White House Diary* (New York: Farrar, Straus & Giroux, 2010), 44, also 137 and 193.

84. "Evening Report," State Department Middle East Desk to Brzezinski, March 22, 1978, JCPL, RAC Collection, ESDN NLC-10-10-1-16-1, 3.

85. Dayan, *Breakthrough*, 168, 173; Lau-Lavie, *Balaam's Prophecy*, 400; and Quandt, *Peace Process*, 216–20.

86. Interview with Mordechai Zippori, former Israeli deputy defense minister, June 17, 2004; and Dayan, *Breakthrough*, 59–68.

87. See, e.g., Foreign Ministry to Washington, "Letter from President Carter to the Prime Minister regarding the Thickening of Settlements," October 26, 1978, Israel State Archives, Foreign Ministry files, Cairo file, het tsadi-6824/7. Carter's growing hostility to Begin is evident in the president's personal journal entries during his trip to Israel in March 1979. See "President's Journal, Middle East Trip," March 8, 1979, JCPL, RAC Collection, ESDN NLC-128-9-9-1-0, 2–35, esp. 17.

88. See, e.g., Quandt to Brzezinski, June 28, 1978, JCPL, NSA file, Brzezinski Material, country file: Israel, box 35, Israel, 5–6/78.

89. Vance to Carter, November 9, 1978, JCPL, RAC Collection, ESDN NLC-15-123-4-8-7, 1.

90. Ibid., 9.

91. Ibid., 10.

92. Carter to Church, April 2, 1979, JCPL, WHCF, subject file: Countries, box CO-24, CO 45 1/1/79–6/30/79.

93. Quandt to Brzezinski, January 3, 1979, JCPL, NSA file, Brzezinski Material, country file: Israel, box 36, Israel, 1–4/79; and "Memorandum of Agreement between the Governments of the United States of America and the State of Israel—Oil," March 26, 1979, http://www.mfa.gov.il/mfa/foreignpolicy/peace/guide/pages/memorandum%20of%20agreement%20between%20the%20governments%20of.aspx.

94. Lau-Lavie, *Balaam's Prophecy*, 413.

95. "Notes Made at Camp David Before Begin and Sadat Arrived," n.d., JCPL, Plains file, subject file: Mid East: Camp David Summit, President's Working Papers, 3.

96. "Memorandum of Agreement between the Governments of the United States of America and the State of Israel," March 26, 1979, http://www.mfa.gov.il/mfa/foreignpolicy/peace/guide/pages/us-israel%20memorandum%20of%20agreement.aspx.

97. Weizman, for example, noted that Begin was apprehensive approaching the Camp David summit and warned his cabinet colleagues that "if the conference does not succeed . . . it will lead to a severe rift with the United States, and . . . would further erode Israel's already precarious position." Weizman, *Battle for Peace*, 340–41. See also "Begin's Objectives in Coming for Bilateral US-Israeli Talks," enclosure to Atherton and Saunders to Vance, February 28, 1979, JCPL, RAC Collection, ESDN NLC-133-61-2-8-6, 6.

98. "Begin's Objectives in Coming for Bilateral US-Israeli Talks," 6.

99. See, e.g., US Ambassador to Tel Aviv Samuel Lewis to Vance, April 5, 1978, JCPL, NSA file, Brzezinski Material, country file: Israel, box 35, Israel, 4/78, item 2c, 8–9; Quandt to Brzezinski, March 3, 1978, JCPL, RAC Collection, ESDN NLC-25-110-5-3-3, 4; "Draft Memorandum of Conversation of First Bilateral Meeting between Presidents Carter and Geisel," Memorandum from the US Embassy in Brasilia to Vance, April 4, 1978, JCPL, RAC Collection, ESDN NLC-16-30-4-25-0, 5–6; and "Trip to Israel and Egypt," Memorandum from Vice President Mondale to Carter, July 4, 1978, JCPL, RAC Collection, ESDN NLC-133-24-1-6-0, 2.

100. See, e.g., Carter, *White House Diary*, 140.

101. Thomas Princen, "Camp David: Problem-Solving or Power Politics as Usual?" *Journal of Peace Research* 28, no. 1 (February 1991): 57–69.

102. Vance advised Carter, "The principle advantages of Summit [*sic*] talks are that we would be able to bring maximum pressure on Sadat and Begin from the outset; and that leaks and public airing of differences would be easier to control." "Strategy for the Middle East Negotiations," Vance to Carter, n.d., JCPL, RAC Collection, ESDN NLC-15-32-4-13-2, 6.

103. Boutros-Ghali, *Egypt's Road to Jerusalem*, 11–12; and Fahmy, *Negotiating for Peace*, 254–60, 265–67.

104. Fahmy, *Negotiating for Peace*, 277–79; and Boutros-Ghali, *Egypt's Road to Jerusalem*, 16, 149–52.

105. Boutros-Ghali, after complaining that "Sadat would not keep his advisers informed," observed that "Sadat was the boss. He could ignore his advisers, bypass the Assembly, override the wishes of the Egyptian people, and he enjoyed demonstrating power." Boutros-Ghali, *Egypt's Road to Jerusalem*, 64, 165.

106. Telhami, *Power and Leadership*, 171.

107. William Quandt, thus, told me that "Sadat was the decider. His foreign ministers were not particularly influential." Interview with William Quandt, February 19, 2008.

108. On the riots, see Tamara Gutner, "The Political Economy of Food Subsidy Reform: The Case of Egypt," *Food Policy* 27, no. 5/6 (October–December 2002): 455–76; Thomas W. Lippman, "Thousands in Egypt Protest Price Rise," *Washington Post*, January 18, 1977 (accessed through LexisNexis, September 12, 2010); and Cooper, *Transformation of Egypt*, 236–37. On the anti-regime and anti-Sadat character of the protests, see Karawan, "Sadat and the Egyptian-Israeli Peace Revisited," 255.

109. "Evening Report," Memorandum for Zbigniew Brzezinski, August 24, 1977, JCPL, RAC Collection, ESDN NLC-10-4-6-22-6, 2.

110. In March 1977, for example, the State Department warned: "Although the military performed well against the rioters in January, there is sufficient grumbling among the officers over economic issues to cast doubt over their willingness to take firm measures in the future against crowds rioting over these same grievances." "Sadat's Need for Progress," Department of State Briefing Paper, March 1977, JCPL, RAC Collection, ESDN NLC-133-157-3-4-3, 7. See also "Camp David Talks: Egyptian Political, Social and Economic Institutions," Memorandum from the American Embassy in Cairo to Vance, September 30, 1978, JCPL, RAC Collection, ESDN NLC-16-45-2-42-7, 11–12.

111. Indeed, he told the Israeli defense minister of a foiled plot in which Libya paid Egyptian officers $750,000 to overthrow Sadat. Weizman, *Battle for Peace*, 323.

112. Interview with William Quandt, February 19, 2008; Cooper, *Transformation of Egypt*, 250–51; and Etel Solingen, *Regional Orders at Century's Dawn: Global and Domestic Influences on Grand Strategy* (Princeton: Princeton University Press, 1998), 177–78.

113. See, e.g., Karawan, "Sadat and the Egyptian-Israeli Peace Revisited," 261.

114. Tim Deal (NSC, International Economics Staff) to Deputy Assistant National Security Advisor David Aaron, October 3, 1978, JCPL, WHCF, subject file: Countries, box CO-24, CO 45 7/1/78–12/31/78. Sadat also requested $20 million in American funding for a mapping project to facilitate Egyptian development. Sadat to Carter, October 18, 1977, JCPL, NSA file, Brzezinski Material, country file: Egypt, box 18.

115. Memorandum of Conversation attached to Brzezinski to Quandt, February 20, 1979, JCPL, WHCF, subject file: Countries, box CO-24, CO 45 1/1/79–6/30/79.

116. "President's Journal, Middle East Trip," March 8, 1979, 8–9.

117. Quandt to Brzezinski, April 5, 1977, JCPL, WHCF, subject file: Countries, box CO-23, CO 45 4/1/77–4/15/77.

118. "Secretary's Meeting with Belgian Prime Minister," October 20, 1977, JCPL, RAC Collection, ESDN NLC-23-22-8-24-8, 9.

119. "Camp David Talks: Egyptian Political, Social and Economic Institutions," 15.

120. Carter Center, *Camp David 25th Anniversary Forum, September 17, 2003* (Atlanta: Carter Center, 2003), 45.

121. Ewan Stein, "The Camp David Consensus: Ideas, Intellectuals, and the Division of Labor in Egypt's Foreign Policy toward Israel," *International Studies Quarterly* 55, no. 3 (September 2011): 745.

122. Interview with William Quandt, February 19, 2008.

123. Article 3, section 3 of the treaty specified: "The Parties agree that the normal relationship established between them will include full recognition, diplomatic, economic and cultural relations, termination of economic boycotts and discriminatory barriers to the free movement of people and goods, and will guarantee the mutual enjoyment by citizens of the due process of law." "Peace Treaty between Israel and Egypt," March 26, 1979.

124. Shimon Shamir, "Israeli Views of Egypt and the Peace Process: The Duality of Vision," in *The Middle East: Ten Years after Camp David*, ed. William B. Quandt, 187–216 (Washington, DC: Brookings Institution, 1988); and Stein, "Continuity and Change," 308–9, 316.

125. Ali E. Hillal Dessouki, "Egyptian Foreign Policy since Camp David," in Quandt, *Middle East*, 94–110.

126. Ali E. Hillal Dessouki, "Egypt and the Peace Process," *International Journal* 45, no. 2 (Summer 1990): 555; and Rami Ginat and Meir Noema, *Egypt and the Second Intifada: Policymaking with Multifaceted Commitments* (Portland, OR: Sussex Academic Press, 2011), 22, 55–56.

127. Hillel Frisch, "Guns and Butter in the Egyptian Army," in *Armed Forces in the Middle East: Politics and Strategy*, ed. Barry Rubin and Thomas A. Keaney (London: Frank Cass, 2002), 102.

128. In the late 1980s and early 1990s, for example, Yitzhak Rabin judged that "it was not likely that Israel's immediate neighbors would be as big a threat as Iran or Iraq," whom he expected to develop nuclear weapons. Quandt, *Peace Process*, 331. See also Yoram Peri, afterword in *The Rabin Memoirs* by Yitzhak Rabin (Berkeley: University of California Press, 1979), 365–66.

129. Sela, *Decline of the Arab-Israeli Conflict*, 297; Nael Shama, *Egyptian Foreign Policy from Mubarak to Morsi: Against the National Interest* (New York: Routledge, 2014), 173; and Stein, "Continuity and Change," 305–6. On Egyptian stagflation, see Simon Bromley and Ray Bush, "Adjustment in Egypt? The Political Economy of Reform," *Review of African Political Economy*. 21, no. 60 (June 1994): 201–13.

130. Fouad Ajami, *The Dream Palace of the Arabs: A Generation's Odyssey* (New York: Vintage Books, 1999), 280; and Sela, "Politics, Identity and Peacemaking," 35.

131. On bilateral frictions, see Stein, "Continuity and Change," 305.

132. Interview with Alan Baker, June 21, 2004.

133. See, e.g., Herbert C. Kelman, "Overcoming the Psychological Barrier: An Analysis of the Egyptian-Israeli Peace Process," *Negotiation Journal* 1, no. 3 (July 1985): 224–25; and Stanley F. Reed, "Shaken Pillar," *Foreign Policy*, no. 45 (Winter 1981–82): 175–85.

134. The trade numbers reported by Egypt and Israel to the IMF, which are reproduced in the Gleditsch "Trade and GDP" data set, are so widely discrepant as to be completely unreliable. For example, in 1984, Egyptian exports to Israel were reportedly $369 million, whereas Israeli imports from Egypt, which should be identical, were reportedly only $700,000. Nonetheless, even using the most optimistic figure ($369 million), this amounted to only 0.36% of Egyptian GDP, or well below the levels of postsettlement Franco-German trade reported in chapter 2. Moreover, the percentage using the most optimistic figure drops each year thereafter, suggesting no significant bilateral exchange. Calculated with figures from Gleditsch, "Expanded Trade and GDP Data"; and the associated data set at http://privatewww.essex.ac.uk/~ksg/exptradegdp.html (accessed May 22, 2014). Trade and GDP figures are in current US dollars. To determine exports as a percentage of GDP, current GDP is calculated by multiplying current GDP per capita by the country's population.

135. See Press-Barnathan, *Transitions to Peace*, 39–40.

136. Victor Lavi, "The Economic Embargo of Egypt by Arab States: Myth and Reality," *Middle East Journal* 38, no. 3 (Summer 1984): 419–32.

137. Vikash Yadav, "The Political Economy of the Egyptian-Israeli QIZ Trade Agreement," *Middle East Review of International Affairs* 11, no. 1 (March 2007): 74–96.

138. Press-Barnathan, *Transitions to Peace*, p. 48. She further notes that the Israeli business community also opposed the QIZ, fearing that it would threaten the US-Israel Free Trade Agreement.

139. Charles Grant, "A New Neighbourhood Policy for the EU," *Centre for European Reform Policy Brief*, March 2011, http://www.cer.org.uk/publications/archive/policy-brief/2011/new-neighbourhood-policy-eu (accessed October 12, 2015), 4. On the limited political significance of the institution, which is like "a balloon that lost its air," see Rosa Balfour, "The Transformation of the Union for the Mediterranean," *Mediterranean Politics* 14, no. 1 (March 2009): 99–105, quote at 99.

140. See, e.g., Eberhard Kienle, *A Grand Delusion: Democracy and Economic Reform in Egypt* (London: I. B. Tauris, 2001); and Jason Brownlee, "Democratization in the Arab World? The Decline of Pluralism in Mubarak's Egypt," *Journal of Democracy* 13, no. 4 (October 2002): 6–14.

141. For this reason, Egypt has not ranked higher on the Polity scale than –2 since the peace treaty was signed.

142. See "A Framework for Peace in the Middle East Agreed at Camp David, Signed September 17, 1978," in Harold H. Saunders, *The Other Walls: The Politics of the Arab-Israeli Peace Process* (Washington, DC: American Enterprise Institute, 1985), 166–68.

143. According to the Israeli government, in 2008 there were 1.488 million Arabs living in the State of Israel, amounting to approximately 20% of the Israeli population. "The Arab Population in Israel," http://www.gov.il/FirstGov/NewsEng/NewsEng_ArabPopulation.htm (accessed October 26, 2012).

144. Stein, "Continuity and Change," 303.

145. See, e.g., Dan Eldar, "The Reversible Peace," *Middle East Quarterly* 10, no. 4 (Fall 2003): 57–65; Efraim Karsh, "The Long Trail of Islamic Anti-Semitism," *Israel Affairs* 12, no. 1 (January 2006): 2, 5–7; and Stein, "Continuity and Change," 310–12.

146. Quoted in Stein, "Continuity and Change," 312.

147. Ibid., 307.

148. The deputy head of the Muslim Brotherhood, Rashad al-Bayoumi, for example, declared in January 2012 that a Brotherhood government "will not recognize Israel under any circumstances" and would let the people decide the fate of the 1979 treaty. Jack Khoury, "Egypt's Muslim Brotherhood Plans to Put Treaty with Israel to a Referendum," *Haaretz*, January 2, 2012, http://www.haaretz.com/print-edition/news/egypt-s-muslim-brotherhood-plans-to-put-treaty-with-israel-to-a-referendum-1.404987 (accessed March 6, 2014).

149. Carter Center, *Camp David 25th Anniversary Forum*, 19.

4. The Israeli-Jordanian Treaty

1. Yehuda Lukacs, *Israel, Jordan, and the Peace Process* (Syracuse, NY: Syracuse University Press, 1997), chap. 1; and Avi Shlaim, *Collusion across the Jordan: King Abdullah, the Zionist Movement, and the Partition of Palestine* (New York: Columbia University Press, 1988).

2. Although his aim may have been an interim step to bringing both the Jewish and Arab areas under his control, this still represents a radical departure from other Arab states. Efraim Karsh, "Israel, the Hashemites, and the Palestinians: The Fateful Triangle," *Israel Affairs* 9, no. 3 (Spring 2003): 4–5.

3. Shlaim, *Collusion across the Jordan*; Mary Wilson, *King Abdullah, Britain and the Making of Jordan* (Cambridge: Cambridge University Press, 1987), 161–67; and Yoav Gelber, *Jewish-Transjordanian Relations, 1921–1948* (London: Frank Cass, 1997). For a dissenting view, see Efraim Karsh, "The Collusion That Never Was: King Abdallah, the Jewish Agency, and the Partition of Palestine," *Journal of Contemporary History* 34, no. 4 (October 1999): 569–85.

4. Abdul Salam Majali, Jawad A. Anani, and Munther J. Haddadin, *Peacemaking: The Inside Story of the 1994 Jordanian-Israeli Treaty* (Norman: University of Oklahoma Press, 2006), 79.

5. Mordechai Gazit, "The Israel-Jordan Peace Negotiations (1948–51): King Abdallah's Lonely Effort," *Journal of Contemporary History* 23, no. 3 (July 1988): 409–24; and Naphtali Lau-Lavie, *Moshe Dayan: A Biography* (London: Valentine, Mitchell, 1968), 79–88.

6. Dennis Ross, *The Missing Peace: The Inside Story of the Fight for Middle East Peace* (New York: Farrar, Straus & Giroux, 2004), 165; and Lukacs, *Israel, Jordan, Peace Process*, 16–17.

7. Lukacs documents nine meetings between Hussein and Israeli prime minister Golda Meir between 1969 and the 1973 war. Lukacs, *Israel, Jordan, Peace Process*, 1. On mutual Israeli-Jordan interests, see Mordechai Gazit, *Tahalich Ha'Shalom: 1969–1973* [The peace process: 1969–1973] (Yad Tabenkin, Israel: Kav Ha'adom, 1984), 155.

8. Gazit, *Tahalich Ha'Shalom*, 112–15; Marvin Kalb and Bernard Kalb, *Kissinger* (Boston: Little Brown, 1974), 199–205; and William B. Quandt, Fuad Jabber, and Ann Mosley Lesch, *The Politics of Palestinian Nationalism* (Berkeley: University of California Press, 1973), 127.

9. The Israelis failed to heed the king's warning and were consequently surprised in early October when Syria and Egypt attacked on Yom Kippur. Lukacs, *Israel, Jordan, Peace Process*, 1–4.

10. Ross, *Missing Peace*, 166.

11. Ian Lustick, "Israel and Jordan: The Implications of an Adversarial Partnership," *Policy Papers in International Affairs*, no. 6 (Berkeley: Institute of International Studies, University of California, 1978).

12. On the Intifada, which also helped weaken Israel's international standing, see Don Peretz, *Intifada: The Palestinian Uprising* (Boulder, CO: Westview, 1990).

13. See, e.g., Daniel Baracskay, *The Palestine Liberation Organization: Terrorism and Prospects for Peace in the Holy Land* (New York: Praeger, 2011), 130–59.

14. Karsh, "Israel, Hashemites, Palestinians," 9–10; and Clinton Bailey, *Jordan's Palestinian Challenge, 1948–1983: A Political History* (Boulder, CO: Westview, 1984).

15. See Bruce Borthwick, "Water in Israeli-Jordanian Relations: From Conflict to the Danger of Ecological Disaster," *Israel Studies*. 9, no. 3 (Spring 2003): 165–86.

16. For a detailed discussion of Israeli and Jordanian mutual interests, see Lukacs, *Israel, Jordan, Peace Process*.

17. Marwan Muasher, *The Arab Center: The Promise of Moderation* (New Haven: Yale University Press, 2008), 27–28.

18. "Treaty of Peace between the Hashemite Kingdom of Jordan and the State of Israel," October 26, 1994, http://www.kinghussein.gov.jo/peacetreaty.html; Ross, *Missing Peace*, 186–87; interview with Israeli Supreme Court justice and former head of the Israeli delegation to the Washington peace talks, Elyakim Rubenstein, June 24, 2008.

19. Polity IV data are from http://systemicpeace.org/polity/polity4.htm (accessed May 2, 2011).

20. Bassel Fawzi Salloukh, "Organizing Politics in the Arab World: State-Society Relations and Foreign Policy Choices in Jordan and Syria" (PhD diss., McGill University, 2000), 81. The East Bank region contained a population of just under 700,000, less than half of Amman's 1,576,000, yet it was allocated thirty-seven parliamentary seats, or more than twice the eighteen seats allocated to Amman. See Ellen Lust-Okar, "Elections under Authoritarianism: Preliminary Lessons from Jordan," *Democratization* 13, no. 3 (June 2006): 463. Population statistics are drawn from the Hashemite Kingdom of Jordan Department of Statistics, "The Preliminary Results of the Population and Housing Census, 2004," http://www.dos.gov.jo/census2004/page1_e.htm (accessed August 23, 2010; no longer available).

21. Laurie A. Brand observes, "On issues of foreign policy, the king, the crown prince, the prime minister, and the chief of the royal court are the decision-making circle. The cabinet, as a body, is not involved, although its members may be consulted for their reactions or comments." *Jordan's Inter-Arab Relations: The Political Economy of Alliance Making* (New York: Columbia University Press, 1994), 65. Another study notes that King Hussein was "the ultimate decision maker in the realm of foreign policy." Ali E. Hillal Dessouki and Karen Abul Kheir, "Foreign Policy as a Strategic National Asset: The Case of Jordan," in *The Foreign Policies of Arab States: The Challenge of Globalization*, ed. Baghat Korany and Ali E. Hillal Dessouki (Cairo: American University of Cairo Press, 2008), 267. See also Salloukh, *Organizing Politics*, 75.

22. Beverley Milton-Edwards, "Façade Democracy and Jordan," *British Journal of Middle Eastern Studies* 20, no. 2 (November 1993): 199; and Quintan Wiktorowic, "Civil Society as Social Control: State Power in Jordan," *Comparative Politics* 33, no. 1 (October 2000): 43–61.

23. Avi Shlaim, "Israeli Politics and Middle East Peacemaking," *Journal of Palestinian Studies* 24, no. 4 (Summer 1995): 30. Majali, Anani, and Haddadin similarly note "success on the Jordanian track was welcomed by all Israelis with the exception of a few ultra-religious groups. The Israeli government did not need to invest in any rigorous publicity campaigns to win support for its plan to make peace with Jordan." Majali, Anani, and Haddadin, *Peacemaking*, 179.

24. BBC News, *On This Day, 1950–2005*, "1994: Israel and Jordan Make Peace," http://news.bbc.co.uk/onthisday/hi/dates/stories/october/26/newsid_3764000/3764162.stm (accessed May 22, 2012); and W. Andrew Terrill, *Global Security Watch—Jordan* (Santa Barbara, CA: ABC-Clio/Praeger, 2010), 58.

25. Tamar S. Hermann, *The Israeli Peace Movement: A Shattered Dream* (New York: Cambridge University Press, 2009), 120n.

26. Hilal Khashan, "Arab Attitudes toward Israel and Peace," Washington Institute Policy Focus no. 40 (August 2000) http://www.washingtoninstitute.org/policy-analysis/view/arab-attitudes-toward-israel-and-peace (accessed May 2014), 7–8.

27. Shlaim, "Israeli Politics," 30. William B. Quandt similarly observes that the king "was ahead of his populace in his readiness to open a new page in relations with Israel." *Peace Process: American Diplomacy and the Arab-Israeli Conflict since 1967*, 3rd ed. (Washington, DC: Brookings Institution, 2005), 334. For the 1994 public opinion survey of 150 Jordanian professionals, see Hilal Khashan, "Partner or Pariah: Attitudes toward Israel in Syria, Lebanon, and Jordan," Policy Papers no. 41 (Washington, DC: Washington Institute for Near East Policy, 1996), 10. The survey indicated that 66% of Jordanian professionals supported peace talks with Israel. Of these professionals, however, 71% opposed normalization of economic relations with Israel (41% strongly opposed) (31).

28. In 1993, almost half of the official population of Jordan (over 1.5 million of Jordan's total population of 3.7 million) consisted of West Bank Palestinians who came under Jordanian jurisdiction when Jordan annexed the West Bank after the 1948–49 Arab-Israeli war or as Palestinian refugees from the 1967 war. This Palestinian population was augmented by nearly 400,000 Palestinians expelled from the Gulf states after Arafat and the PLO supported Saddam Hussein during the Gulf War. Jean-Marc F. Blanchard and Norrin M. Ripsman, *Economic Statecraft and Foreign Policy: Sanctions, Incentives, and Target State Calculations* (London: Routledge, 2013), 47; Howard Adelman, "The Palestinian Diaspora," in *The Cambridge Survey of World Migration*, ed. Robin Cohen (Cambridge: Cambridge University Press, 1995), 414–16; and Don Peretz, *Palestinians, Refugees, and the Middle East Peace Process* (Washington, DC: United States Institute of Peace, 1993), 14–17.

29. Laura Zittrain Eisenberg and Neil Caplan, "The Israel-Jordan Peace Treaty: Patterns of Negotiation, Problems of Implementation," *Israel Affairs* 9, no. 3 (Spring 2003): 100.

30. Paul L. Scham and Russell E. Lucas observed that "the Balqa refugee camp—a barometer of Palestinian opinion in Jordan—witnessed demonstrations against the accord." Paul L. Scham and Russell E. Lucas, " 'Normalization' and 'Anti-Normalization' in Jordan: The Public Debate," *Middle East Review of International Affairs* 5, no. 3 (September 2001): 57.

31. Khashan, "Partner or Pariah," 10. This 1993 study did not include non-Palestinian Jordanians nor nonprofessional Palestinians. Nonetheless, since the study canvassed urban professionals—the most cosmopolitan and, therefore, those most likely to support peacemaking—we can surmise that the rest of Jordan's Palestinian population was at least comparably opposed to peace with Israel.

32. Majali, Anani, and Haddadin, *Peacemaking*, 71, 81–84. Khashan's polling data also confirmed that the more religious the respondent, the less likely he/she was to support the peace process. Khashan, "Partner or Pariah," 14.

33. Eisenberg and Caplan, "Israel-Jordan Peace Treaty," 87.

34. On the vote, see Terrill, *Global Security Watch—Jordan*, 58. On the king's domination of the legislature, see Curtis R. Ryan, "Hashimite Kingdom of Jordan," in *The Government and Politics of the Middle East and North Africa*, 5th ed., ed. D. E. Long, B. Reich, and M. Gasiorowski (Boulder, CO: Westview, 2007), 304; and Salloukh, *Organizing Politics*, 81.

35. Salloukh, *Organizing Politics*, 393–95; Scham and Lucas, " 'Normalization' and 'Anti-Normalization'," 145–46; and interview with Asher Susser, Tel Aviv University, May 7, 2008.

36. Nigel Ashton: *King Hussein of Jordan: A Political Life* (New Haven: Yale University Press, 2008), 301.

37. Russell E. Lucas, "Jordan: The Death of Normalization with Israel," *Middle East Journal* 58, no. 1 (Winter 2004): 94–95.

38. The ban was prompted by a five-thousand-strong demonstration in Amman against the treaty days before its official signature. For a nondemocratic regime with a small population, that represented a considerable protest. The Islamic Action Front, the political arm of the Muslim Brotherhood, had planned larger protests for the following day but were prevented by the strictly enforced ban. "Jordanian Police Stage Security Crackdown after Large Moslem Demo," *Jerusalem Post*, October 27, 1994 (accessed through LexisNexis, September 27, 2010); "Opposition Protests

in Amman against Peace Treaty," *BBC News*, October 27, 1994 (accessed through LexisNexis, September 27, 2010). On other forms of protest, see Scham and Lucas, "'Normalization' and 'Anti-Normalization.'"

39. "Opposition Statement Rejects Peace Treaty; Massive Protests Planned," *BBC News Summary of World Broadcasts*, October 27, 1994 (accessed through LexisNexis, September 27, 2010).

40. P. V. Vivekanand, "Majority of Jordanians Support Washington Declaration, Poll Finds," *Jordan Times*, August 25–26, 1994, 1.

41. Interview with Eynat Shlein-Michael, second secretary for Political Affairs and acting commercial attaché at the Israeli embassy in Amman, 1995–97, February 14, 2008; interview with Asher Susser, May 7, 2008; and Danishai Kornbluth, "Jordan and the Anti-Normalization Campaign, 1994–2001," *Terrorism and Political Violence* 14, no. 3 (Autumn 2002): 91.

42. Interview with Tuvia Israeli, director, Jordan Department, Israeli foreign ministry, June 18, 2008.

43. On the Arab boycott, see Gil Feiler, *From Boycott to Economic Cooperation: The Arab Boycott of Israel* (London: Taylor & Francis, 1998).

44. See Kristian S. Gleditsch, "Expanded Trade and GDP Data," *Journal of Conflict Resolution* 46, no. 5 (October 2002): 712–24; and the associated data set at http://privatewww.essex.ac.uk/~ksg/exptradegdp.html (accessed May 22, 2014), which utilizes IMF data. Zero trade might be a slight underestimate, but it clearly implies that the two states did not trade significantly before the treaty.

45. Galia Press-Barnathan, *The Political Economy of Transitions to Peace: A Comparative Perspective* (Pittsburgh, PA: University of Pittsburgh Press, 2009), 57; and "Treaty of Peace between the Hashemite Kingdom of Jordan and the State of Israel," article 7.

46. For discussions of the prospects for economic cooperation between Israel and Jordan at the time of the treaty, see Nadav Halevi, *Trade Links between Israel and Jordan: Prospects and Considerations* (Tel Aviv: Armand Hammer Fund for Economic Cooperation in the Middle East, 1994); and Arie Arnon, Avia Spivak, and J. Weinblatt, "The Potential for Trade between Israel, the Palestinians, and Jordan," *World Economy* 19, no. 1 (January 1996): 113–34.

47. Muhammad Azhar, "Phosphate Exports by Jordan," *Arab Studies Quarterly*. 22, no. 4 (Fall 2000): 59–80; and World Bank, *Peace and the Jordanian Economy* (Washington, DC: International Bank for Reconstruction and Development, 1994), 22.

48. Ambassador Shamir, for example, noted that Jordanian business interests, and even the Jordanian government, "feared that Israelis would buy out all of Jordan." Interview with Shimon Shamir, Israeli ambassador to Jordan, 1995–97, June 25, 2008; interview with former Canadian ambassador to Jordan Mike Molloy, November 7, 2008; and Patrick Clawson and Zoe Danon Gedal, *Dollars and Diplomacy: The Impact of US Economic Initiatives on Arab-Israeli Negotiations*, (Washington, DC: Washington Institute for Near East Policy, 1999), 12.

49. See Lucas, "Jordan," 95.

50. Asher Susser, "Jordan," in *Middle East Contemporary Survey*, vol. 19, *1995*, ed. Bruce Maddy-Weitzman (Boulder, CO: Westview Press, 1997), 391–92; and Kornbluth, "Anti-Normalization Campaign," 88–93.

51. Howard Rosen, "Free Trade Agreements as Foreign Policy Tools: The US-Israel and US-Jordan FTAs, in *Free Trade Agreements: US Strategies and Priorities*, ed. Jeffrey J. Schott (Washington, DC: Institute for International Economics, 2004), 60; and Steven E. Lobell, "The Second Face of American Security: The US-Jordan Free Trade Agreement as Security Policy," *Comparative Strategy* 27, no. 1 (2008): 1–13.

52. The idea actually came from Jordanian businessman Omar Salah and Israeli businessman Dov Lautman, who lobbied the US State Department and the White House. This occurred after the treaty's signature, though. Markus E. Bouillon, "The Failure of Big Business: On the Socio-Economic Reality of the Middle East Peace Process," *Mediterranean Politics* 9, no.1 (Spring 2004): 9–10. Moreover, far from representing the Jordanian business community, Salah was initially shunned in Jordan, and the products produced in Irbid, the first QIZ, were initially boycotted in Jordan. Jessica Steinberg, "An Unusual Commute Leads to a Different Kind of Partnership," *New York Times*, September 20, 2000, http://partners.nytimes.com/library/tech/00/09/biztech/technology/20steinberg.html (accessed May 18, 2014). Thus, the QIZ

cannot be interpreted as evidence that the Jordanian business community anticipated economic gains through peacemaking.

53. Interview with Elyakim Rubenstein, June 24, 2008; interview with then Israeli ambassador to Canada and former legal adviser to the Israeli foreign ministry and member of the Israeli negotiating delegation Alan Baker, August 22, 2008; and interview with Justice Aun al-Khasawneh of the International Criminal Court, December 16, 2008. All three participated in these consultations.

54. Ross, *Missing Peace*, 186–87.

55. See, e.g., Itamar Rabinovich, *Waging Peace: Israel and the Arabs, 1948–2003* (Princeton: Princeton University Press, 2004), 59.

56. Martin Indyk, *Innocent Abroad: An Intimate Account of American Peace Diplomacy in the Middle East* (New York: Simon & Schuster, 2009), 94.

57. Interview with Shimon Shamir, June 25, 2008.

58. Interview with Daniel Kurtzer, former US ambassador to Israel and Egypt and member of the Near East bureau of the US State Department, November 11, 2012. Ambassador Shamir also emphasized that "a stable Jordan is a constant Israeli interest." Interview with Shimon Shamir, June 25, 2008.

59. Yoram Peri, afterword, in *The Rabin Memoirs* by Yitzhak Rabin, (Berkeley: University of California Press, 1979), 365–66.

60. Efraim Inbar, *Rabin and Israel's National Security* (Washington, DC: Johns Hopkins University Press, 1999), 137–39.

61. Quandt, *Peace Process*, 331; and Indyk, *Innocent Abroad*, 168n.

62. Interview with Shimon Shamir, June 25, 2008.

63. Dessouki and Kheir, "Foreign Policy," 254.

64. See, e.g., Eisenberg and Caplan, "Israel-Jordan Peace Treaty," 99.

65. Indyk, *Innocent Abroad*, 94.

66. Indyk, *Innocent Abroad*, 94. King Hussein had been worried since Arafat's 1970 uprising that PLO nationalism might attempt to overthrow the Jordanian monarchy. Asher Susser, *Israel, Jordan, and the Palestinians: The Two-State Imperative* (Waltham, MA: Brandeis University Press, 2012), 177.

67. Interview with Daniel Kurtzer, November 11, 2012. Deputy chief of the Jordanian embassy in Washington Hamid Walid told me that "from an analytical point of view of the border and demographic factors, Jordan had to be on board in the Oslo agreement." Interview with Hamid Walid, Jordanian embassy, Washington, DC, February 20, 2008.

68. M. Akif Kumral, "Hashemite Survival Strategy: The Anatomy of Peace, Security and Alliance Making in Jordan," master's thesis, Naval Postgraduate Institute, Monterey, CA, June 2000, http://www.dtic.mil/cgi-bin/GetTRDoc?Location=U2&doc=GetTRDoc.pdf&AD=ADA379647 (accessed March 13, 2012), 6.

69. Clawson and Gedal, *Dollars and Diplomacy*, 35; Interview with Jordanian ambassador to the United Nations Mohammed al-Allaf, November 5, 2007; and Asher Susser, "Jordan: Al-Mamlaka al-Urdunniyya al-Hashimiyya," in *Middle East Contemporary Survey 1993*, vol. 17, ed. Ami Ayalon (Boulder, CO: Westview Press, 1995), 473. The American appeal was not terribly successful, and Jordanians feel they did not receive economic rewards for the peace treaty that were in any way comparable to those given to Egypt for its treaty with Israel. Interview with Hamid Walid, February 20, 2008.

70. Indyk, *Innocent Abroad*, 127; and Majali, Anani, and Haddadin, *Peacemaking*, 248.

71. Indyk, *Innocent Abroad*, 128–29.

72. King Hussein of Jordan, "Remarks on the Peace Process, Amman, 9 July 1994," *Journal of Palestine Studies* 24, no. 1 (Autumn 1994): 135.

73. Ross, *Missing Peace*, 171–75.

74. Indyk, *Innocent Abroad*, 127.

75. Anthony H. Cordesman, *After the Storm: The Changing Military Balance in the Middle East* (Boulder, CO: Westview, 1993), 288–89.

76. Risa Brooks, *Political-Military Relations and the Stability of Arab Regimes*, Adelphi Paper 324 (London: International Institute Strategic Studies, 1998), 31.

77. King Hussein of Jordan, "Remarks on the Peace Process, Amman, 9 July 1994," 135; Rabinovich, *Waging Peace*, 60; Aaron David Miller, *The Much Too Promised Land: America's Elusive Search for Arab-Israeli Peace* (New York: Bantam Books, 2009), 215; interview with Mohammed al-Allaf, November 5, 2007; and interview with Hamid Walid, February 20, 2008. Justice al-Khasawneh confirmed that "the Iraq war was a major issue. . . . The Jordanian government thought, in the aftermath of the Iraq War, that it had lost almost all of its traditional allies. Therefore, Jordan believed that its salvation lay on this path [i.e., a peace treaty with Israel]." Interview with Aun al-Khasawneh, December 16, 2008.

78. Indyk, *Innocent Abroad*, 19; and Terrill, *Global Security Watch—Jordan*, 81.

79. Inbar, *Rabin and Israel's National Security*, 50–51.

80. See, e.g., the degree of interest and coordination discussed throughout Majali, Anani, and Haddadin's *Peacemaking*.

81. Interview with former United States envoy to the Middle East, Dennis Ross, February 14, 2008.

82. This paragraph draws from Blanchard and Ripsman, *Economic Statecraft and Foreign Policy*, chap. 2.

83. Ziad Swaidan and Mihai Nica, "The 1991 Gulf War and Jordan's Economy," *Middle East Review of International Affairs* 6, no. 2 (June 2002): 70; Curtis R. Ryan, "Jordan in the Middle East Peace Process: From War to Peace with Israel," in *The Middle East Peace Process: Interdisciplinary Perspectives*, ed. Ilan Peleg (Albany: SUNY Press, 1998), 167; and Press-Barnathan, *Transitions to Peace*, 60.

84. Mohamad Amerah, Mohammad Khasanweh, Nabih Nabhani, and Fawzi Sadeq, *Unemployment in Jordan: Dimension and Prospects* (Amman: Centre for International Studies, 1993), 8.

85. Curtis R. Ryan, "Peace, Bread, and Riots: Jordan and the International Monetary Fund," *Middle East Policy* 6, no. 2 (October 1998): 54–66.

86. World Bank, *Peace and the Jordanian Economy*, 8–9; and Press-Barnathan, *Transitions to Peace*, 61–62.

87. Majali, Anani, and Haddadin, *Peacemaking*, 128–29.

88. Ashton, *King Hussein of Jordan*, 304–5.

89. King Hussein of Jordan, "Remarks on the Peace Process, Amman, 9 July 1994," 134; and Indyk, *Innocent Abroad*, 130.

90. Ziv Rubinovitz, "Blue and White 'Black September': Israel's Role in the Jordan Crisis of 1970," *International History Review* 32, no. 4 (December 2010): 687–706; and Ashton, *King Hussein of Jordan*, 148–54.

91. Counselor Shlein-Michael thus stressed that "every Jordanian government knows that Jordanian stability is a fundamental Israeli interest." Interview with Eynat Shlein-Michael, February 14, 2008. Deputy Chief of Mission Walid thus recalled of the treaty that, whereas for Egypt peace with Israel was a national security issue, "for Jordan it was a critical issue of survival of the people and state." Interview with Hamid Walid, February 20, 2008.

92. Ross, *Missing Peace*, 165–66; interview with Tuvia Israeli, November 5, 2007; and interview with Dennis Ross, February 14, 2008. Ross also emphasized that King Hussein was eager to fulfill his grandfather's destiny by making peace with Israel. It seems implausible that such an emotional motivation would trump the more practical motivations for peacemaking outlined in this section—especially for a practical man like King Hussein, who had no compunction about joining the Arab preparations for war against Israel in 1967 in the anticipation of sharing in the spoils of victory. See Karsh, "Israel, Hashemites, Palestinians," 8.

93. Interview with Mohammed al-Allaf, November 5, 2007; and Terrill, *Global Security Watch—Jordan*, 58.

94. Former Jordanian foreign minister (2002–4) Marwan Muasher recalled: "One most important aspect of a treaty for Jordan was existential in nature. Jordan is not a Palestinian homeland. Since Israel agreed to an Eastern border, therefore, Jordan was clearly not the Palestinian homeland." Interview with senior vice-president of the World Bank (External Affairs) Marwan Muasher, September 23, 2008. See also Joseph Nevo, "The Jordanian-Israeli Peace: The View from Amman," in *The Middle East Peace Process: Vision Versus Reality*, ed. Joseph Ginat, Edward Joseph Perkins, and Edwin G. Corr (Norman: University of Oklahoma Press, 2002), 172.

95. Interview with Dennis Ross, November 14, 2008. See also, Susser, *Israel, Jordan, Palestinians*, 188; and Indyk, *Innocent Abroad*, 126, 140–41n. Indeed, Indyk reports that Rabin made this threat explicitly to King Hussein: "Unless he was now ready to negotiate a full peace treaty with Israel, there would be no role for Jordan in the peace process" (95).

96. Efraim Halevy, *Man in the Shadows* (London: Weidenfeld & Nicolson, 1966), 82–83.

97. Interview with Asher Susser, May 7, 2008. Susser is an Israeli political scientist who was personally involved in peacemaking due to his contacts with the Jordanian leadership.

98. Interview with former Mossad director (1998–2002; deputy director, 1990–95) Efraim Halevy, June 24, 2008.

99. Interview with Tuvia Israeli, November 5, 2007; interview with Asher Susser, May 7, 2008; and Scham and Lucas, " 'Normalization' and 'Anti-Normalization,' " 62–63.

100. See, e.g., King Hussein's angry March 9, 1997, letter to Israeli prime minister Benjamin Netanyahu, reproduced in Avi Shlaim, *Lion of Jordan: The Life of King Hussein in War and Peace* (New York: Knopf, 2008), 574–75; Lukacs, *Israel, Jordan, Peace Process*, 200–202; and interview with Efraim Halevy, June 24, 2008.

101. Interview with Mohammed al-Allaf, November 5, 2007; interview with Shimon Shamir, June 25, 2008; Lucas, "Jordan," 97–99; and Majali, Anani, and Haddadin, *Peacemaking*, 314–19. On the political consequences of the Mashal assassination attempt, see P. R. Kumaraswamy, "Israel, Jordan, and the Masha'al Affair," *Israel Affairs* 9, no. 3 (Spring 2003): 113–15.

102. Operation Cast Lead was Israel's December 2008 military operation to stop Hamas rocket attacks from the Gaza Strip against Israeli civilian targets.

103. "After 3 Years, Jordan Appoints New Ambassador to Israel," *Al-Monitor*, September 30, 2012, http://www.al-monitor.com/pulse/politics/2012/09/king-abdullah-believes-netanyahu.html# (accessed February 22, 2014); and "Peace Monitor," *Journal of Palestine Studies* 30, no. 2 (Winter 2001): 140.

104. Ariel Ben Solomon and Daniel K. Eisenbud, "Jordanian Parliament Calls to Expel Israeli Envoy," *Jerusalem Post*, May 8, 2013, http://www.jpost.com/Diplomacy-and-Politics/Jordanian-parliament-asks-govt-to-expel-Israeli-ambassador-312480 (accessed May 19, 2014); and "Jordan MPs Vote to Expel Israeli Ambassador in Jerusalem Holy Site Row," *Guardian*, February 26, 2014, http://www.theguardian.com/world/2014/feb/26/jordan-expels-israeli-ambassador-jerusalem-holy-site-row (accessed May 19, 2014).

105. On the evolving Israeli national security environment, which features improving relations with "first ring" states, such as Jordan and Egypt, but serious threats from "second ring" states with nuclear aspirations, namely Iraq and Iran, see Efraim Inbar, *Israel's National Security: Issues and Challenges since the Yom Kippur War* (Abingdon, UK: Routledge, 2008), 108–14.

106. Quote from Terrill, *Global Security Watch—Jordan*, 75. On the importance of the United States to Jordanian grand strategy, see Robert B. Satloff, "The Jekyll-and-Hyde Origins of the US-Jordanian Strategic Relationship," in *The Middle East and the United States: Historical and Political Reassessment*, ed. David W. Lesch (Boulder, CO: Westview Press, 1996), 114–24, esp. 115–19; and Terrill, *Global Security Watch—Jordan*, chap. 4.

107. See, e.g., Dessouki and Kheir, "Foreign Policy," 278; International Crisis Group, "Red Alert in Jordan: Recurrent Unrest in Maan," International Crisis Group Middle East Briefing, February 19, 2003, http://www.crisisgroup.org/~/media/Files/Middle%20East%20North%20Africa/Iran%20Gulf/Jordan/B005%20Red%20Alert%20In%20Jordan%20Recurrent%20Unrest%20In%20Maan.pdf ; and Bill Spindle and Suha Philip Ma'ayeh, "Jordanians Call for End to Monarchy," *Wall Street Journal*, November 16, 2012, http://online.wsj.com/news/articles/SB10001424127887324556304578122784202064810 (accessed May 2014).

108. Press-Barnathan, *Transitions to Peace*, 58.

109. Bouillon, "Failure of Big Business," 9; and interview with Asher Susser, May 7, 2008.

110. There are wide discrepancies in the IMF data on Israeli-Jordanian trade, as the figures reported by the two countries do not agree. Gleditsch, "Expanded Trade and GDP Data," 712–24; and the associated data set at http://privatewww.essex.ac.uk/~ksg/exptradegdp.html (accessed May 22, 2014).

111. Post-2000 trade figures in this chapter are from International Monetary Fund, *Direction of Trade Statistics* [Custom Table], https://www.imf.org/external/pubs/cat/longres.cfm?sk=19305.0

(accessed January 7, 2014). Trade as a percentage of GDP is calculated with GDP per capita figures from The World Bank, World Development Indicators (year). *GDP per capita* [data file], http://data.worldbank.org/indicator/NY.GDP.PCAP.CD (accessed May 22, 2014) and population figures from The World Bank, World Development Indicators (year). *Population* [data file], http://data.worldbank.org/indicator/SP.POP.TOTL?page=2 (accessed May 22, 2014). These figures must be taken with a grain of salt, given that Israeli figures differ. Nonetheless, it is clear that bilateral trade never amounted to very much. See also Vikash Yadav, "The Political Economy of the Egyptian-Israeli QIZ Trade Agreement," *Middle East Review of International Affairs* 11, no. 1 (March 2007): 77–78.

112. Yadav, "QIZ Trade Agreement," 77–78.

113. Avraham Sela, "Politics, Identity and Peacemaking: The Arab Discourse on Peace with Israel in the 1990s," *Israel Studies* 10, no. 2 (Summer 2005): 29.

114. See, e.g., Sela, "Politics, Identity, Peacemaking," 35; and Kornbluth, "Anti-Normalization Campaign," 91.

115. Lucas, "Jordan," 101.

116. "The Free Arab Voice," February 12, 2001, http://www.freearabvoice.org/ArabZion istConflictInJordan.htm (accessed March 11, 2013); interview with Marwan Muasher, September 23, 2008; and interview with Mike Molloy, November 7, 2008.

117. Interview with Eynat Shlein-Michael, November 14, 2008.

118. Bouillon, "Failure of Big Business," 9.

119. Kornbluth, "Anti-Normalization Campaign," 80.

120. I thank Assaf David for bringing this to my attention.

121. Clawson and Gedal, *Dollars and Diplomacy*, 35–36.

122. "Arms Control and Regional Security in the Middle East (ACRS)," http://cns.miis.edu/inventory/pdfs/acrs.pdf (accessed March 13, 2012); and "Middle East Peace Process Arms Control and Regional Security (ACRS) Working Group," fact sheet, July 1, 2001, Online Archives of the US Department of State, http://2001-2009.state.gov/t/pm/rls/fs/4271.htm (accessed February 21, 2014).

123. "Polity IV Project, *Political Regime Characteristics and Transitions, 1800–2010,*" http://www.systemicpeace.org/inscr/inscr.htm (accessed March 10, 2012); and Monty G. Marshall, Keith Jaggers, and Ted Robert Gurr, "Political Regime Characteristics and Transitions, 1800–2010: Dataset Users' Manual," http://www.systemicpeace.org/inscr/p4manualv2010.pdf, pp. 13–16 (accessed March 10, 2012).

124. Quintan Wiktorowicz, "The Limits of Democracy in the Middle East: The Case of Jordan," *Middle East Journal* 53, no. 4 (Autumn 1999): 615–17; Salloukh, *Organizing Politics*, 393–94; and Ashton, *King Hussein of Jordan*, 334. Notably, the king had high-profile treaty opponent Layth Shubaylat imprisoned for "defaming the monarchy and instituting sedition." Kornbluth, "Anti-Normalization Campaign," 92; and Ryan, "Jordan in the Middle East Peace Process," 173–74.

125. Clawson and Gedal, *Dollars and Diplomacy*, 40; and interview with Tuvia Israeli, November 5, 2007.

126. Interview with Tuvia Israeli, November 5, 2007.

127. On the Israeli attitude toward peace with Jordan, see Ashton, *King Hussein of Jordan*, 323. This arm's-length relationship is, in large measure, fueled by obstacles to intersocietal conflict in the form of Jordanian economic and cultural shunning of those who normalize with Israel and Israeli security restrictions and the difficulty with which Israel grants visas to Jordanians who wish to travel to Israel, which impede cultural, educational, and social exchanges. Interview with Tuvia Israeli, June 18, 2008; Assaf David, "Jordanian-Israeli Relations," October 28, 2009, *Middle East Progress*, http://www.middleeastprogress.org/?p=4485&preview=true (accessed February 22, 2014).

128. Mark Tessler and Jodi Nachtwey, "Islam and Attitudes toward International Conflict: Evidence from Survey Research in the Arab World," *Journal of Conflict Resolution* 42, no. 5 (October 1998): 632–33; and Kornbluth, "Anti-Normalization Campaign," 84–86.

129. According to a 2000 survey of Arab states, only 27% of Jordanian students and businesspeople surveyed reported that they "want peace" with Israel, while 70.5 "did not want it."

Hilal Khashan, "Arab Attitudes toward Israel and Peace," Policy Focus, no. 40, August 2000, Washington Institute for Near East Policy, 27. In a 1998 poll, over 87% of Jordanian students questioned opposed normalization with Israel. Clawson and Gedal, *Dollars and Diplomacy*, 12.

130. Sela, "Politics, Identity, Peacemaking," 39.

131. Marc Lynch, *State Interests and Public Spheres: The International Politics of Jordan's Identity* (New York: Columbia University Press, 1999), 205–15.

132. Lucas, "Jordan," 108.

133. Interview with Mohammed al-Allaf, November 5, 2007.

134. Press-Barnathan, *Transitions to Peace*, 58.

135. Ashton, *King Hussein of Jordan*, 335.

5. Other Twentieth-Century Cases

1. Paul F. Diehl and Gary Goertz, *War and Peace in Enduring Rivalries* (Ann Arbor: University of Michigan Press, 2000), 145–46.

2. Ronald Bruce St. John, "The Ecuador-Peru Boundary Dispute: The Road to Settlement," *IBRU Boundary and Territory Briefing* 3, no. 1 (January 1999): 3; and Georg Maier, "The Boundary Dispute between Ecuador and Peru," *American Journal of International Law* 63, no. 1 (January 1969): 30.

3. St. John, "Ecuador-Peru Boundary Dispute," 3–4.

4. Ibid., 9–17; Monica Herz and João Pontes Nogueira, *Ecuador vs. Peru: Peacemaking amid Rivalry* (Boulder, CO: Lynne Rienner, 2002), 30–31; and L. A. Wright, "A Study of the Conflict between the Republics of Peru and Ecuador," *Geographical Journal* 98, no. 258 (November–December 1941): 269.

5. Isaiah Bowman, "The Peru-Ecuador Boundary Dispute," *Foreign Affairs* 20, no. 4 (July 1942): 757–58. On the role of the guarantors, see Beth A. Simmons, "Territorial Disputes and Their Resolution: The Case of Ecuador and Peru," *Peaceworks*, no. 27 (Washington, DC: United States Institute of Peace, 1999), 8.

6. Specifically, a US Army aerial survey indicated that the Cenepa River, rather than being small and inconsequential, was actually 190 kilometers long and constituted a second *divortium aquarum* between the Santiago and Zamora Rivers, in contradiction to article 8 of the Rio Protocol. Ronald Bruce St. John, "Conflict in the Cordillera del Condor: The Ecuador-Peru Dispute," *IBRU Boundary and Security Bulletin* (Spring 1996): 79; and David Scott Palmer, "Overcoming the Weight of History: 'Getting to Yes' in the Peru-Ecuador Border Dispute," *Diplomacy & Statecraft* 12, no. 2 (June 2001): 33.

7. St. John, "Cordillera del Condor," 80.

8. Ibid., 81.

9. Herz and Nogueira, *Ecuador vs. Peru*, 36–47; and David R. Mares and David Scott Palmer, *Power, Institutions, and Leadership in War and Peace: Lessons from Peru and Ecuador, 1995–1998* (Austin: University of Texas Press, 2012), 36–41.

10. Alan K. Henrikson, "Facing across Borders: The Diplomacy of Bon Voisinage," *International Political Science Review* 21, no. 2 (April 2000): 139.

11. Mares and Palmer, *Power, Institutions, Leadership*, 139, 142–43. It has proved impossible for me to access Ecuadorian public opinion polls on this issue.

12. Diana Jean Schemo, "3 Years after War, Ecuador and Peru Agree to Peace Talks," *New York Times*, January 20, 1998, http://www.nytimes.com/1998/01/20/world/3-years-after-war-ecuador-and-peru-agree-to-peace-talks.html (accessed September 2, 2013).

13. When asked their opinion of the treaty between Peru and Ecuador in October 1998 those who responded "I approve of it totally" and "It was not what I wanted, but I approve of it" totaled 45%, whereas those who responded "I don't like it, I don't approve of it, but we must accept it" and "It must be rejected" totaled 52%. In November those numbers were 43% approving it; 54% disapproving it. In December, those who disapproved still formed a 52% to 46% majority. Only in January 1999 did those who approved of the treaty (52%) outnumber those who disapproved (46%). Apoyo Opinión y Mercado, *Informe de Opinión* (Lima: Apoyo Opinión y Mercado, 1999).

14. Palmer, "Overcoming Weight of History," 41; and "Ecuador-Peru: Five Dead in Protests against Peace Accord," Inter Press Service News Agency, October 26, 1998, http://ipsnews2.wpengine.com/1998/10/ecuador-peru-five-dead-in-protests-against-peace-accord (accessed October 4, 2013).

15. On the softening of Ecuadorian attitudes in which 49% of the population continued to see Peru as an enemy state, see Simmons, "Territorial Disputes," 17–18.

16. IMF trade data, as reported by Gleditsch, has some wide discrepancies between trade figures reported by the two countries. For example, Ecuadorian exports to Peru in 1998 are reported to be $199 million (or less than 0.5% of Ecuadorian GDP), whereas Peruvian imports from Ecuador are reported to be only $72 million (or less than 0.2% of GDP). There is greater agreement on Peruvian exports to Ecuador, which amounted to about $100 million, or less than 0.01% of GDP. Even with the more optimistic numbers, bilateral trade was quite low and not terribly important for either country. Unless otherwise indicated (for years before 1945 and after 2000), all trade and GDP figures in this chapter are calculated in current dollars with figures from Kristian S. Gleditsch, "Expanded Trade and GDP Data," *Journal of Conflict Resolution* 46, no. 5 (October 2002): 712–24; and the associated data set at http://privatewww.essex.ac.uk/~ksg/exptradegdp.html (accessed May 22, 2014). Where there is a discrepancy between the trade figures reported by the two partners, I have selected figures only for years where the disagreement does not exceed 10% of the reported total and have then averaged the figures reported for each country. To determine exports as a percentage of GDP, current GDP is calculated by multiplying current GDP per capita by the country's population.

17. Henrikson, "Facing across Borders," 139.

18. This amount was insignificant for countries with an annual GDP of $18 billion (Ecuador) and $59 billion (Peru). Mares and Palmer, *Power, Institutions, Leadership*, 126, 163.

19. Simmons, "Territorial Disputes," 18.

20. St. John, "Ecuador-Peru Boundary Dispute," 42n.

21. Clare Ribando, *Organization of American States: A Primer* (Washington, DC: Library of Congress Congressional Research Service, 2005), http://oai.dtic.mil/oai/oai?verb=getRecord&metadataPrefix=html&identifier=ADA457489 (accessed October 30, 2013), 2. See also Richard E. Feinberg, *Summitry in the Americas: A Progress Report* (Washington, DC: Institute for International Economics, 1997); and Andrew Fenton Cooper and Thomas Legler, "A Model for the Future?" *Journal of Democracy* 12, no. 4 (October 2001): 124.

22. Mauricio Baquero-Herrera, "The Andean Community: Finding Her Feet within Changing and Challenging Multidimensional Conditions," *Law and Business Review of the Americas* 10, no. 3 (Summer 2004): 577–612, esp. 577–78.

23. Palmer, "Overcoming Weight of History," 35–38; and Simmons, "Territorial Disputes," 8–9, 13. On the utility of US military-to-military contacts with Peru and Ecuador to defuse tensions in 1998, see Donald E. Schulz, "The United States and Latin America: Shaping an Elusive Future," *Small Wars and Insurgencies*, vol. 11, no. 3 (Winter 2000): 71.

24. Palmer, "Overcoming Weight of History," 39–40.

25. Ronald Bruce St. John, "Ecuador-Peru Endgame," *IBRU Boundary and Security Bulletin* (Winter 1998–99): 84. See also Manpreet Sethi, "Novel Ways of Settling Border Disputes: The Peru-Ecuador Case," *Strategic Analysis* 23, no. 10 (January 2000): 1776.

26. Luis I. Jacome H., "The Late 1990s Financial Crisis in Ecuador: Institutional Weakness, Fiscal Rigidities, and Financial Dollarization at Work," IMF Working Paper WP/04/12, January 2004, International Monetary Fund, http://www.imf.org/external/pubs/ft/wp/2004/wp0412.pdf (accessed October 5, 2013), 37.

27. Sethi, "Settling Border Disputes," 1775. See also International Crisis Group, "Ecuador: Overcoming Instability?" *Latin American Report* 22 (August 7, 2007): 7–9.

28. Simmons, "Territorial Disputes," 11.

29. Sethi, "Settling Border Disputes," 1775.

30. Ibid., 127–28. See also Alejandra Ruiz-Dana, "Peru and Ecuador: A Case Study of Latin American Integration and Conflict," in *Regional Trade Integration and Conflict Resolution*, ed. Shaheen Rafi Khan (New York: Routledge, 2009), 176.

31. Post-2000 trade figures in this chapter are from IMF Direction of Trade Statistics [Custom Table], International Monetary Fund, https://www.imf.org/external/pubs/cat/longres.

cfm?sk=19305.0 (accessed January 7, 2014). Exports as a percentage of GDP in this chapter are calculated using the following sources on GDP per capita and population: World Bank, World Development Indicators (year), GDP per capita [data file], http://data.worldbank.org/indica tor/NY.GDP.PCAP.CD (accessed May 22, 2014); and World Bank, World Development Indicators (year), Population [data file], http://data.worldbank.org/indicator/SP.POP.TOTL?page=2 (accessed May 22, 2014).

32. See, e.g., Edward D. Mansfield, Jon C. Pevehouse, and David H. Bearce, "Preferential Trading Arrangements and Military Disputes," *Security Studies*. 9, no. 1 (Autumn 1999): 92–118.

33. Juan Jose Taccone and Uziel Noguiera, *Andean Report 2002–2004*, no. 2, (Buenos Aires: Inter-American Development Bank, Institute for the Integration of Latin America and the Caribbean, June 2005), 52.

34. Mares and Palmer, *Power, Institutions, Leadership*, 129. According to the Polity IV data set, Ecuador has registered only a +5 on the "democ" scale since 2007, making it, at best, an "open anocracy" rather than a full democracy. "Polity IV Project: Political Regime Characteristics and Transitions, 1800–2012," http://www.systemicpeace.org/inscr/inscr.htm (accessed December 8, 2013).

35. In a 2001 Apoyo public opinion poll, for example, 54% of decided Chilean respondents reported a favorable opinion of Ecuador (51% "somewhat favorable" and 3% "very favorable"), while 70% of decided respondents judged Peru's relations with Ecuador to be good (66% "fairly good" and 4% "very good"). Apoyo Opinion y Mercado, "USIA Poll no. 2001-I200154: Economic Conditions/President Toledo/US/Terrorism/International Coalition [PEUSIA2001-I200154]," Lima, December 14–26, 2001, http://www.ropercenter.uconn.edu/CFIDE/cf/action/catalog/abstract.cfm?type=&start=&id=&archno=PEUSIA2001-I200154&abstract= (accessed May 25, 2014).

36. Rudolf Lill, "The Historical Evolution of the Italian Frontier Regions," *West European Politics* 5, no. 4 (1982): 109–122; and Roberto G. Rabel, *Between East and West: Trieste, the United States, and the Cold War, 1941–1954* (Durham: Duke University Press, 1988), 2–3, 9.

37. Zara Steiner, *The Lights that Failed: European History, 1919–1933* (Oxford: Oxford University Press, 2005), 86–90; and John C. Campbell, *Successful Negotiation: Trieste 1954* (Princeton: Princeton University Press, 1976), 4–5.

38. On the treaties of Rapallo and Rome, see Alan Sharp, *The Versailles Settlement: Peacemaking after the First World War, 1919–1923* (London: Palgrave MacMillan 2008), 150. On Mussolini's efforts to curtail the Kingdom of Yugoslavia, see Patricia Knight, *Mussolini and Fascism* (New York: Routledge, 2003), 87; and Martin Blinkhorn, *Mussolini and Fascist Italy* (New York: Routledge, 2006), 60.

39. Srdjan Trifkovic, "Rivalry between Germany and Italy in Croatia, 1942–1943," *Historical Journal* 36, no. 4 (December 1993): 880–81.

40. Christopher Seton-Watson, "Italy's Imperial Hangover," *Journal of Contemporary History* 15, no. 1 (January 1980): 170–71.

41. United Nations, "Treaty of Peace with Italy," February 10, 1947, articles 3 and 4, United Nations Treaty Series, vol. 49, https://treaties.un.org/doc/Publication/UNTS/Volume%2049/v49.pdf.

42. Josef L. Kunz, "The Free Territory of Trieste," *Western Political Quarterly* 1, no. 2 (June 1948): 99–112; M. K. G., "The Trieste Dispute," *World Today* 10, no. 1 (January 1954): 6–18; and M. K. G., "Trieste: Background to a Deadlock," *World Today* 8, no.10 (October 1952): 429–39.

43. Bogdan C. Novak, *Trieste, 1941–1954: The Ethnic, Political, and Ideological Struggle* (Chicago: University of Chicago Press, 1970), 429–31; and Campbell, *Successful Negotiation*, 11.

44. Rabel, *Between East and West*, 156–57.

45. According to Polity IV, in 1953–54, Italy received a perfect +10 on the Polity scale; Yugoslavia received a –7, ranking it as an autocracy.

46. Pierangelo Isernia, "Italian Public Opinion and the International Use of Force," in *Public Opinion and the International Use of Force*, ed. Philip Everts and Pierangelo Isernia (London: Routledge, 2001), 90.

47. See, e.g., US Ambassador to Rome Clare Booth Luce to Secretary of State John Foster Dulles, April 19, 1954, document 185, United States State Department, *Foreign Relations of the*

United States (FRUS), 1952–1954, vol. 8 (Washington, DC: US Government Printing Office, 2000), 411.

48. Novak, *Trieste*, 384–88.

49. Campbell, *Successful Negotiation*, esp. 149–50.

50. See, e.g., Glenda Sluga, "Trieste: Ethnicity and the Cold War, 1945–54," *Journal of Contemporary History* 29, no. 2 (April 1994): 285–303.

51. Campbell, *Successful Negotiation*, 10.

52. Jean-Baptiste Duroselle, *Le Conflit de Trieste 1943–1954* (Brussels: Institut de Sociologie de l'Université Libre de Bruxelles, 1966), 412–14. See also "Memorandum by the Assistant Secretary of State for European Affairs (Merchant) to the Deputy Under Secretary of State (Murphy)," September 9, 1954, document 264, *FRUS*, vol. 8, 525–26; Sir Anthony Eden, *Full Circle: the Memoirs of Sir Anthony Eden* (London: Cassell, 1960), 206–7; and Rabel, *Between East and West*, 156–59. Rabel (156) comments that "this promise of economic assistance helped seal the bargain."

53. "The Acting Secretary of State to the President, at Denver," September 3, 1954, document 256, *FRUS*, vol. 8, 517. See also Novak, *Trieste*, 450.

54. Campell, *Successful Negotiations*, 20n; and Rabel, *Between East and West*, 161; and Ettore Greco, "Italy, the Yugoslav Crisis and the Osimo Agreement," *International Spectator* 29, no. 1 (January–March 1994): 17–18. For the text of the treaty, see http://www.triestfreeport.org/wp-content/uploads/2010/09/orig.-Treaty-OSIMO-1975.pdf.

55. Greco, "Italy, Yugoslav Crisis, Osimo Agreement," 18.

56. Ibid., 22–26.

57. Jack Raymond, "Yugoslavia, Italy Better Relations: Plans for More Trade Follow Trieste Accord," *New York Times*, November 21, 1954, 35.

58. Greco, "Italy, Yugoslav Crisis, Osimo Agreement," 16.

59. See, e.g., William Wallace, *Regional Integration: The West European Experience* (Washington, DC: Brookings Institution, 1994), 100. Even its later and more coherent iteration, the Organization for Security and Cooperation in Europe, remained a weak organization relying on consensus and lacking any independent decision-making capacity. See Seth G. Jones, *The Rise of European Security Cooperation* (Cambridge: Cambridge University Press, 2007), 83; and Nuray Ibryamova, "The OSCE as a Regional Security Actor: A Security Governance Perspective," in *The Security Governance of Regional Organizations*, ed. Emil J. Kirchner and Roberto Dominguez (New York: Routledge, 2011), 98.

60. Polity IV ranks Slovenia as a +10 on the Polity scale beginning in 1991. It lists Croatia as a +9 on this scale as of 2005.

61. I thank Alexandra Vuldzheva for translating Bulgarian-language sources for this mini–case study.

62. René, Ristelhueber, *A History of the Balkan Peoples* (New York: Twayne, 1971), 130–32; and James Pettifer, "The New Macedonian Question," *International Affairs* 68, no. 3 (July 1992): 477.

63. Patrick Moore, "Macedonia: Perennial Balkan Apple of Discord," *World Today* 35, no. 10 (October 1979): 421.

64. Richard C. Hall, *The Modern Balkans: A History* (London: Reaktion Books, 2011), 78.

65. Tom Gallagher, *Outcast Europe: The Balkans, 1789–1989: From the Ottomans to Milosevic* (London: Routledge, 2001), 156.

66. "Treaty of Peace with Bulgaria 1947," *American Journal of International Law* 42, no. 3 (July 1948): 179.

67. On Moscow's dominance of Eastern Europe, especially "quiescent states" such as Bulgaria, see Andrew C. Janos, "From Eastern Empire to Western Hegemony: East Central Europe under Two International Regimes," *East European Politics and Societies* 15, no. 2 (March 2001): 225–29.

68. Deyan Martinovski, *Makedonskiat Vapros v Bulgaro-Yugoslavskite Otnoshenia 1948–1968* [The Macedonian question in Bulgarian-Yugoslav relations 1948–1968] (Sofia: Institute for Historical Research, 2010), 9.

69. On several occasions, such as Dimitrov's 1948 proposal for a Balkan federation, when Stalin objected to policies pursued by Dimitrov, the Bulgarian leader hastily backed down to

avoid the consequences of challenging Moscow. See, e.g., Vesselin Dimitrov, *Bulgaria: The Uneven Transition* (London: Routledge, 2001), 23; Robert Gellately, *Stalin's Curse: Battling for Communism in War and Cold War* (Oxford: Oxford University Press, 2013), 319–20; and Ivo Banac, ed., *The Diary of Georgi Dimitrov, 1933–1949* (New Haven: Yale University Press, 2003), 435.

70. Nassya Kralevska-Owens, *Communism versus Democracy: Bulgaria 1944 to 1997* (Sofia: Asi Print, 2010), 127.

71. R. J. Crampton, *A Concise History of Bulgaria* (Cambridge: Cambridge University Press, 1997), 187.

72. Fred Warner Neal, *Titoism in Action: The Reforms in Yugoslavia after 1948* (Berkeley: University of California Press, 1958), 221–22.

73. Ryan C. Amacher, *Yugoslavia's Foreign Trade: A Study of State Trade Discrimination* (New York: Praeger, 1972), 31, 39.

74. Richard Felix Staar, *Communist Regimes in Eastern Europe*, 4th ed. (Palo Alto, CA: Hoover Institution Press, 1982), 325–26.

75. Center for Macedonians Abroad and Society for Macedonian Studies, *Macedonia: History and Politics* (Athens: Ekdotike Athenon, 1994), 38. See also, John Phillips, *Macedonia: Warlords and Rebels in the Balkans* (New Haven: Yale University Press, 2004), 36–38.

76. Dimitar Petkov, "Bulgaro-Yugoslavskite Otnoshenia Mart 1953–Oktomvri 1956" [Bulgarian-Yugoslav political relations, March 1953–October 1956] *Istoricheski Pregled* [Historical Review], no. 1–2 (2008): 175.

77. Moore, "Macedonia," 423–24; and Stephan E. Palmer and Robert R. King, *Yugoslav Communism and the Macedonian Question* (Hamden, CT: Archon Books, 1971), 163.

78. Paul Hoffmanns, "Yugoslavs Experience New Hostility from the Soviet Bloc and Suspect Moscow Inspired It," *New York Times*, September 10, 1968, 13.

79. Bulgaria scored a –7 on Polity IV's "democ" scale until 1990, while Yugoslavia scored –7 until 1980 and –5 until 1991.

80. Loring M. Danforth, *The Macedonian Conflict: Ethnic Nationalism in a Transnational World* (Princeton: Princeton University Press, 1995), 68–69.

81. "Only 8% of Bulgarians support Macedonia's EU bid unconditionally: Sitel," Focus News Agency, December 11, 2012, http://www.focus-fen.net/index.php?id=n294474 (accessed January 7, 2013).

82. Stefanos Katsikas, *Negotiating Diplomacy in the New Europe: Foreign Policy in Post-Communist Bulgaria* (London: I. B. Tauris, 2011), 163–64.

83. Ibid.; and Emil Giatzidis, *An Introduction to Post-Communist Bulgaria: Political, Economic and Social Transformation* (Manchester, UK: Manchester University Press, 2002), 152–53.

84. Katsikas, *Negotiating Diplomacy*, 164.

85. Polity IV ranked Bulgaria as at least +8 on the Polity scale since 1990. It has ranked Macedonia as a +9 since 2002.

86. Katsikas, *Negotiating Diplomacy*, 164.

87. Karen E. Smith, *European Union Foreign Policy in a Changing World*, 2nd ed. (Cambridge, UK: Polity Press, 2008), 26.

88. A public opinion survey published in December 2013 showed that 62% of Bulgarian respondents favored Macedonian EU membership. "62% of Bulgarite iskat Sarbia v ES, 57%-Makedonia, samo 28%-Turtsia" [62% of Bulgarians want Serbia in the EU, 57% want Macedonia, only 28% want Turkey], *24 chasa* [24 hours], December 6, 2013, http://www.24chasa.bg/Article.asp?ArticleId=2547721 (accessed May 9, 2014).

89. See, e.g., Peter van Ham, "Central Europe and the EU's Intergovernmental Conference: The Dialectics of Enlargement," *Security Dialogue* 28, no. 1 (1997): 75–76; and "Text of the Proposal for an Additional Protocol to the Convention for the Protection of Human Rights and Fundamental Freedoms, Concerning Persons Belonging to National Minorities," February 1993, http://stars.coe.fr/ta/ta93/EREC1201.HTM#1.

90. For studies of Russo-Turkish relations in different eras, see William Edward David Allen and Paul Muratoff, *Caucasian Battlefields: A History of the Wars on the Turco-Caucasian Border 1828–1921* (Cambridge: Cambridge University Press, 2010); Michael A. Reynolds, *Shattering Empires: The Clash and Collapse of the Ottoman and Russian Empires, 1908–1918* (Cambridge:

Cambridge University Press, 2011); and Bülent Gökay, *Soviet Eastern Policy and Turkey, 1920–1991: Soviet Foreign Policy, Turkey and Communism* (London: Routledge, 2006).

91. J. A. R. Marriott, *The Eastern Question: An Historical Study in European Diplomacy* (Oxford: Oxford University Press, 1918), 3.

92. Mustafa Aydin, "Determinants of Turkish Foreign Policy: Historical Framework and Traditional Inputs," *Middle Eastern Studies* 35, no. 4 (October 1999): 164.

93. Alan Bodger, "Russia and the End of the Ottoman Empire," in *The Great Powers and the End of the Ottoman Empire*, ed. Marian Kent, 73–105 (London: Frank Cass, 1996); and V. Necla Geyikdai, *Foreign Investment in the Ottoman Empire: International Trade and Relations, 1854–1914* (London: I. B. Tauris, 2011), 49–50, 97, 137.

94. William Hale, *Turkish Foreign Policy, 1774–2000* (London: Frank Cass, 2000), 34–35; and Michael A. Reynolds, *Shattering Empires: The Clash and Collapse of the Ottoman and Russian Empires, 1908–1918* (Cambridge: Cambridge University Press, 2011), 108–9.

95. Reynolds, *Shattering Empires*, 170–85.

96. Arnold J. Toynbee and Kenneth P. Kirkwood, *The Modern World: Turkey* (New York: Scribner, 1927), 124–25.

97. Polity IV ranks Russia as a −1 (anocracy) in 1921on its Polity scale; thus, it cannot be classified as democratic. It ranks Turkey in 1921 as a −66 on the Polity scale, a special case of anocracy. "Polity IV Project."

98. Reynolds, *Shattering Empires*, 168–69.

99. Bülent Gökay, *A Clash of Empires: Turkey between Russian Bolshevism and British Imperialism 1918–1923* (London: Tauris Academic Studies, 1997), 64–65; and Paul Dumont, "L'axe Moscou-Ankara," *Cahiers du Monde russe et soviétique* 18, no. 3 (July–September 1977): 172–73.

100. Reynolds, *Shattering Empires*, 186; and Hale, *Turkish Foreign Policy*, 36.

101. Bodger, "Russia and the End of the Ottoman Empire," 80. The IMF trade and GDP data is available only starting in 1946 and, consequently, is not useful for this case.

102. Ibid., 81.

103. See, e.g., Peter Kenez, *Civil War in South Russia, 1919–1920: The Defeat of the Whites* (Berkeley: University of California Press, 1977), 178–212.

104. Hale, *Turkish Foreign Policy*, 50–51.

105. Necmeddin Sadak, "Turkey Faces the Soviets," *Foreign Affairs* 27, no. 3 (April 1949): 450.

106. Dumont, "L'axe Moscou-Ankara," 170. See also Gökay, *Clash of Empires*, 102.

107. Dumont, "L'axe Moscou-Ankara," 169.

108. See, e.g., Adam B. Ulam, *Expansion and Coexistence: Soviet Foreign Policy, 1917–73* (New York: Praeger, 1975), 126–36; and Adam B. Ulam, *The Bolsheviks: The Intellectual and Political History of the Triumph of Communism in Russia* (Cambridge: Harvard University Press, 1998), 465–67. On the importance of state building and regime survival as a motive for Lenin's New Economic Policy during the immediate post-Revolution era, see Robert Service, *Lenin: A Biography* (London: Macmillan, 2010), 421; and Mark Sandle, *A Short History of Soviet Socialism* (New York: Routledge, 2007), 114–17.

109. George F. Kennan, *Soviet Foreign Policy, 1917–1941* (Westport, CT: Greenwood Press: 1960), 67.

110. J. C. Hurewitz, "Russia and the Turkish Straits: A Revaluation of the Origins of the Problem," *World Politics* 14, no. 4 (July 1962): 605–6.

111. Harry N. Howard, "The Soviet Union and the Middle East," *Annals of the American Academy of Political and Social Science* 263, (May 1949): 181; Hurewitz, "Russia and the Turkish Straits," 505–7; Jamil Hasanli, *Stalin and the Turkish Crisis of the Cold War, 1945–1953* (Lanham, MD: Rowman & Littlefield, 2011), 26–27, 45–47, 198; and Mustapha Aydin, "Determinants of Turkish Foreign Policy: Changing Patterns and Conjunctures during the Cold War," *Middle Eastern Studies* 36, no. 1 (January 2000): 106–9.

112. Aydin, "Changing Patterns and Conjunctures," 111–13.

113. In 1924, for example, Soviet exports to Turkey accounted for only 6% of all Soviet exports (and a much lower share of Soviet GDP). This made Turkey a smaller market than Germany, Great Britain, and "the Border States and Poland." Turkish exports to the USSR, moreover, were inconsiderable, ranking less than Germany, Great Britain, the United States,

"the Border States and Poland," and Scandinavia, constituting a small part of the 13% of Soviet imports produced by "other countries." "Soviet Commerce Gains: Volume of Exports Approaches That of the Last Pre-War Year," *New York Times*, May 24, 1924, ProQuest Historical Newspapers, *New York Times* (1851–2010), 5. Although the two countries signed a trade treaty in 1927, it restricted Turkish exports to Russia to an annual value of £750,000 and placed heavy bureaucratic impediments in the way of Turkish trade. See "Soviet-Turkish Trade Treaty to be Signed," *Times* (London), March 3, 1927, 13; "Turco-Soviet Trade Agreement," *Times* (London), March 14, 1927, 13; and "Turkey and the Soviet," *Times* (London), July 4, 1929, 15.

114. On the Treaty of Kars, see Charlotte Hill, *State Building and Conflict Resolution in the Caucasus* (Leiden, Netherlands: Koninklijke Brill, 2010), 159.

115. Selim Deringil, *Turkish Foreign Policy during the Second World War: An "Active" Neutrality* (Cambridge: Cambridge University Press, 1989), 89–91. In the absence of public opinion data for these years, there is little information on Turkish attitudes toward Russia during the 1920s and 1930s. There is less information about Soviet public opinion, except to say that it was politically irrelevant. As Jamil Hasanli notes, "account has to be taken of the fact that in the 1930s and 40s the notion of 'public opinion' as it was used in the Soviet Union was of a formal nature, and state bodies were behind the actions of the public." Jamil Hasanli, *Stalin and the Turkish Crisis of the Cold War, 1945–1953* (Lanham, MD: Lexington Books, 2011), 101.

116. David D. Laitin and Said S. Samatar, *Somalia: Nation in Search of a State* (Boulder, CO: Westview, 1987), 73.

117. Daniel D. Kendie, "Toward Northeast African Cooperation: Resolving the Ethiopia-Somalia Disputes," *Northeast African Studies* 10, no. 2 (2003), 74; and Michael P. Colaresi, *Scare Tactics: The Politics of International Rivalry* (Syracuse, NY: Syracuse University Press, 2005), 47–53. For the text of the Somali constitution, see "Constitution of the Somali Republic," in *Constitutions of Nations*, vol. 1, *Africa*, 3rd rev. ed., ed. Amos J. Peaslee (The Hague, Netherlands: Martinus Nijhoff, 1965), 776–803.

118. Kendie, "Northeast African Cooperation," 76; and Jeffrey A. Lefebvre, *Arms for the Horn: US Security Policy in Ethiopia and Somalia, 1953–1991* (Pittsburgh, PA: University of Pittsburgh Press, 1991), 114–20.

119. Steven David, "Realignment in the Horn: The Soviet Advantage," *International Security* 4, no. 2 (Fall 1979): 72.

120. Lefebvre, *Arms for the Horn*, 114–16.

121. Ibid., 176–80; and David, "Realignment in the Horn," 80.

122. Lefebvre, *Arms for the Horn*, 245–46.

123. Gebru Tareke, "The Ethiopia-Somalia War of 1977 Revisited," *International Journal of African Historical Studies* 33, no. 3 (2000): 666.

124. Ibid., 667.

125. Lefebvre, *Arms for the Horn*, 245.

126. Ibid., 245; and Patrick Gilkes, "Somalia: Conflicts within and against the Military Regime," *Review of African Political Economy*, no. 44 (1989): 55.

127. "Polity IV Project."

128. Actually, it lists Somali exports to Ethiopia at zero and Ethiopian exports to Somalia at near zero (ranging from zero in 1983 to $310,000 in 1982).

129. For a critical analysis of the OAU, see Gino J. Naldi, *The Organization of African Unity: An Analysis of Its Role*, 2nd ed. (New York: Bloomsbury Academic, 1999).

130. Lefebvre, *Arms for the Horn*, 258–66; William Reno, *Warfare in Independent Africa* (Cambridge: Cambridge University Press, 2011), 190–96; and Daniel Compagnon, "Somali Armed Movements," in *African Guerrillas*, ed. Christopher Clapham, 73–90. (Oxford: James Currey, 1998).

131. Gebru Tareke, *The Ethiopian Revolution* (New Haven: Yale University Press, 2009), 309.

132. International Crisis Group, "Somalia: To Move beyond the Failed State," *Africa Report*, no. 147 (December 23, 2008), 1–2.

133. S. C. M. Paine, *The Sino-Japanese War of 1894–1895: Perceptions, Power, and Primacy* (Cambridge: Cambridge University Press, 2003), 265–90.

134. On the Port Arthur massacre, see Masahiro Yamamoto, *Nanking: Anatomy of Atrocity* (Westport, CT: Praeger, 2000), 25; and Paine, *Sino-Japanese War*, 213–14.

135. The indemnity was 450,000,000 taels, greater than the Chinese government's annual revenue, and annual payments totaled about one-fifth of the government's annual budget. Joseph Esherick, *The Origins of the Boxer Uprising* (Berkeley: University of California Press, 1987), 311.

136. See, e.g., Bruce A. Elleman, *Wilson and China: A Revised History of the Shandong Question* (New York: M. E. Sharpe, 2002), 68–69.

137. For general sources on the rivalry during the 1930s and 1940s, see David M. Gordon, "Historiographical Essay: The China-Japan War, 1931–1945," *Journal of Military History* 70, no. 1 (January 2006): 137–82; James C. Hsiung, "Introduction: Theory and the Long Running Tussle," in *China and Japan at Odds: Deciphering the Perpetual Conflict*, ed. James C. Hsiung (New York: Palgrave MacMillan, 2007), 6–8; and Ian Nish, "An Overview of Relations between China and Japan, 1895–1945," *China Quarterly*, special issue, "China and Japan: History, Trends and Prospects," no. 124 (December 1990): 613–22. On the Japanese treatment of Chinese civilians during their campaign of expansion, see Joshua A. Fogel, *The Nanjing Massacre in History and Historiography* (Berkeley: University of California Press, 2000); Peter Li, "The Nanking Holocaust: Memory, Trauma and Reconciliation," in *The Search for Justice: Japanese War Crimes*, ed. Peter Li, 227–43 (New Brunswick, NJ: Transaction, 2003); Fei Fei Li, Robert Sabella, and David Liu, eds., *Nanking 1937:Memory and Healing* (New York: M. E. Sharpe, 2002), 76–77; and Iris Chang, *The Rape of Nanking: The Forgotten Holocaust of World War II* (New York: Basic Books, 1997).

138. Chalmers Johnson, "The Patterns of Japanese Relations with China, 1952–1982," *Pacific Affairs* 59, no. 3 (Autumn 1986): 410–14; and Chai-Jin Lee, "The Making of the Sino-Japanese Friendship Treaty," *Pacific Affairs* 52, no. 3 (Autumn 1979): 420–21.

139. For the text of the treaty, see *Peking Review*, August 18, 1978, 7–8, http://www.marxists.org/subject/china/peking-review/1978/PR1978-33.pdf (accessed December 8, 2013).

140. Joseph Y. S. Cheng, "China's Japan Policy in the 1980s," *International Affairs* 61, no. 1 (Winter 1984–85): 91.

141. See, e.g., Robert A. Scalapino, "China and the Balance of Power," *Foreign Affairs* 52, no. 2 (January 1974): 349–85, esp. 356–58; Robert S. Ross, "International Bargaining and Domestic Politics: US-China Relations since 1972," *World Politics* 38, no. 2 (January 1986): 261–64; Gerald Segal, "China and the Great Power Triangle," *China Quarterly*, no. 83 (September 1980): 493–98; and Harry Harding, "China's Cooperative Behavior," in *Chinese Foreign Policy: Theory and Practice*, ed. Thomas W. Robinson and David L. Shambaugh (Oxford: Oxford University Press, 1994), 398.

142. Yang Kuisong, "The Sino-Soviet Border Clash of 1969: From Zhenbao Island to Sino-American Rapprochement," *Cold War History* 1, no. 1 (August 2000): 21–52; and Cheng, "China's Japan Policy in the 1980s," 92–93.

143. Kuisong, "The Sino-Soviet Border Clash of 1969"; and William Burr, "Sino-American Relations, 1969: The Sino-Soviet Border War and Steps towards Rapprochement," *Cold War History* 1, no. 3 (April 2001): 73–112.

144. Yinan He, "Remembering and Forgetting the War: Elite Mythmaking, Mass Reaction, and Sino-Japanese Relations, 1950–2006," *History and Memory* 19, no. 2 (Fall–Winter 2007): 49–50; Daniel Tretiak, "The Sino-Japanese Treaty of 1978: The Senkaku Incident Prelude," *Asian Survey* 18, no. 12 (December 1978): 1235–36; Robert G. Sutter, "China and Japan: Trouble Ahead?" *Washington Quarterly* 25, no. 4 (Autumn 2002): 37; and Ming Wan, *Sino-Japanese Relations: Interaction, Logic, and Transformation* (Washington, DC: Woodrow Wilson Center Press, 2006), 86.

145. Wan, *Sino-Japanese Relations*, 86–87; and Tretiak, "Sino-Japanese Treaty of 1978," 1239–40, 1247.

146. Johnson, "Japanese Relations with China," 412–13.

147. Tretiak, "Sino-Japanese Treaty of 1978," 1236. See also Hong N. Kim, "The Fukuda Government and the Politics of the Sino-Japanese Peace Treaty," *Asian Survey* 19, no. 3 (March 1979): 301; and Johnson, "Japanese Relations with China," 416.

148. Fukui Haruhiro, "Tanaka Goes to Peking: A Case Study in Foreign Policymaking," in *Policymaking in Contemporary Japan*, ed. T. J. Pempel (Ithaca: Cornell University Press, 1977), 62–63; and Lee, "Sino-Japanese Friendship Treaty," 432–433. For a more circumscribed view of the US role, see Tretiak, "Sino-Japanese Treaty of 1978," 1236–37.

149. Tretiak, "Sino-Japanese Treaty of 1978," 1239.

150. "Polity IV Project." In contrast, Japan scored a perfect 10 on the Polity scale.

151. As a twenty-first century analysis of Chinese foreign policy observed, "it should be noted at the outset that China is not a democracy and that public opinion does not have much direct impact on policy, particularly in the area of foreign policy." Joseph Fewsmith and Stanley Rosen, "The Domestic Context of Foreign Policy: Does 'Public Opinion' Matter?" in *The Making of Chinese Foreign and Security Policy in the Era of Reform*, ed. David M. Lampton (Stanford: Stanford University Press, 2001), 155. Andrew J. Nathan and Robert S. Ross similarly note that the lines of authority in Chinese foreign policy run downward from above, where powerful leaders, such as Mao Zedong and Deng Xiaoping predominate and the public has little role. See *The Great Wall and the Empty Fortress: China's Search for Security* (New York: Norton, 1997), 124–25. I thank Jean-Marc F. Blanchard of Shanghai Normal University for bringing these sources to my attention.

152. Yung H. Park, "The Tanaka Government and the Mechanics of the China Decision," in *China and Japan: A Search for Balance since World War I*, ed. A. Cook and H. Conroy (Santa Barbara, CA: ABC-Clio, 1978), 395. For public opinion polls showing a strong Japanese public affinity for China, see Mindy L. Kotler, Naotaka Sugawara, and Tetsuya Yamada, "Chinese and Japanese Public Opinion: Searching for Moral Security," *Asian Perspective* 31, no. 1 (January 2007): 96.

153. There is a large discrepancy in the IMF data between Chinese exports to Japan in 1978 ($4.5 billion) and Japanese imports from Japan in that year ($2 billion).

154. Once again, there is a discrepancy in the data, with the Chinese reporting almost $5.5 billion in 1978 (still under 0.7% of Japanese GDP). See also Cheng, "China's Japan Policy in the 1980s," 98.

155. Ibid., 91.

156. Ibid., 98.

157. Margaret M. Pearson, for example, comments as late as the mid-1990s, after central control of the Chinese business environment abated somewhat: "Although China's new business elite is distanced structurally and ideologically from state authority, there is no compelling evidence that it has tried to influence government policy as an independent class, or that there is even sufficient cohesiveness for it to do so." *China's New Business Elite: The Political Consequences of Economic Reform* (Berkeley: University of California Press, 1997), 115.

158. Of course, since there really has not been a state-to-nation imbalance issue involving China and Japan in the post–World War II era, once Japan was evicted from Chinese lands it controlled, this needs further clarification. In essence, the post–World War II rivalry cannot be explained by a state-to-nation imbalance, so its termination should not require one.

159. On Japanese concerns over Chinese dominance, see Glenn D. Hook, Julie Gilson, Christopher W. Hughes, and Hugo Dobson, *Japan's International Relations: Politics, Economics and Security*, 2nd ed. (London: Routledge, 2005), 197–201; Christopher B. Johnstone, "Paradigms Lost: Japan's Asia Policy in a Time of Growing Chinese Power," *Contemporary Southeast Asia* 21, no. 3 (December 1999): 365–85; and Denny Roy, "Hegemon on the Horizon? China's Threat to East Asian Security," *International Security* 19, no. 1 (Summer 1994): 149–68. On Chinese concerns, see Russell Ong, *China's Security Interests in the 21st Century* (New York: Routledge, 2007), 59–75; and Denny Roy, *China's Foreign Relations* (Lanham, MD: Rowman & Littlefield, 1998), 162–65. On the troubled bilateral relationship in general, see Leszek Buszynski, "Sino-Japanese Relations: Interdependence, Rivalry and Regional Security," *Contemporary Southeast Asia* 31, no. 1 (April 2009): 143–71.

160. On the island dispute, see Jean-Marc F. Blanchard, "The US Role in the Sino-Japanese Dispute over the Diaoyu (Senkaku) Islands, 1945–1971," *China Quarterly*, no. 161 (March 2000): 95–123; and Zhongqi Pan, "Sino-Japanese Dispute over the Diaoyu/Senkaku Islands: The Pending Controversy from the Chinese Perspective," *Chinese Journal of Political Science* 12, no. 1 (April 2007): 71–92. On the maritime boundary dispute more generally, see Mark J. Valencia, "The East China Sea Dispute: Context, Claims, Issues, and Possible Solutions," *Asian Perspective* 31, no. 1 (Summer 2007): 127–67.

161. Chris Buckley, "China Claims Air Rights over Disputed Islands," *New York Times*, November 23, 2013, http://www.nytimes.com/2013/11/24/world/asia/china-warns-of-action-against-aircraft-over-disputed-seas.html?_r=0 (accessed April 7, 2014).

162. Johnson, "Japanese Relations with China," 419–25.

163. He, "Remembering and Forgetting the War," 44.

164. Kazuyuki Katayama, "Development of Japan-China Relations since 1972," *International Journal of China Studies* 2, no. 3 (December 2011): 651.

165. See, e.g., Christopher R. Hughes, "Japan in the Politics of Chinese Leadership Legitimacy: Recent Developments in Historical Perspective," *Japan Forum* 20, no. 2 (July 2008): 248–49; Mingde Wang and Maaike Okano-Heijmans, "Overcoming the Past in Sino-Japanese Relations," *International Spectator* 46, no. 1 (March 2011): 129; S. Zhao, "A State-Led Nationalism: The Patriotic Education Campaign in Post-Tiananmen China," *Communist and Post-Communist Studies* 31, no. 3 (1998): 287–302; Allan S. Whiting, *China Eyes Japan* (Berkeley: University of California Press, 1989), 67–79; and Jessica Chen Weiss, *Powerful Patriots: Nationalist Protest in China's Foreign Relations* (New York: Oxford University Press, 2014).

166. For example, in a public opinion poll conducted in 2008, only 19% of Japanese respondents reported that they trusted China (compared to 78% who did not). Chinese respondents to the same survey were more positive but were still split, as 56% stated that they trusted Japan, while 42% said they did not. Joseph Yu-shek Cheng, "China's Japan Policy: Seeking Stability and Improvement in Uncertainties," *China: An International Journal* 9, no. 2 (September 2011): 269. Peter Hayes Gries, however, notes widespread Chinese anger at Japan stemming from the Japanese defeat of China in the Sino-Japanese wars and Japanese atrocities during World War II. "Nationalism, Indignation, and China's Japan Policy," *SAIS Review* 25, no. 2 (Summer–Fall 2005): 111–13.

167. According to Polity IV, China has received a –7 (authoritarian) on the Polity scale every year since the treaty.

168. Chinese exports to Japan exploded from either $3 billion or $5 billion in 1978 to about $55 billion in 2000, or more than 1.1% of Chinese GDP. In the same period, Japanese exports to China jumped from either $3 billion or $5.5 billion to about $62 billion, or 1.9% of Japanese GDP. Trade has continued to climb since then. This is not as integrated as the Franco-German relationship, in which both countries produce about 4% of their GDP through bilateral exports, but it is still significant.

Peacemaking between Regional Rivals

1. See Benjamin Miller, "Explaining Variations in Regional Peace: Three Strategies for Peace-making," *Cooperation and Conflict* 35, no. 2 (June 2000): 155–91; and Benjamin Miller, *States, Nations and the Great Powers* (Cambridge: Cambridge University Press, 2007).

2. The inclusion of the Anglo-German (1919) case would add a second case of peacemaking between democracies, but it would be a weak one, given that the Weimar German regime was a brand-new regime at the time of the Paris Peace Conference, whereas democratic peace theorists usually require an interim period (for some, three years, for others, a peaceful transition of power) for a state to be considered fully democratic. See, e.g., Bruce M. Russett, *Grasping the Democratic Peace* (Princeton: Princeton University Press, 1993), 14–16. Moreover, as I indicate in the introduction, the inclusion of the Anglo-German case would unfairly stack the deck in favor of a top-down transition, as the Treaty of Versailles was imposed on defeated Germany by the victors in the immediate aftermath of the war rather than negotiated freely by both democracies after more time had elapsed.

3. See Gary Goertz, Bradford Jones, and Paul F. Diehl, "Maintenance Processes in International Rivalries, *Journal of Conflict Resolution* 49, no. 5 (October 2005): 742–69, esp. 744 and 755; and D. Scott Bennett, "Integrating and Testing Models of Rivalry Duration," *American Journal of Political Science* 42, no. 4 (October 1998): 1209–10.

4. Elsewhere, I have written on peacemaking between the three Western democracies and Weimar Germany and the impact of the Palestinian Authority's democratic election in January 1996 on the Israeli-Palestinian peace process. In both cases, state attitudes were much more conciliatory than societal attitudes, and to the extent that peace processes advanced, it was owing to state actions rather than public preferences. See Norrin M. Ripsman, *Peacemaking by*

Democracies: The Effect of State Autonomy on the Post–World War Settlements (University Park: Penn State University Press, 2002); and Norrin M. Ripsman, "Peacemaking and Democratic Peace Theory: Public Opinion as an Obstacle to Peace in Post-Conflict Situations," *Democracy and Security* 3, no. 1 (January 2007): 89–113.

5. For related arguments, see Miller, *States, Nations, Great Powers*; Benjamin Miller, "When and How Regions Become Peaceful: Potential Theoretical Pathways to Peace," *International Studies Review* 7, no. 2 (2005): 229–67; Jonathan Rynhold, "The German Question in Central and Eastern Europe and the Long Peace in Europe after 1945: An Integrated Theoretical Explanation," *Review of International Studies* 37, no. 1 (January 2011): 249–75; and Charles Kupchan, *How Enemies Become Friends: The Sources of Stable Peace* (Princeton: Princeton University Press 2010).

6. In this regard, see Steven E. Lobell and Norrin M. Ripsman, eds., *The Political Economy of Regional Peacemaking* (Ann Arbor: University of Michigan Press, 2016).

7. Amitav Acharya, *Constructing a Security Community in Southeast Asia: ASEAN and the Problem of Regional Order* (London: Routledge, 2001); and Etel Solingen, *Regional Orders at Century's Dawn: Global and Domestic Influences on Grand Strategy* (Princeton: Princeton University Press, 1998), 3.

8. Douglas Dion, "Evidence and Inference in the Comparative Case Study," in *Necessary Conditions: Theory, Methodology, and Applications*, ed. Gary Goertz and Harvey Starr (Lanham, MD: Rowman & Littlefield, 2003), 95–112; Jack S. Levy, "Case Studies: Types, Designs, and Logics of Inference," *Conflict Management and Peace Science* 25, no. 1 (February 2008): 8–9; and Alexander L. George and Andrew Bennett, *Case Studies and Theory Development in the Social Sciences* (Cambridge: MIT Press, 2005), 23–24.

9. Robert Gilpin, *War and Change in International Politics* (Cambridge: Cambridge University Press, 1981); and William Wohlforth, "The Stability of a Unipolar World," *International Security* 24, no. 1 (Summer 1999): 5–41. This differs from the economic version of the theory advanced by Stephen Krasner, Charles Kindleberger, and others. Stephen D. Krasner, "State Power and the Structure of International Trade," *World Politics* 28 (April 1976): 317–47; and Charles P. Kindleberger, *The World in Depression, 1929–1939* (Berkeley: University of California Press, 1973), chap. 14. I thank Jack Levy for bringing this distinction to my attention.

10. This builds on Kenneth A. Oye, "Explaining Cooperation under Anarchy: Hypotheses and Strategies," *World Politics* 38, no. 1 (October 1985): 4–11; and Duncan Snidal, "The Limits of Hegemonic Stability Theory," *International Organization* 39, no. 4 (Autumn 1985): 579–614.

11. See Michael W. Doyle, *Ways of War and Peace: Realism, Liberalism, and Socialism* (New York: Norton, 1997), 230–50; Erik Gartzke, "The Capitalist Peace," *American Journal of Political Science* 51, no. 1 (January 2007): 166–91; and John Mueller, "Capitalism, Peace, and the Historical Movement of Ideas," *International Interactions* 36, no. 2 (June 2010): 169–84. For an empirical critique of the argument that conquest no longer pays, see Peter Liberman, *Does Conquest Pay? The Exploitation of Occupied Industrial Societies* (Princeton: Princeton University Press, 1998).

12. Edward Vose Gulick, *Europe's Classical Balance of Power* (New York: Norton, 1967).

13. See, e.g., Reinhold Niebuhr, *The Structure of Nations and Empires* (New York: Scribner's, 1959), 197.

14. David A. Lake, "Why 'isms' Are Evil: Theory, Epistemology, and Academic Sects as Impediments to Understanding and Progress," *International Studies Quarterly* 55, no. 2 (June 2011): 465–80.

15. On eclectic theories, see John A. Hall and T. V. Paul, "Preconditions for Prudence: A Sociological Synthesis of Realism and Liberalism," in *International Order and the Future of World Politics*, ed. T. V. Paul and John A. Hall, 67–77 (Cambridge: Cambridge University Press, 1999); and Rudra Sil and Peter J. Katzenstein, *Beyond Paradigms: Analytic Eclecticism in the Study of World Politics* (London: Palgrave Macmillan, 2010).

16. See Gideon Rose, "Neoclassical Realism and Theories of Foreign Policy," *World Politics* 51, no. 1 (October 1998): 144–72; Randall L. Schweller, "Unanswered Threats: A Neoclassical Realist Theory of Underbalancing," *International Security* 29, no. 2 (Fall 2004): 159–201; Jeffrey W. Taliaferro, Steven E. Lobell, and Norrin M. Ripsman, "Introduction: Neoclassical Realism, the State, and Foreign Policy," in *Neoclassical Realism, the State, and Foreign Policy*, ed. Steven E. Lobell, Norrin M. Ripsman, and Jeffrey W. Taliaferro, 1–41 (Cambridge: Cambridge University

Press, 2009); and Norrin M. Ripsman, Jeffrey W. Taliaferro, and Steven E. Lobell, "The Future of Neoclassical Realism," in Ripsman, Taliaferro, and Lobell, *Neoclassical Realism, the State, and Foreign Policy*, 280–99.

17. On this point, see Norrin M. Ripsman, Jeffrey W. Taliaferro, and Steve E. Lobell, *Neoclassical Realist Theory of International Politics* (Oxford University Press, 2016).

18. Norrin M. Ripsman, "The Curious Case of German Rearmament: Democracy and Foreign Security Policy," *Security Studies* 10, no. 2 (Winter 2001): 31–32.

19. Norrin M. Ripsman, "The Politics of Deception: Forging Peace Treaties in the Face of Domestic Opposition," *International Journal* 60, no. 1 (Winter 2004–5): 211–14.

20. Phoebe Greenwood, "Gaza Protests Accuse Palestinian Authority of Betrayal in Talks with Israel," *Guardian*, January 28, 2011, http://www.theguardian.com/world/2011/jan/28/gaza-protests-palestinian-papers-leak (accessed May 13, 2014).

21. See Jean-Marc F. Blanchard and Norrin M. Ripsman, *Economic Statecraft and Foreign Policy: Sanctions and Incentives and Target State Calculations* (London: Routledge, 2013), 25–31; and Peter B. Evans, "The Eclipse of the State? Reflections on Stateness in an Era of Globalization," *World Politics* 50, no. 1 (October 1997): 62–87.

22. On spoilers of a peace process, see Stephen John Stedman, "Spoiler Problems in Peace Processes," *International Security* 22, no. 2 (Fall 1997): 5–53. On the concept of veto players, see George Tsebelis, *Veto Players: How Political Institutions Work* (Princeton: Princeton University Press, 2002).

23. In a similar vein, the literature on peacebuilding suggests that state building is an important component of any attempt at building peace in failed states. Roland Paris and Timothy D. Sisk, "Introduction: Understanding the Contradictions of Postwar Statebuilding," in *The Dilemmas of Statebuilding: Confronting the Contradictions of Postwar Peace Operations*, ed. Roland Paris and Timothy D. Sisk, 1–20 (Abingdon, UK: Routledge, 2009).

24. This supports the argument made, for different reasons, by Javier Solana and Benita Ferrero-Waldner, "Statebuilding for Peace in the Middle East: An EU Action Strategy," European Council, Council of the EU, S378/07, http://www.consilium.europa.eu/ueDocs/cms_Data/docs/pressdata/en/reports/97949.pdf.

25. On the FPE, see Taliaferro, Lobell, and Ripsman, "Introduction," 23–28; Margaret G. Hermann, Charles F. Hermann, and Joe D. Hagan, "How Decision Units Shape Foreign Policy Behavior, in *New Directions in the Study of Foreign Policy*, ed. Charles F. Hermann, Charles W. Kegley, and James N. Rosenau, 309–36 (Boston: Allen and Unwin, 1987); and David A. Lake, *Power, Protection, and Free Trade: International Sources of US Commercial Strategy, 1887–1939* (Ithaca: Cornell University Press, 1988).

26. For a similar argument in the economic sanctions literature, see Bruce W. Jentleson and Christopher A. Whytock, "Who 'Won' Libya? The Force-Diplomacy Debate and Its Implications for Theory and Policy," *International Security* 30, No. 3 (Winter 2005–6): 47–86.

27. I. William Zartman, *Ripe for Resolution: Conflict and Intervention in Africa* (New York: Oxford University Press, 1985); and Marieke Kleiboer, "Ripeness of Conflict: A Fruitful Notion?" *Journal of Peace Research* 31, no. 1 (February 1994): 109–16.

28. Joseph Kostiner and Chelsi Mueller, "Egyptian and Saudi Intervention in the Israeli-Palestinian Conflict (2006–09): Local Powers' Mediation Compared," in *International Intervention in Local Conflicts: Crisis Management and Conflict Resolution since the Cold War*, ed. Uzi Rabi (London: I. B. Tauris, 2010), 202, 210.

29. See, e.g., Stephen G. Brooks and William C. Wohlforth, *World Out of Balance: International Relations and the Challenge of American Primacy* (Princeton: Princeton University Press, 2008).

30. Charles-Philippe David and Stéphane Roussel, "Middle Power Blues: Canadian Policy and International Security after the Cold War," *American Review of Canadian Studies* 28, no. 1 (November 2009): 135–36.

31. Krasner, "State Power."

32. For a contrary perspective, see Kenneth A. Schultz, "The Politics of Risking Peace: Do Hawks or Doves Deliver the Olive Branch?" *International Organization* 59, no. 1 (Winter 2005): 1–38.

33. These failed talks are discussed in Helena Cobban, *The Israeli-Syrian Peace Talks: 1991–96 and Beyond* (Washington, DC: United States Institute for Peace, 1999); and Itamar Rabinovitch, *The Brink of Peace: The Israeli-Syrian Negotiations* (Princeton: Princeton University Press, 1998).

34. Dennis Ross, *The Missing Peace: The Inside Story of the Fight for Middle East Peace* (New York: Farrar, Straus & Giroux, 2004), 765–67; and interview with former United States envoy to the Middle East, Dennis Ross, February 14, 2008.

35. See Ripsman, *Peacemaking by Democracies.*

36. Classical realists who argue that the public is more bellicose than its leaders after wars include Niebuhr, *Structure of Nations and Empires*, 197; and Walter Lippmann, *Essays in the Public Philosophy* (Boston: Little, Brown, 1955), 18–21. See also Ripsman, "Peacemaking and Democratic Peace Theory."

37. On the importance of state capacity and legitimacy in shielding the state, see Jean-Marc F. Blanchard and Norrin M. Ripsman, *Economic Statecraft and Foreign Policy: Sanctions and Incentives and Target State Calculations* (London: Routledge, 2013).

38. Ripsman, *Peacemaking by Democracies*, chap. 4.

39. Johan Galtung, "On the Effects of International Economic Sanctions: With Examples from the Case of Rhodesia," *World Politics* 19, no. 3 (April 1967): 378–416.

40. Galia Press-Barnathan, *The Political Economy of Transitions to Peace: A Comparative Perspective* (Pittsburgh, PA: University of Pittsburgh Press, 2009), 66.

41. See, e.g., Norrin M. Ripsman, "Neoclassical Realism and Domestic Interest Groups," in *Neoclassical Realism, the State, and Foreign Policy*, ed. Steven E. Lobell, Norrin M. Ripsman, and Jeffrey W. Taliaferro (Cambridge: Cambridge University Press, 2009), 182–185.

42. I thank an anonymous reviewer for suggesting this line of inquiry.

Index

Page numbers in italics refer to figures or tables

Syrian-Israeli relations, 8
Syrian surprise attack on Israel, 88, 182n9
Syrian threat to Jordan, 96

Tanaka, Kakuei, 128
temporary peace agreements, *33*, 125, 132, *133*, 134, 137
territorial disputes: border changes, 43–44, 46, 50, 72, 85–86, 108–110; border wars, 124–125; core territory, 5–7, 18; principles *uti possidetis juris*, 108; religious, 159n5
third parties, 22–23, 30, 143–151, 160n18. *See also individual nations*
Three Power Prohibited and Limited Industries Agreement, 40, 41
Three Powers (United States, Great Britain, France), 15, 35, 36
Tito, Josip, 115
top-down approach: assessments of peacemaking, 54, 61–62, 79–80, 101, 106–107; balance of power/ balance of threat theory, 45–49, 73; *versus* bottom-up approach, 17, 129–130; bottom-up simultaneous, 146; hegemonic influence, 27–29, 49–51, 74–77, 97–99; realists, 26–27; reassurance signaling theory, 29; regional stabilization, 26–32; societal hostility, 129–131; state-preservation motives, 29–32, 51–53, 77–79, 99–101, 138, 145, 160n14, 195n108; successes, 135, 138–139; threats, 73; transition phase, 45–54, 73–80, 95–101
trade. *See* bilateral trade
transition phase. bottom-up dynamics, 36–45, 67–73, 90–95; causes, 35–54, *61*, 67–80, *85*, 90–101, *107*, *131*, *137*; strategy matching, 145–147; top-down dynamics, 45–54, 73–80, 95–101
Transjordan. *See* Jordan
Treaty of Berlin, 117
Treaty of Brest-Litovsk, 122
Treaty of Friendship (1925), 132
Treaty of Friendship, Alliance, and Commerce (1832), 109
Treaty of Friendship and Cooperation (1974), 125
Treaty of Friendship and Neutrality (1925), 123
Treaty of Kars (1921), 124
Treaty of Moscow (1921), 122, 124, 132
Treaty of Osimo (1975), 115, 132
Treaty of Paris, 114, 115
Treaty of Peace and Friendship (1978), 128
Treaty of Rapallo (1920), 113
Treaty of Rome (1924), 113

Treaty of Rome (1957), 39, 41
Treaty of San Stefano, 117
Treaty of Versailles (1919), 11, 113, 158n29, 199n2
Treaty on a Final Settlement with Respect to Germany (1990), 5
Trieste agreement, 115, 132
Trieste territory, 113–115
Turkey, 113, 122, 123, 124, 195n97, 196n115
Turkish-Russian relations. *See* Russian-Turkish relations
Two Plus Four agreement (1990), 60

Union for the Mediterranean, 82, 104
United States: debt forgiveness, 97; defense spending, 172n140; economic incentives, 50–51, 76–77, 93, 115; foreign policy, 162n37; hegemonic influence, 28, 49–51, 57, 74–79, 81, 104, 111; military power, 50–51, 57; peace-building programs, 3–4; public opinion, 162n37
United States Agency for International Development (USAID), 3, 155n1
United States-Canada partnership, 56
United States-Cuba relations, 10
United States Development Program, 3
United States-Soviet relations, 10, 18
uti possidetis juris (territorial disputes principles), 108

Vance, Cyrus, 68, 76, 79, 179n102
Velasco, José María, 109
von Bismarck, Otto, 34

Waltz, Kenneth, 140
war: strategies to end war, 142–143; theory, 17, 140–*141*, 156n14, 158n32
warm peace, 4–5, 44
water supply, 89
Weizman, Ezer, 69, 71
Western European Union, 42
Wilson, Woodrow, 25, 113

Yalta Conference, 117
Yom Kippur War (1973), 65, 74, 88, 182n9
Yugoslavia, 114–116, 119–120, 194n79
Yugoslavian-Bulgarian relations. *See* Bulgarian-Yugoslavian relations
Yugoslavian-Italian relations. *See* Italian-Yugoslavian relations
Yugoslavian-Macedonian relations, 120
Yugoslavian-Soviet relations, 119

Zhou Enlai, 127–128
Zippori, Mordechai, 177n65